THE GOLDEN TOUCH: FRANKIE CARLE

THE GOLDEN TOUCH: FRANKIE CARLE
by Gene Catrambone

Library of Congress Catalog No. 80-80901

Copyright © 1981 by Gene Catrambone

All rights reserved

Libra Publishers; Inc.
391 Willets Road
Roslyn Heights, New York 11577

Manufactured in the United States of America
ISBN: 0-87212-124-0

To
my wonderful wife, Mary,
and loving children, Penny,
Whitey, Jane, David, and Jill

Contents

Prologue	ix
Foreword	xi
Preface	xiii
List of Illustrations	xvii

Chapter 1	Substance of the Man	1
Chapter 2	Persistence of Challenge	9
Chapter 3	Force of Nature	18
Chapter 4	Inclination of Adolescence	28
Chapter 5	Saga of Springfield	46
Chapter 6	Expansion of Horizon	81
Chapter 7	Frustration of Failure	95
Chapter 8	Renewal of Hope	108
Chapter 9	Elusiveness of Fame	121
Chapter 10	Seed of Recognition	137
Chapter 11	Recurrence of Challenge	171
Chapter 12	Triumph of the Man	187

Appendix:	Frankie Carle Music	210
Appendix:	Discography	234
Picture Credits		254
Index		255

PROLOGUE

In the apartment of newlyweds Danny and Nellie Fisher in Harold Robbins' novel, *A Stone for Danny Fisher* (Alfred A. Knopf, 1953), Danny says:

I sat down in the parlor and turned on the radio. Soft music filled the room. It was the right kind of music to start a new day: Frankie Carle's "Sunrise Serenade."

Danny Fisher utters a sentiment with which countless numbers have concurred for over forty years.

FOREWORD

The life story of Frankie Carle is not only a saga of a man's music, but, indeed, a story of the American dream come true. It proves that in this great land of ours, if one works hard enough and long enough, almost anything is possible. Success does not come easily. It takes purpose, patience and perseverance.

While Frankie's young friends played baseball in the streets of his native Providence, Frankie spent endless hours practicing at his piano.

Frankie never forgot his roots. He would return home to be with his family and friends on holidays—especially at Christmas time. Each time he returned to Providence he would visit me while I was Governor of the State of Rhode Island. He would perform at the Governor's Christmas party for State employees and play his famous tunes to the delight of his audience.

Frankie is generous to a fault in sharing his great talent with others. A devoted family man; a legend in the world of music; a great human being and one I am proud to call friend. Indeed, I could go on and on but I prefer to have you read the book.

John O. Pastore
Former Governor, State of Rhode Island
United States Senator (Retired)

PREFACE

Millions of us are still around—that is, people of a generation who were fortunate enough to live in the era of the big bands. I cannot speak for those millions in saying "one more time," particularly in the case of Frankie Carle. A generation preceding and following mine can very well utter the same sentiment—that's how long Frankie Carle had pleased people with his music, one way or another. And do not be misled by my reference to the big bands. This is not the story of that era. Frankie Carle goes before and beyond it. But the laurels he finally received as a triple-threat occurred in the closing stages of that era. Thus, *The Golden Touch* is an account of Francis Nunzio Carlone who has performed in and contributed to music since 1916 and waited 30 years before enjoying the success that was long overdue when it did occur.

For the record, I was not among the insiders during any of the "ages" in music through which Frankie Carle passed. Nor was I among the insiders during the heyday of that fabulous Big Band Era. But I lived music in that era. I was one waiting in the long theater lines. I was not one performing on the stage. Occasionally I was "crashing" the stagedoor to meet the leaders, singers, and sidemen. I was not one coming out. I was one dancing on the ballroom floors, not providing the music to dance by. I was a reader of the *Down Beats* and *Metronomes*. I was not a writer for them. I was a follower of the bands. I was a receiver, not a giver, but I lived strongly in the era and contend that "they also serve who only stand and wait." And that standing and waiting game meant a whole bunch to me because it was paying my dues to belong to the "time," to belong to the "hep" crowd, one of thousands of crowds who displayed a kind of enthusiasm and following, the likes of which may never happen again.

When I discovered the name of Frankie Carle, I was disappointed that the older boys in the neighborhood already knew it. I was disappointed because this bit of wisdom was going to show them, finally, that I was really "hep" on the goings on and, hence, rightfully belonged to the crowd. My particular crowd, along with a concentration of numerous others, nested in an area already boasting a host of horn tooters playing with big bands, Jimmy Zito being one of the more renown. The Hull House was a stone's throw away and everybody knew who emerged from that place. But the older boys were right: I could not buy my membership with so scanty an initiation fee. But how could they have already known Frankie Carle?

It was in the summer of 1939 when I first heard Gray's recording of "Sunrise Serenade" at the Chateau at Devil's Lake, Wisconsin. I found myself humming that tune continuously as I footed the high bluffs. I had heard the Gray rendition the night before, when my aunt and uncle made the momentous decision that I was really old enough to go alone to the Chateau by the lake, about one-half mile down from our campsite. But more important, that tune captured my imagination and from that moment on, popular music replaced the kid games as the love in my life.

We had a piano in our household, but none of the children studied piano. My "Pa" used to play the contraption by ear, and did rather well, but the piano rolls took the place of the 14 hands of the children occupying the flat. An older sister and a younger brother would sometimes pounce on the keys, and after that Devil's Lake outing, I, too, demanded equal time. I persisted, pecking the keys until I would finger a semblance of "Sunrise Serenade." I never learned the piano, but, by golly, I could still finger "Sunrise"—forty years later! That tune was my baptism into music consciousness. I joined the ranks of the public, who, at that time, had already effected a craze in popular music.

The present account of Frankie Carle, from 1916 to 1947, is an outgrowth of a newspaper feature I did in 1973 for the *Las Virgenes Enterprise*. Frankie had come out of retirement in the fall of 1972 to do the Cavalcade of Bands tour with Freddy Martin, Bob Crosby and Margaret Whiting. It was just before the tour that I met Frankie for the first time.

Knowing my waning familiarity with the big bands and understanding my respect for Frankie Carle's music, the *Enterprise* publisher assigned me to do the feature. In the several years that followed, Frankie and I talked much. The information Frankie couldn't provide, we queried others about, digging deeply into mounds of memorabilia. I must acknowledge a host of very cooperative folks and organizations who responded to sundry queries and solicitations, and thank them here: Mac J. and Maria Benoit, Chuck Cecil, Mrs. Augustus Benvenuti, James Cagney, the late Bing Crosby, Bob Crosby, Morty Geist, Butler Gillman, Vincent Gamelli, Henry Jacobson, Harry James, Horace Heidt, Sammy Kaye, Frankie Laine, the late Guy Lombardo, William Lackenbauer, Hack O'Brien, the late Olga Dunbar (through the courtesy of her husband Dr. Clinton McGrew), Freddy Martin, Lyle "Spud" Murphy, the Honorable John Pastore, Joe Perry, Ralph "Slim" Overman, George Simon, Hal Totten, Fred Wade, Lawrence Welk, Margaret Whiting, Gene Gressley, Evie Vale, Ken Smith, Bob Switzer, Robert Mathieu (Dept. of Health, R. I.), MCA Records, CBS Records, and the numerous friends who shared with me their nostalgia and love for Frankie Carle.

To each his own reverie. As for me and countless others, play it again, Frankie.

Gene Catrambone, 1979

List of Illustrations

Festivity at St. Anne's Catholic Church	6
Nicholas Colangelo's Favorites	27
May Yohe's Shelatone Orchestra	39
McEnelly Band, 1924	47
Mrs. Frankie Carle	55
Mound City Blue Blowers	62
Typical Billing	65
McEnelly Poster, 1925	67
Frankie Carle Recognition	68,69
Billing in a Depression Year	79
Mal Hallet Orchestra, 1933	82
Carle with Hallett	93
Hallett's Kentucky Hotel Orchestra, 1934	94
Carle Returns to Springfield	96
Carle, Piano Teacher	97
Frankie Carle 1935 Band	98
Bayside Review	99,100
Carle Billings, circ. 1935	104
Vitaphone Movie Short	114
"Georgianna" & "Deep In Your Eyes" Songsheets	119
Carle Seven Gables Orchestra, 1938	124
Glen Gray and "Sunrise Seranade"	136
Horace Heidt Troupe, 1939-40	140
Carle Billing with Heidt	141
The Heidt Herald	147
"Song Hits" Award	152
Carle's "Lover's Lullaby" & "Falling Leaves"	155
Entertaining the Troops	163,164
Heidt/Carle Pact	168
Heidt Personnel	169
Heidt Finale	170
Frankie Carle 'Rouge' Debut, 1944	174
Theater/Radio Debut	177
Playing the Camps and Boys Town	181
Widespread Popularity	183

Carle Gives Ginny Sims Record #5,000,000	190
Billboard Poll	198
Palladium Life	200
Movie Scene	201
The Orpheum, a Record	202
The Fabulous Theater Shows	203
The Bill & Talent	204
"Oh! What It Seemed To Be"	205
Well Deserved Plaudits	206
Extracurricular Performances	207
Terrace Room & Steel Pier	208
The Cocoanut Grove	209

THE GOLDEN TOUCH: FRANKIE CARLE

CHAPTER 1

Intermittent puffs on his pipe.

A rather short, staccato, nasal laugh for a full-framed-but-not-fat hunk of a man.

And the brief salutation ended, as I entered his study.

Frankie Carle, 76-year-old virtuoso, straightens up in a captain's chair, slaps both knees with his hands—the hands of the Golden Touch—and with that gesture, another of many visits begins.

"Gene," he says, "see this"—a way he often opened our talks when there was something he wanted particularly to show me. "This is my second music book. From Italy. Love it. Still use it."

After numerous similar visits, I was convinced that the stability and perseverance of Frankie Carle lay in the person of Frankie Carle. His music and his artistry emanated from a philosophy of simplicity, evidenced by "choice" mementoes which bedecked the walls and tables of his den in his Westlake Village home in the western end of Los Angeles County.

An upright stood against one wall; a couch against the opposite wall. An antique pull-down-cover desk sat in front of the only window which looked out to an enclosed private street. The remaining side of the room was wall-length closet, overloaded with hundreds of records, albums, music sheets, stacked boxes, and sundry other memorabilia, salvaged from his recent move from a large house in Tarzana to a smaller Village Glen townhouse in Westlake Village. "I threw so much stuff out," he would say habitually every time the occasion called for a bit of evidence to corroborate an incident he might have just vaguely remembered. Then he would grimace, "Where's that damned thing!"

But in clear view were the mementoes that touched the man deeply, his appreciation for these things, just short of reverence, being always obvious. He smiled; he was quite proud to be their possessor. He referred to them as though they were the ultimate achievement of his long celebrated life. No *Variety* front-page headline in 72-point blurting out "Carle Woos 'Em at the Capitol" in glass hung on the wall. (The Capitol was the scene of Frankie's first theater engagement with his big band.) Plaudits of that vintage lay buried in cardboard boxes, crammed and tucked away on the floor of the closet, a floor that was wall-to-wall boxes except for 50 or 60 record albums. Frankie Carle revered most, the plain certificates of appreciation from such organizations and agencies as the Sister Kenny Foundation, Boys' Town, the Veterans Administration, the Army, the Navy, the State of Rhode Island, and many others; and, if one can imagine, a Providence Public School diploma! The diploma apparently was a prized possession, for it was the diploma that effected a rather lengthy elocution.

One of my very early visits with Frankie Carle, some years ago now, perplexed me. "What's this," I thought, "A romance with a grade school diploma?" For a time afterwards, when I would reconsider that early bit of intelligence Frankie imparted, I would shake my head—not so much in disbelief as in shock of misunderstanding.

This man—this man who wrote "Sunrise Serenade," "Falling Leaves," "Lover's Lullaby," "Oh What It Seemed to Be," and over 100 other songs; who distinguished himself at the piano, performing for 56 years and leading a band for almost 20 years; who had become a household name, appearing in crossword puzzles as simply:———, pianist, and being mentioned by name in novels, in Joe Palooka, even in the Racing Form (horses named after him because of his interest in racing); who had been foremost in the thoughts of parents who envisioned their children playing the piano; whose name Hollywood implanted in the sidewalk; who had earned a berth in Rhode Island's Hall of Fame; and who had enjoyed the ultimate respect and success in his work—this man showed me his Providence Public School diploma which hung in the middle of the wall, and upon which he began to elucidate.

I was not too enthusiastic, but not rude, as he persisted, emotionally, to delineate the contents line for line. My eyes ping-ponged during the rhetoric, getting glimpses of a plaque for Song of the Year, a three-panel array of 8 x 10's commemorating Frankie Carle Night at Dodger Stadium, a sketch personally done by Walt Disney, and other testimonials. I wanted to absorb details of the plaque, or the Sister Kenny certificate, or the picture of Father Flanagan; but I was patient with the grade school diploma from Providence Public School.

Since that time, however, I have come to appreciate Frankie's regard for that document. My fuller understanding of its import makes me admire the man, not the composer-piano player who for me had become legend, but the man whom I have never known. There is nothing simpler than a grade school diploma; that is, of course, in a modern day context. In the context of an offspring of first-wave immigrant parentage in 1916, well, that is something else. Frankie's appreciation for that piece of parchment is typical, not atypical, of the man.

Frankie Carle, born Francisco Nunzio Carlone on March 25, 1903, to a struggling immigrant family, understood what it was to be poor. In an incomplete and unpublished 20-page "Memoir," Frankie wrote:

> We were so poor that during my school days, I had to go in woods to find branches, wood, etc. so that we could build a fire at home to keep warm. My sisters, brothers, and I did not know what milk or butter tasted like, until I went to work to help my folks provide these items.
>
> Financially, there was no money available for sweets of any kind. There was just about enough money for food, and we did not get much of that. And there was no one we could turn to for financial help. We were just poor, and that was that.

All his life he was sensitive to the basic needs of others. He never hesitated to give his time, talent, or money unselfishly to charities, even when he was not so fortunate. He believed that everyone—whether he be an aspiring musician or singer or a wayward in Boys' Town—should be given a chance. He had encouraged many young talents and had interceded in whatever small or large way he could for young talents to get a chance. He had helped materially in other causes.

The certificates on the wall attested to some causes—but how many more, God knows. Frankie dismissed the subject of charities lightly. But I remember, on one occasion, the emptied envelopes clearly visible in the heap in the waste basket revealed that the contents had been removed and tended to. Envelopes for mailing stacked on his desk were pre-addressed. I caught glimpses—Blind Children, Indian Children, Korean Children, North Vietnamese Children, and some others. I remembered, having gone over a full box of miscellaneous stuff in Frankie's garage, other evidence of earlier contributions—like Operation Help, a Catholic charity for children; a St. Anthony's Guild of Paterson, New Jersey; a Jewish hospital in Denver and another in Los Angeles; even a leper colony. Then I further remembered something of a casual reference Frankie had made about Dora, his mother.

Dora was particularly special to Frankie. He always said she was responsible for his success. Dora never wanted anything from Frankie's success but that he be a good man, have faith, and be thankful to God that things turned out well. He should never forget poor kids, for he himself was one of a houseful and a neighborhoodful of poor kids. Before Dora died in 1944, Frankie had promised her that he would help poor children. Frankie has never reneged. Neither has he ever reneged on his faith in God. Always a man of faith, regardless of the demands of his work over the years, he has attended church regularly. In his "Memoir," Frankie was explicit when he included "faith in God" among the influences responsible for his success:

> Regardless of all the persons I mentioned who helped me up the ladder of success, to whom I'm eternally grateful, I honestly believe my success could not have been achieved without the help of God. In one short sentence, I was blessed with the gift of music by our Lord, because of my faith in Him. That probably was so, since I started as an altar boy in St. Anne's Catholic Church in my hometown at the age of five.

Frankie Carle is uncomplicated, like his music. He is comfortable to be with; he is candid and genuinely sincere, even to a point of *naivete*. He is never condescending and always attentive to what is said to him, regardless of who says it. He has a sense of humor, a hearty laugh, a broad smile—a smile so characteristic of the man that for some time he was known as "Smiling Frankie Carle."

To the people he worked with or with whom he became acquainted over the years, Frankie is a warm personable human being. Unconsciously, he evokes respect from a variety of personalities in his capacity as leader, as featured soloist or sideman, or as one in a crowd. Butler "Butch" Gillman, who played sax, clarinet, and xylophone in the Edwin J. McEnelly band with Frankie, writes: ". . . a better person, and one who takes an interest in other human beings and never forgets his friends . . . well, he's going to be awfully hard to find." Bing Crosby, a later 1920-ish contemporary of Frankie, in speaking of Frankie's unique style, adds "very pleasant man, too, very appealing personality." Lawrence Welk, another of the giants in the industry who go back a good number of years, divulges, "I have always held him in the very highest esteem . . . he is one of the finest men in our profession." Lyle "Spud" Murphy, who sidemanned with Frankie in the early 1930's Mal Hallett group and, at this writing, is president of the American Society of Music Arrangers (ASMA), remembers Frankie as "a man of his word and one on whom you could always rely to fulfill his musical obligation." Guy Lombardo, the grand-daddy of popular music, thinks the man with the Golden Touch and a five-feet, seven-inch build simply a "wonderful little guy," while Sammy Kaye expresses "my admiration for his musicianship and [his] being such a great fellow."

H.L. "Hack" O'Brien, drummer in Frankie Carle's orchestra in the 1930's and later, through Frankie, with Horace Heidt, tells of Frankie's "sincere friendliness and interest in his musicians." O'Brien relates an incident which exemplifies the kind of man Frankie Carle is. When the Carle band was playing the State Theatre in Hartford, Connecticut, O'Brien came to work the matinee, feeling sick. Frankie learned of O'Brien's

Festivity at St. Anne's Catholic church where Frankie served as an altar boy. Frankie appears behind sailor on left forefront.

illness during the show and very shortly after the show, he went to O'Brien and said, "Come on, cab's waiting for us." The taxi took them straight to a doctor, a friend of Frankie's, for some immediate attention. "Now how many big-time band leaders do you know," pondered O'Brien, "that would take the time and trouble to do that for a sideman?"

O'Brien continued with a compliment which was again reflected in another observation many, many years later. Writes O'Brien, "If you're a musician, you know that's a fine compliment to your leader when a musician says, 'He is still a sideman.'" Morty Geist, Juilliard-schooled saxaphonist and clarinetist, who debuted with Art Mooney before joining Frankie in 1950, recalls a like impression. Writes Geist, "Although he achieved great success, the one fact that stood out was that he never ceased to be a sideman. He treated us as he would have liked to have been treated." It was no surprise then, 40 years after O'Brien's observation, when Frankie Carle did the Cavalcade of Bands tour in 1972, that Freddy Martin observed, "Every musician in the band put out for him every moment he was on stage." And concluded Martin, best summing up the person of Frankie Carle, poignantly even if tritely, "To know him, as the saying goes, is to love him."

Frankie Carle is a composite of a warm human being and a remarkable talent, a combination more anomalous than indigenous to the coterie of celebrated personalities. And too often this rarity among men is relegated to a lesser priority of exposure in magazines and books—so it seems. The prowess of the athlete, the escapades of the rascal, the hangups of the misfit, or the trivia of the celebrated, command more linotype than the contributor, who, in a manner of speaking, "keeps his house in order."

Several years ago, two so-called journalists approached Frankie for a feature story on some aspect of Frankie's life. The feature would have reached a readership from coast to coast. Frankie Carle's name is still familiar to a great number of people in this country and abroad. But the so-called publishers wanted neither Frankie Carle the songwriter-pianist nor

Frankie Carle the bandleader. What they did want, however, was Frankie Carle the rascal. Who and when were his conquests? What were some of the tantalizing debaucheries in his follies? And the so-called journalists were serious! The audacity of these pseudo-journalists to intimate such behavior was downright slanderous. Frankie frowned at this indignation and, after telling me of the incident, he shrugged his shoulders and said, "Oh, well, what can you do, Gene? I told them to get lost. Who needs that?"

It was obvious that he was insulted. It also was ironic that the incident occurred very shortly after he and his wife Ede celebrated their 50th wedding anniversary in 1975.

To be sure, nature has coupled a good human being with an extraordinary talent. Before we trace that talent, however, let us understand in general, Frankie Carle's place in the history of popular music. Frankie Carle is music; he is part of that omnipresent commodity which imbues our every day of existence. He has created over 100 songs; he has sold over an estimated 100 million records. If music can influence our moods, provoke reveries, or effect myriad human responses, then the music of Frankie Carle can do these things. Music, like no other contrivance of man, can so readily suggest the circumstance of a former experience or preface the mood of a forthcoming one; Frankie Carle's music, or he himself, ascribes to this principle.

Frankie Carle was part of the music scene in America in varying degrees and in different roles from 1916 through the Cavalcade of Bands in 1972. Frankie Carle is history, and his history is a 56-year participation in, and contribution to, popular music. That's where he fits.

"Yep, one of my very first books," he iterated, putting down his pipe and reaching over to get the book from the sheet stand on the piano. The book: *Methods,* Beniamino Cesi (G. Ricordi & Co., 1912).

CHAPTER 2

The Frankie Carle orchestra made its debut in New York in February 1944 at the Cafe Rouge in the Pennsylvania Hotel (now the Statler). Actually, Frankie Carle made his debut as a leader during World War I, after serving a very short apprenticeship in Nicholas Colangelo's Favorites. The Hotel Pennsylvania was the right place, but trends indicated that 1944 was a wrong time for the debut of a big band. And Frankie Carle was an artist at the piano, a sideman, not a leader. At least his history up to that time indicated that he was not a leader.

"I suggested he not form a big band," writes Horace Heidt, who headed one of the greatest music organizations of all time (twelve separate divisions, with a staff for each!). "I thought it a mistake to bury himself with a lot of saxes and brass. I thought four pieces called Frankie Carle's 'Sunrise Serenaders' would bring him as much money as a full band, less headaches for him, and the people could hear Frankie's Golden Touch all the time."

Frankie had established a name for himself as a featured pianist with Heidt, and long before Heidt, with Edwin McEnelly and Mal Hallett. But the latter two were more regional than they were national. Frankie had further distinguished himself as a songwriter; not, however, before Glenn Miller pressed "Sunrise Serenade" on Bluebird in 1939 and Frankie's receiving Song Hits award (*Song Hits* magazine) in 1940. "Lover's Lullaby" and "Falling Leaves," also in 1940, cemented Frankie's reputation as a songwriter, fifteen years after he wrote his first song. A featured pianist and songwriter, yes. A bandleader? No.

Could Frankie Carle succeed as a bandleader in 1944? He failed in attempts in the second, the third, and fourth decades of the 20th Century, notwithstanding some local success in the New England area in 1938 and 1939.

In 1917 a fourteen-year old Frankie Carle left Nicholas Colangelo's Favorites, a local dance band in Providence, to form his own group, a five-piece outfit. His group never got beyond weddings and local parties, except for two occasions at local ballrooms. In 1919 the Frankie Carle orchestra no longer existed, and Frankie was playing piano in a silent movie house.

Before the Edwin J. McEnelly days in the early 1920's, Frankie fronted a band in vaudeville, the Shelatone band, but it was not his band.

In his ten years with McEnelly, Frankie led the band occasionally toward the end of his association with Jerry Cook and McEnelly. But that was not his band.

Frankie was a sideman in Mal Hallett's orchestra twice: from March, 1933, to October, 1934, and from September, 1936, to October, 1937. In both tenures he acted in the role of an assistant, leading but not a leader. After his first tenure with Hallett—climaxed with a nervous breakdown—Frankie attempted another band of his own. Success was not in the cards. By that time, Frankie had lost much of the aspiration to lead again. He stood by as big bands like those of Benny Goodman, the Dorsey Brothers, Benny Carter, Glen Gray, Bob Crosby, and many others were molding an epoch in music across the country.

There was no future for Frankie Carle, bandleader; nor did it seem there was a future for Frankie Carle, songwriter! Frankie composed an average of five songs a year. In 1936 he struggled to complete one, "If You Please," which, like the others, was no roaring success.

After giving up his 1935-36 band, Frankie rejoined Hallett. This time he lasted 15 months. But, alas, he submitted to that recurring urge to lead a band in his own style. In 1938 and 1939, when the big bands were "catching" on, Frankie was at it again. He enjoyed local raves but suffered financial disaster.

By mid-1939 Frankie could only envy other piano players in the thick of the big band craze—players like Bob Zurke, Howard Hall, Lou Bush, Van Nordstrand, Chummy MacGreggar, others. Big bands were here—Count Basie, Artie Shaw, Gene Krupa, Glenn Miller, Jimmy Dorsey, more. But Frankie Carle was folding his band. He became even more frustrated when publishers turned down his songs.

Then, Horace Heidt came into Frankie's life, and Frankie, once more, became a sideman. With Heidt, Frankie "starred," until a nervous breakdown cut him down. But Frankie came back, and eventually led the Horace Heidt band; one more time he led a band that was not his. When Heidt suggested that Frankie was ready for his own Frankie Carle combo, Frankie could only recall the pangs of previous failures. Was it the failures as bandleader that challenged Frankie Carle in 1944? "I don't know," recollected Frankie in 1977, "I just wanted to lead my own band, play my own style."

The year, 1944, was more precarious than opportune for a big band. Big bands were facing growing competition from single performers and smaller combos. Heidt foresaw obstacles; he warned Frankie against the venture of a big band.

The decline of the big bands was rapid toward the end and after World War II. The decline was understandable for many reasons—reasons, however, to be treated here only in general to show the imminent trend into which Frankie Carle was launching his big band.

I

The curtailment of popular music caused by the ASCAP*BMI feud and the Petrillo ban of the early forties had a detrimental effect on music in general and on the bands in particular.* The

---

*In 1941 the American Society of Authors, Composers and Publishers (ASCAP) demanded more remuneration from the radio networks for airing songs of ASCAP members. The networks not only rebuffed ASCAP but banned ASCAP tunes, creating in the process their own agency, Broadcast Music, Inc. (BMI). The competition lasted for about a year, effecting a dearth of great big-band music on the air during that time. No sooner had the fires of ASCAP-BMI cooled, then Caesar Petrillo, president of the American Federation of Musicians (AFM), directed all AFM musicians to stop recording. Petrillo demanded that recording companies pay musicians when their records were aired and when played in juke boxes. Thus, from the fall of 1942 to the fall of 1943 no instrumentals were recorded until Capital and Decca came to terms with AFM. Victor and Columbia settled late in 1944.

emotions of a wartime society often precluded attendance at ballrooms and other places for girlfriends and wives of many servicemen. After the war, attendance at these places dropped considerably. Then, the romantic ballad, i.e., the single vocal, gained an advantage over a "jump" number. The best-selling recordings became the sweet numbers as opposed to the instrumentals. The theaters would soon be abandoning the stage show. In other words, the avenues on which big bands thrived in 1939, 1940, 1941, 1942 and 1943 were beginning to wear. No one can really surmise to what heights—or what prolonged prominence—the big band era might have achieved if World War II had never happened. But World War II did happen, and Frankie Carle did venture a big band while the war was yet being waged, but the "time" was not good for that kind of venture.

George Simon (*The Big Bands,* MacMillan, 1974) sets the dates of the big band era with Benny Goodman ushering the way from late 1935 to 1946, when the swinging giants like Goodman, Barnet, Herman, James, and others disbanded. Woody Herman once commented on the Merv Griffin television program (October 8, 1975) that the "1950's buried the bands." (This writer prefers to think that the big bands died with Miller in 1944.)

Maybe 1946 is a liberal cutoff for the big band era if we gauge the public's response to the big band sound, basically instrumental, as opposed to that of the single vocal. We have to agree, further, that records which sell a million copies are an indication of public response. (By today's standard, a million copies in the 1930's and 1940's would be the equivalent of five million.) Judging from the list of "million-sellers" compiled by Chuck Cecil, d j, KGIL radio, San Fernando Valley, we see that the instrumental was losing rapidly by the time the Frankie Carle band appeared on the scene. A brief history of the million-sellers shows this trend.

The only million-seller in the early 1930's, before 1935 and Benny Goodman, was Clyde McCoy's "Sugar Blues" in 1934. There were no million-sellers in 1935 or 1936; only two in

1937—Bing Crosby's "Sweet Leilani," a vocal, and Tommy Dorsey's "Marie," an instrumental. In 1938 six tunes hit the million-seller list. They included Arthur Fiedler and the Boston Pops' "Jalousie," and Glahe Musette's "Beer Barrel Polka." The others were Harry James' "One O'Clock Jump," Artie Shaw's "Begin the Beguine," Tommy Dorsey's "Boogie Woogie," and Ted Weems' "Heartaches." In 1939 ten numbers made the million club, seven basically instrumental, and three vocal. The vocals were Gene Autry's "That Silver-haired Daddy of Mine," Bonnie Baker's (with Orrin Tucker) "Oh Johnny, Oh Johnny!", and a novelty—call it vocal—Kay Kyser's "Three Little Fishies." The instrumentals included Harry James' "Ciribiribin;" Glenn Miller's "Little Brown Jug," "Sunrise Serenade," and "In the Mood;" Guy Lombardo's "Easter Parade;" Woody Herman's "Woodchoppers' Ball;" and Cab Calloway's "The Jumpin' Jive." Hence, in the decade of the 1930's that gave prominence to the big bands, instrumentals enjoyed a better than 5-1 margin over the vocals. (In retrospect, one wonders why the margin was not far greater, particularly since some of the greatest big band sounds came out of the 1937, 1938, and 1939 years. One wonders further why Benny Goodman, the King himself, was not represented at least a dozen times on the illustrious million-seller list.)

From 1940, a year which produced five of the million-sellers (Glenn Miller's "Tuxedo Junction" and "Pennsylvania Six Five Thousand," Johnny Long's "In a Shanty in Old Shanty Town," and Artie Shaw's "Summit Ridge Drive" and "Star Dust"), through 1942, the big band sound continued to dominate the music scene, but did give some ground to the vocals. Of the 22 million-sellers in that three-year period, 16 were basically instrumental, six vocal. The instrumentals with a mixture of vocal in them, in addition to the five above, were Glenn Miller's "I've Got a Gal in Kalamazoo," "American Patrol," and "Chattanooga Choo Choo;" Harry James' "You Made Me Love You;" Freddy Martin's "Tchaikovsky Piano Concerto (Tonight We Love);" Horace Heidt's "Deep in the Heart of Texas;" and Kay Kyser's "Who Wouldn't Love You?", "Jingle Jangle Jingle,"

"Praise the Lord and Pass the Ammunition," and "Strip Polka." The six vocals included Kate Smith's "Rose O'Day" (1941), Vaughn Monroe's "Racing with the Moon" (1942), Elton Britt's "There's a Star Spangled Banner Waving Somewhere" (1942), Frank Sinatra's "There Are Such Things" (1942), and—counting as basically vocal—Helen O'Connell's and Bob Eberly's (with Jimmy Dorsey) "Maria Elena" and "Green Eyes" (1941). Thus, the instrumental-vocal margin from 1935 through 1943 was reduced to slightly better than 3-1.

In 1943, the year Frankie Carle was to leave Heidt, the million-seller list was even more disconcerting to the producers of big band records. Only four of the million-sellers made the list and all four were vocals: Mills Brothers' "Paper Doll," Dick Haymes' "You'll Never Know," Bing Crosby's "Sunday, Monday, or Always" and "Pistol Packin' Mama." The ratio was reduced even further.

From 1944 through 1946, the years in which Frankie Carle was trying to make it as a big band, only five instrumentals hit the million mark—Spike Jones' "Cocktails for Two" (1944), Guy Lombardo's "Humoresque," Carmen Cavallaro's "Chopin's Polonaise" (1945), Woody Herman's "Laura" (1945), and Louis Jordan's "Choo Choo Ch' Boogie" (1946)—while 32 vocals made it. Thus, then, from the point of view of million sellers, the instrumental approach was at a definite disadvantage.

It was no wonder that great bands were disbanding by 1946. Perry Como, Bing Crosby, The Ink Spots, The Andrews Sisters, The Mills Brothers, and Al Jolson captured the million-sellers. The vocals were bigger than the bands, with vocals multiplying farther into the 1940's (Frankie Laine, Art Lund, Peggy Lee, Dinah Shore, Margaret Whiting, Evelyn Knight, Vic Damone, and Nat Cole).

Frankie Carle had his work cut out for him when he decided in 1944 to go with the big band—big band connoting, of course, instrumental, whether swing, sweet, or jazz. Obviously, in Frankie Carle, eliminate jazz; his *forte* was sweet, with doses of swing, although his artistry at the keyboard was apparent in any classification.

By the end of World War II in 1945, the year Como, Crosby, and Jolson monopolized the million-sellers, the Frankie Carle band had been playing the circuit (theaters, ballrooms) for more than one year. The Frankie Carle band was confronting a new society of millions of ex-servicemen, a different teen-age population, a changing face in music, and the advent of a revolution in entertainment—television.

II

Servicemen, particularly the generation of them who supported the big bands in dance halls, in theaters, and in procurement of "78" disc collections, returned to civilian life no longer thoroughly big band-impassioned as they had been. This generation came home from a two-or three-or four-year absence ready and eager to build themselves futures or to resume occupations. Many pursued trades or professions. The GI Bill offered them opportunities for trades or college, a reality undreamed of for most of them in a post-Depression, pre-war society. It was not that the returning servicemen disliked the music they had grown up with, but rather that they rearranged their priorities. In their vigorous pursuits, I suspect, the generation who grew up with the big bands continued to play the records already in their collections, rather than add to them. Actually, there was really not much to add—even though some good swing continued. Goodman, Barnet, *et al.* disbanded. Miller was gone; subsequent leaders of the Miller style did not recapture the Miller followers or recruit the new public's enthusiasm.

The aspect of the ballrooms and the taste in music in vogue reveal something of the decline of interest in the big bands in the new, post-war society. The former, usually crowded in the late 1930's and early 1940's, were not frequented so much as they had been. Again, returning servicemen rearranged priorities. Big band followers who had frequented ballrooms two, three, even four times a week in pre-war days no longer enjoyed the pleasure so often. The new generation of teens that had made its entrance was not attracted to ballrooms regularly as its predecessor had been.

The big bands themselves were finding it more difficult to exist. The ballrooms began closing their doors. The theaters that booked bands continued the practice for a time after the war, but it was on its way out. (Remember how in the 1930's and 1940's some of us went to the theaters only because of the bands that were featured?). Television became available in 1946, and in short order revolutionized entertainment. Uncle Miltie, Sid Caesar and Imogene Coca, Ed Sullivan, boxing, ballgames, what else, captured viewing audiences in numbers never before heard of. Had Miller and Goodman toured the country every day for a whole year, they still would not have come close in attendance figures to the viewing audience television commanded in one performance.

Bands—swing, sweet, jazz, whatever—were changing. The beat was different, so it seems, or the tempo, or the tune, or maybe just the public's attitude. Big band sounds were still around, even in the 1950's, even in the 1960's, even now—but not the response to them. The inevitable occurred. Change. And the change failed to rekindle the public in the same way as the change in the mid-1930's had done. Be-bop, for example, like boogie woogie earlier, enjoyed a temporary popularity. Though be-bop was a logical progression in swing, it was not swing.* Kentonesque, with some really great musicianship to offer a new society, was not to evoke a response of the magnitude of that of the late 1930's and early 1940's. Vocalist June Christy, I conjecture, was perhaps more successful than the instrumentals. On the jazz scene, followers were experiencing an uneasiness with jazz groups. By the late 1940's and into the 1950's the situation was so very bad that jazzmen themselves

---

*There is disagreement among authorities who treat this subject. For example, "bop" has been defined as a "degenerated form of swing and not jazz at all" and as "a sudden eruption within jazz." Cf. Marshall Stearns, *The Story of Jazz* (New York: Oxford Press, 1958) and LeRoi Jones, *Blues People* (New York: William Morrow and Co., 1963).

tore into their own.**

Thus, Frankie Carle launched a big band in a new society. Could he make the grade in the big band business under the conditions permeating the post-war atmosphere? What were his chances of success in the theaters and ballrooms when a beachhead to obsolescence had begun for big bands in these places? And what were his chances in recordings when the vocals were already monopolizing the record sales? Yet Frankie Carle, who knew of "band flops" for 25 years, dared the venture in 1944.

Big bands with basically sweet rather than swing books had an inside chance for prolonged obsolescence, assuming sweet music (sometimes called "straight" music), can linger in any period of experimentation or change (Lawrence Welk and Guy Lombardo, for example.) And straight or sweet was the essence of Frankie Carle. "I wanted to play music that people would recognize readily," admitted Frankie.

At least, then, Frankie Carle did have that inside chance of proving himself and his style of music; and that, in part, was what the Hotel Pennsylvania debut in February 1944 was all about. That debut meant a beginning and an ending—the beginning of another challenge and the ending of one that had begun 28 years earlier in 1916.

**One of the more profound though terse analyses of the situation came from Chubby Jackson, who did not blame a public but the jazzmen themselves. "Jazz is being plagued by a cult of young, non-thinking, imitative musicians who'd do themselves more good by staying home and practicing than by creating bizarre night club spectacles..." q.v. *Down Beat,* October 20, 1950.

CHAPTER 3

Nicholas Colangelo's Favorites was setting up, getting ready for one of its regular Monday, Wednesday, and Saturday night dances at Columbus Hall on Westminster Street in Providence, Rhode Island. The year, 1916.

Broadway was the biggest entertainment going in 1916. Fanny Brice joined veteran W.C. Fields and Will Rogers in the "Ziegfeld Follies." Tin Pan Alley songs, ragtime, waltzes, and the cake walk were in vogue. Words like "swing," as a reference to music, and "jazz," a localism, were unheard of in the Nicholas Colangelo dance band. Waltzes were the band's *forte*. Victor and Columbia recording companies, still in their infancies, were recording, but their features were the singers. Henry Burr and Billy Murray—who were to appear later in the 1920's with Edwin J. McEnelly—had already appeared on Columbia and Victor labels by 1916. Nicholas Colangelo was but a small part of dancing America at this time, even if the Favorites were far removed from the excitement generated on Broadway or in New Orleans or in Chicago. The members of the Nicholas Colangelo's Favorites were all musicians of an 1890 vintage, their leader a classical musican from Europe.

Colangelo was padding the foot pedals on the piano so that the pedals would reach the dangling feet of a thirteen-year-old wide-eyed youth who sat high on a swivel piano seat. The piano seat had already been padded so that the youth's hands would be positioned correctly on the keyboard. The men in this 13-piece band were middle-aged, presenting a noticeable contrast to the youth at the piano, a serious-faced Francis Carlone. He jumped on and off the piano seat as Colangelo made the necessary adjustments. Francis Carlone really did not want to play that night; Francis Carlone did not want to play any night. But he resigned himself to his fate.

"Try it now, Frankie," suggested Colangelo, and Frankie positioned his small husky frame upon the stool, nodding approval that all was okay. A look of fright subsided somewhat as he fingered the keyboard.

"It's all right now, Uncle."

Nicholas Colangelo was not really an uncle. He was a first cousin to Frankie's mother Dora. Dora and all the Carlones called Nicholas Uncle Nick. Nicholas had been Frankie's piano teacher since 1908. He had not planned on Frankie's debut with the band at that particular time, although Nicholas was confident that his young pupil could handle the job well. Frankie's start in the band occurred rather abruptly, brought about by a combination of influences and incidents which spelled destiny for a disinterested Providence youngster.

A youthful Francis Carlone no more thought of music than did his father, Angelo Carlone. But Dora loved music; she loved the idea of music in the family. She remembered the enjoyment in her growing-up years when her sister Daisy practiced and played tunes on the upright in their home in New York. Dora loved to sing and would often do her chores singing, as her mother had done before her. Dora's brother Charlie was a vocalist in the wings in silent movie houses. Dora, who harbored a dream that her offspring would play music, envisioned that reality when Uncle Nick, newly arrived from Italy, came to visit the Carlones in 1908. However, young Francis Carlone had no such visions; he showed more enthusiasm for baseball with the team from Vesi Street Elementary School or for boxing at the gymnasium which another relation—an aunt's brother-in-law—managed.

One must understand the role of music in an Italian household to appreciate Dora's drive, that music in some form had to be a part of the Carlone family. Music in Italian families, particularly the poorer families, is paradoxical. It would be the rule and not the exception that a household budget include some sacrifice for music. Though a family may enjoy few amenities, the one item it desired most was the musical instrument. The essentials of the household would be the stove, the table, the bed, and the musical instrument—in something like that order. Music was culture, and in the eyes of the immigrant Italian parent, paramount. This was particularly true in the family of Dora George.

For an offspring to pursue the study of music, the mother-father relationship had in its favor another tradition so very characteristic of immigrant parents: insistence on obedience to the hierarchy in the family, i.e., obedience to every directive in all matters from anyone of the immediate family, or relation, who was older. Culture and conduct, two typical disciplines practiced by many immigrant parents, were omnipresent in the George family when Dora was growing up and after she married Angelo, persisted in the Carlone household. And it was the mother to whose charge these aspects of life were delegated almost instinctively. Obedience to mother's direction was automatic, unquestionably so if the father was satisfied with the efficacy of mother's performance in running the home. Angelo Carlone had no complaints with Dora on this account.

It would have been impossible for Dora Carlone not to solicit the indulgence of a close relative now that Colangelo had come to live in America. Dora's predilection for music in the family was not matched by her husband Angelo, but it *was* by Uncle Nick. He was the pride of the George clan. Nicholas studied extensively in Europe. He graduated from the Conservatory of Milan and studied at conservatories in Paris, Berlin, and Vienna. He was an accomplished musician, and when he came to America, it was comparatively easy for him to adapt to a more popular style of music and at the same time to make a livelihood. Nicholas played all instruments, but he favored the cornet. Having taught and played in the old country, he continued the practice in America. He formed the Nicholas Colangelo's Favorites and provided dance music around Providence for several years. Nicholas was a musician, a music teacher; Dora had a son. Nothing more need be said, especially since Uncle Nick agreed to teach Frankie and charge no fee.

When music lessons for five-year-old Frankie were discussed, he shared none of the enthusiasm of Dora or Nicholas. He wanted his baseball and boxing, two activities he engaged in regularly for most of his growing-up years. However, these activities were not cultural. Dora accepted them only insofar as they were not deterrents. Husband Angelo had no preference; he agreed to whatever the boy wanted to do, so long as

Dora approved. When Frankie tried to disregard a practice session at the piano in favor of the other activities, it was Angelo Carlone who would intercede on his behalf. "Oh, Dora," he would whine, "Let the boy do what he wants." But after Dora would vehemently oppose the Rough Rider's carefree attitude in these matters, Angelo Carlone would turn to his son and say, very authoritatively, "You do what your mother says." Frankie invariably did. Dora Carlone was more adamant than Angelo was tough.

Angelo Carlone had been a cocky, self-asserting youth when, at 16, he left home—Compo Basso, Italy, a farm community near Naples—to come to America. After shifting around Providence for two years in odd jobs, he joined the Army. As a soldier on a pass to New York, Angelo met Dora George. Dora was one of five children. Her parents had emigrated from Abruzzi, Italy. Dora, however, had been born in New York. Having similar backgrounds, Angelo and Dora found it easy to communicate with each other. Their courtship was brief and they married—he at 18, she at 17.

Angelo was a big man, standing 6 feet 3 inches and scaling 260 pounds. His burly build was carried on in Frankie's two brothers Louie and Lucky; Frankie, on the other hand, reached only 5 feet 7 inches. Angelo served with the Rough Riders and returned to civilian life a decorated man. Settling in Providence, he took a job as a molder in an iron foundry. The pay was meager, but the Carlones survived—as did their neighbors in this immigrant community. Children came quickly—Jenny, Frankie, Etta, Evelyn, Louise, Ann, Esther. It was just after Ann was born that Angelo suffered an accident on the job which led to the loss of a leg. A "cocksure" Angelo disregarded a safety precaution by not wearing unlaced shoes on the job. He was unable to get his shoe off quickly enough when molten iron spilled; consequently, he lost most of his foot. The incident was both tragic and ironic. Dora purposely had budgeted enough money for the purchase of special unlaced shoes, but Angelo—typically—thought such a requirement a lot of nonsense. Instead, "he used the money for booze," remembered

Frankie. "Pa was always in the saloon, playing cards with the men. He liked his Scotch." Over a period of time, doctors found it necessary to perform piece-meal amputations, first cutting above the ankle, then later up to the knee.

The job at the foundry became too risky for Angelo; he was forced to seek other employment. Frankie was thirteen years old at this time. "There was no unemployment compensation in those days," Frankie continued. "Ma was really concerned. Pa wasn't," he chuckled, "He was quite a guy."

Eager to work outdoors, to work with this hands, Angelo happily accepted a job digging ditches for the Rhode Island Gas Company.

Angelo's attitude never changed. He was carefree and careless; Dora was just the opposite. But their union was a happy one from the beginning, ten children having come out of it. Esther, Louie, and Lucky were born after the accident. Another child came after Lucky, but lived only a few months.

Since it seemed almost certain that five-year-old Frankie was to study music, the next question was, which instrument? Uncle Nick knew all instruments. Frankie thought about the violin more than any other instrument, primarily because a school chum Arthur Addeo, whose father owned the saloon which Angelo frequented, had begun violin lessons. But Dora was partial to the piano, even if the Carlones did not have one. Besides, Dora's sister Daisy had intimated the possibility of her coming to live with the Carlones, and Daisy played a piano. The possibility was sufficient for Dora; thus the piano was the unquestionable choice. Did this mean, then, that Frankie had a temporary reprieve until such time as Aunt Daisy would come to live with the Carlones? Certainly not.

Uncle Nick favored the European *solfeggio* method, a method of instruction which emphasized reading. The pupil learned to sight-read and to beat a tempo. "You just sing the notes and beat the time," said Frankie, as he simulated a demonstration. "The first six months I did nothing but learn to read music," he recalled. "I didn't touch a piano. We didn't have one. We were poor." He continued, "the next six, I learned the keyboard and so well that I never have to look at it. I learned to read music as most kids learn to read books. That's probably why I can play 2,000 pieces from memory."

It was almost a year later that Aunt Daisy came to live with the Carlones, and with her came a piano.

Nicholas Colangelo was a music teacher of the old school. He knew his music and showed unrestrained provocation when his young pupil had not mastered a lesson. On occasions, Frankie would experience a tap on the hands with a small rod, particularly when Nicholas expected better manipulation of notes or chords than his pupil had demonstrated. Lessons occurred twice a week, eventually encompassing harmony, theory, and composition.

"My mother would get me up at 7 in the morning," remembered Frankie. "I'd practice before going to school—even when I came home for lunch. After school, Ma kept me at the piano for at least an hour before I went out to play. She kept two things close by—a clock and a strap."

On one occassion, Dora had reason to use the strap. When Frankie was nine years old and considered to be old enough to go downtown alone, Dora would let him go to Uncle Nick's studio for lessons. At least Dora thought Frankie was going to piano lessons. For a whole month, Frankie did not go to Uncle Nick but instead went to see nickelodeon movies. "I fooled Mother when she asked me to play the lesson because I read well," related Frankie. "But one day my 'Uncle' phoned to ask why I had not been coming for lessons. Boy, did I get it." After that incident, Dora accompanied her son to Uncle Nick's. The reprimand was Dora's doing. Angelo chuckled at the incident. "If a kid studying music doesn't practice," offered Frankie, "that's Mama or Papa's fault."

During the early years of Frankie's piano lessons, Dora persisted in two demands. Frankie accompanied his mother, without question, to concerts, especially when such great artists as Sergei Rachmaninoff and Artur Rubinstein were performing. "I've seen them all," sighed Frankie. "Ma saw to that." Not too enthusiastic at first, Frankie eventually began to enjoy the concerts. Listening to such great artists may have contributed to the awakening of an apparently dormant talent, that of distinguishing keenly between tone qualities. He really had no other comparison in piano technique to make, other than with great classical artists, for Dora never allowed Frankie to listen to popular pianists on records or go to see them in person. Later in this career, Frankie was grateful for this restriction. It was probable, it would seem, that since he did not have any popular pianist to imitate, he developed his own style.

Thus, a routine in music instruction began early, even though Frankie had inclinations to other activity. During his eight years in grammar school, an agile and exceptionally well-coordinated Francis Carlone enjoyed all the play peculiar to young boys. He was literally forced to surrender to the discipline demanded in piano instruction. Dora saw to that. Besides, if Frankie disobeyed Mother, he had Father to contend with, and did not Father constantly remind him to "listen to your mother?" By his own admission, Frankie would often fret and cry when he could not go out with the boys to participate in athletic competition. Francis was never aware of the apparent contradiction of forces within him during the later years of grammar school. On the one hand, he could not wait until the school bell rang, mostly to get out and play ball or go to the gym to box. On the other hand, while in the confines of the classroom, he daydreamed about music, a subject for which he showed a preference. One of his teachers seemed to sense that Francis showed some trace of musical talent. In his "Memoir," Frankie noted:

> One teacher whom I've never forgotten all these years was Miss Irene Walsh, who gave me encouragement and help, for it seemed to her that I had a gift of music ability.
>
> I wasn't the best student in class, for I day-dreamed most of the time about music. My best three subjects were geography, history, and I was especially good in music. Miss Walsh used to keep me after school to teach me some of the fine points in music, which was a great help towards the future for me in the music world.

But Francis had much energy to burn; he wanted to move about. He loved physical challenges and found great enjoyment in baseball and boxing. It was at the gymnasium or on the ball field that the son of Angelo Carlone was evident. The aggressiveness of the pugilist under the wing of the mother's relative at the gym was quite contrary to the quiet disciplined demeanor of the prodigy under "Uncle Nick." And Dora was the liaison, of course favoring Francis Carlone, piano player. She did understand growing boys, however. Dora realized that her son needed diversion and compromised, permitting him to spend some time in doing what he found enjoyable with his friends. Frankie played ball. He did well, too, as an infielder and pitcher. The game did not seem to be dangerous; he never came home bruised or bleeding. Dora never objected, so long as he continued with his piano instruction and practice and never came home with any evidence of injury.

Frankie would also spend much time at the National Club, a fighters' gymnasium, the one managed by Dora's relative, several times removed. And any relative was good enough for Dora; she felt secure that kinfolk were there to look after her son.

Many of the professional fighters of the day trained at the National Club, and Frankie, being related to the "boss", enjoyed unlimited freedom of the club. Whenever he could, he would work out, getting hints from most of the professionals. Titleholder Jack Delaney and Johnny Dundee worked out there. "I got pointers from Delaney," recalled Frankie. "He was one of the best at the time."

By the time Frankie was 12 years old, he had compiled 10 straight ring victories. In his boxing career, he had fought thirty bouts in the 118-pound class, under the name of Frankie Young. Dora did not share Angelo Carlone's pride and enthusiasm in the young pugilist, but she had no cause to complain. As a matter of fact, Dora really did not understand what Frankie was engaged in, but the lack of injury appeased her displeasure in father Angelo's excitement when Frankie informed him of the victory or details of the bout. But then it happened.

Frankie was paired against a "scrawny little black kid named Billy Cook," as he recalled it. "He not only knocked me cold," related Frankie Young, "but gave me a beautiful shiner." That night when Frankie went home, Dora took one look at his eye and her mind was made up. The boxing career of Frankie Young came to an immediate end, despite Angelo's protestations to the contrary. Angelo surveyed the face of his fighter son and could only call the shiner what it was—"a beaut!"

Very shortly after Frankie's boxing career halted, Angelo Carlone suffered the accident in the foundry. The outlook for the Carlone family was not bright. Now thirteen years old, Frankie would have to help out. Boxing was obviously out of the question. Frankie played the piano well, and "Uncle Nick" had a dance orchestra. One dollar a week would certainly be some help, even if it represented three working nights. Nothing more need be said.

Thus, a thirteen-year-old disinterested Providence youngster hopped on and off the piano stool as Nicholas Colangelo adjusted the height of the seat to permit short dangling feet to reach the piano pedals. This night, Francis Carlone was to play in public for the first time with Nicholas Colangelo's Favorites. That was in the spring of 1916, at Columbus Hall, on Westminster Street in Providence, Rhode Island.

Francis Carlone, 13, at the piano in Nicolas Colangelo's Favorites, 1916. Uncle Nick is at the far right (with mustache).

CHAPTER 4

Dora Carlone was one of the proudest mothers in Providence when Frankie received his diploma in June 1917. In her experience, not many youngsters growing up in New York's Little Italy had sustained eight years of formal instruction. Frankie's graduation was a cultural breakthrough and a fulfillment of her obligation to her way of life. She was proud, but at the same time anxious. The young folks completing their elementary school in those days went on to jobs out of pure necessity. She had hoped Frankie would go on with schooling. He did for a period of time, but did not finish. At this time in his life, he really began to think seriously about music; but he also wanted to earn money. He knew well the financial straits of the large Carlone family. He first began to earn a salary during summer vacation at the ages of twelve and thirteen in the Wauskuck Woolen Mills in Providence as a yarn carrier. Also, at thirteen, he played three nights per week with Nicholas Colangelo's Favorites. At fourteen, in addition to the night work, he worked as a stockroom boy at the Outlet Company, lying that he was sixteen to get the job. Lasting not too long at the Outlet Company, he secured another department store job, at the Boston Store, selling bed sheets and pillows. But during the time of the latter two jobs, the piano meant more to Frankie. He was practicing longer hours, doing more with music, even playing the newer kind i.e., not classical. Frankie continued with Uncle Nick during the last year of elementary school and toward the end of 1917.

In 1917, newer music, jazz, notably that of the Old Dixieland Jazz Band and the William C. Handy orchestra, appeared on Victor and Columbia labels. By the time Frankie was 14 years old, Dora's earlier edict that Frankie was not to listen to popular music had long since been rescinded. He was adept at picking up the newer jazz tempo. And since he was devoting many more hours to the piano, no kind of music escaped him. Scott Joplin was already legendary in ragtime piano, and Frankie could expertly manipulate the keys in ragtime. He could even "imitate a pianola to perfection," remembered Henry Jacobson, one of the original five in Frankie's first band. Hence, a unique talent was becoming evident at this time in Frankie's life, and this Providence youth unconsciously accepted whatever keyboard harmony challenged that talent.

The concerts to which Dora had been taking Frankie, through the elementary school years, had already assumed a different flavor, one of welcome anticipation rather than of perfunctory participation. His tenure in trade school, a school of design (in which field he showed some aptitude), was short-lived, and though Dora desired Frankie to pursue education further, she appreciated his increased devotion to piano practice and instruction. However much more he was becoming attentive to his music, Frankie still wanted to work, especially since Angelo Carlone earned a smaller salary after the foundry accident.

I

When Frankie turned fifteen, Nicholas Colangelo cancelled his ballroom lease. Not quite pleased with the various jobs and other avenues of training he had experienced, Frankie now wanted only a career in playing the piano. He sought piano playing jobs in orchestras around Providence. "No one seemed to want to hire me," recollected the young piano player. "Being a youngster, and of Italian descent—and in those days we were considered a low class of people—it was difficult breaking into the field of music."

In the spring Frankie went to see his chum Arthur Addeo whom he had not seen for almost two years. In that time Addeo had organized a band of his own, but "even he couldn't use me," commented Frankie, shaking his head dejectedly. "He really thought I couldn't play."

Thus, in early 1918, the Providence youth of fifteen made up his mind to form his own band. But that venture would have to be postponed, for there surfaced another interlude before a Francis Carlone group could be organized. Frankie related the event in his "Memoir."

> My mother decided to take a trip to New Jersey [West Hoboken, now Union City] to visit a few relatives, and I went along with her. I tried to find work. I went to New York and walked into the music publishing house of Harry Von Tilzer. I auditioned for a Mr. Harry Bloom. He didn't have any openings, but he told me to see a Pat Rooney in some small studio, who was looking for a pianist to play for his dance team. I was given the job and was told to report for final rehearsal on Monday, for the act was supposed to open in Kansas City. And when he said we'd be traveling on a vaudeville circuit all the way to the West Coast, it scared me. I never went back to rehearse.

A few days later, Frankie returned to New York and secured a job in a nightclub as the pianist for a singing waiter. What Frankie did not know was that the owner—"with one eye," he added—apparently had gangland connections, for the clientele was a mixture of the respectable citizenry and mob-affiliates. Frankie remained there for almost two weeks, splitting the tips with the singing waiter. "One night," remembered the pianist, "some gangster, flanked by bodyguards, came into the place. Before you knew it, the shooting started. People scattered. I ran to the kitchen and out of the place—and never went back!"

Frankie no longer entertained the notion of working in New York; West Hoboken was less dangerous. As noted in his "Memoir:"

> I landed a job as pianist in a silent movie theater. It was the Strand Theater. I stayed there three months until my mother and I left to go back home.

It was early summer when Frankie and Dora returned to Providence. Having been unsuccessful in securing a job with a band before his jaunt to Jersey and then experiencing trauma in New York, Frankie proceeded to look for musicians, to try organizing his own group. Finding musicians was not easy. Jazz had begun to appear in clubs in New York, in Chicago, and in Kansas City, and had attracted many music-oriented youths. Some musicians he tried to recruit did not read music; Frankie wanted players who could read music especially arranged for dancing. Frankie was so accustomed to reading music that he could not readily accept departure from the practice. He really intended to organize a band with at least ten members, but he settled for six, including himself. It was at this time that Francis Carlone changed his name to Frankie Carle, and, as all young talents are wont to do, he selected a rather colorful name for his group.

The drummer of the group was Henry Jacobson of Providence, three years Frankie's senior. Jacobson, of Fall River, Massachusetts, as of this writing, retired from a career as a successful corporate executive. He imparts his recollections of that first Carle band:

> We were known as "Frankie Carle's Red Flame Syncopators" and I had a circular painting on the head of my bass drum, showing the name and a fire, flame, etc. Incidentally, I have a brother who played the saxophone with another band, and he used to kid me about playing with "Frankie Carle's Stinkopators."

The Red Flame Syncopators included Ray Whittaker, violin, Harry Ivonelli, trombone, John Accevedo, trumpet, Pete Condullo, bass, Jacobson, and Frankie.

As a leader, Frankie would now experience a new dimension in music. Did he have the proper temperament and attitude to nurture an *esprit de corps?* Did he have what it takes to gain the respect and discipline necessary in a dance band? He could handle a piano, but the piano was inanimate. Yes, indeed, the attributes of bandleadership were present at the outset of the Red Flame Syncopators.

"He was the nicest person I played for," said Jacobson, "always pleasant, always had a nice smile and always most considerate." The point of Frankie's sincere concern for others was borne out previously by Hack O'Brien who was speaking of a Frankie Carle in the 1930's. Jacobson, in speaking of Frankie ten years earlier, writes:

> In the days I played, none of us could afford a car and our transporation was by trolley cars. Drummers were required to get a pass for the bass drum, store it with the motorman, and pay an extra fare for same. I mention the foregoing because of all the fellows I played for, Frankie was the only one who used to give me 50 cents extra to cover the extra expense.

As a person, a precocious seventeen-year old Frankie Carle showed admirable character; as a musician, he displayed exceptional talent. Jacobson attests to that talent:

> To appreciate his expertise, you would have to live with him as I did for several nights each week. In those days, we used to get our names on a music publisher's list, and in return for pushing their numbers, would get free orchestrations. We would bring these on the job, give the piano part to Frankie, and he would play a solo without having seen the number before. This greatly impressed me because I had a brother-in-law who also played the piano and he had to really practice a new number before playing.

Play the number without having seen it before? Yes, remember a nine-year old Frankie who fooled his mother by playing a lesson from Uncle Nick when Frankie had not gone to Uncle Nick?

"I also remember that Frankie once showed me a syncopated beat on the drum," continued Jacobson, "which I used a lot, and at times he would duplicate it on the piano, and right in tune."

Hence the first Carle band seemingly possessed what was necessary—a considerate leader with a talent recognized and appreciated by his sidemen. These qualities, to be sure, would evoke enthusiasm, hard work, and response.

The prodigy of Nicholas Colangelo and the charge of Dora Carlone was on his own in the trial of the Red Flame Syncopators. Dora's anxiety persisted not so much that Frankie no longer continued formal education, but that he might become frustrated if the band venture failed. The venture relied on one thing only, bookings. Dora encouraged Frankie, even if many weeks went by without a booking. She fully realized how much a career in music meant to Frankie. Even father Angelo had come to understand that this, perhaps, was what his boy really wanted to do. Did not Angelo always express the attitude, "Let the boy do what he wants!"?

Unfortunately, the Red Flame Syncopators enjoyed fewer bookings than their leader anticipated. They played numerous weddings, special occasion parties, and some dances, but nothing on a continuing basis.

The Red Flame Syncopators enjoyed two comparatively noteworthy successes just after World War I ended. The first was a dance in a local but very popular ballroom, the Colonial Ballroom, in Central Falls. The ballroom was filled to capacity, and people who came to dance were not disappointed. Judging by the crowd and the apparent fun-time they were enjoying, Frankie was optimistic for the future of the band. "A lot of people told us we were good," remembered Frankie, "but . . ." And he shrugged his shoulders.

The second big occasion occurred in Providence, and although this occasion followed the first by a matter of weeks, it would be fallacious to presume that the Syncopators landed the job on the strength of their performance in Central Falls. This second occasion was a "Welcome Home" dance for the doughboys of the 13th Infantry Rhode Island. It was the biggest event of the year. Every dignitary in Providence and environs attended. The people complimented the Red Flame Syncopators freely. The Syncopators became very confident that they had established a foothold. So they thought. Much to the dismay of Frankie and his Syncopators, however, the going was downhill thenceforth. The Syncopators worked fewer jobs and these jobs, by comparison with the Central Falls and the 13th Infantry affairs, were disconcertingly small.

It was a long, cold winter. Pete Condullo bought a used car which the musicians used for transportation. Although the Syncopators literally froze getting to a job, the car was a blessing. Everybody was running out of money, what little there was in the first place. But an incident with the car on the way to Fall River just about cinched the fate of the Red Flame Syncopators. On a very cold and windy day the automobile stalled on the road, "directly across from a fire station," remembered Frankie. Condullo checked the gas tank—by lighting a match to see down the tank. Fortunately the tank did not explode, but a streak of flame—like a 'blow' torch—routed the onlookers who scattered in all directions. The infrequency of the bookings, the freezing conditions of travel, and the general disappointment of six enthusiastic syncopators contributed to the waning desire to continue. Then, having come close to disaster on their way to Fall River, the Red Flame Syncopators suspected futility, and in 1919 the group dissolved.

Dora, meanwhile, observed that the Red Flame Syncopators were less and less engaged, but she would never make an issue of the dearth of bookings.

And as Frankie covered up disappointment with an exuberance over his accepting another job, so Dora played the game with jubilation that he was again to play piano in a silent movie house. Frankie began at the Casino Theater in Central Falls, a job that lasted for six months and one that paid more money than he had theretofore been able to command.

Thus, Frankie's first venture as a bandleader flopped. The Casino Theater did not challenge Frankie's talent, but he was satisfied, for, at least, he was bringing home some money. He fulfilled his obligation at the Casino, but as the months moved on, he became restless. The routine—the monotony—eventually prevailed, and Frankie, eager to get back to the music he wanted to play, came back as a sideman, the second time a sideman in his four-year professional life. This time, he joined Ray Welch in 1920.

II

Ray Welch was a guitarist who had played with various groups in and around Providence before he organized his own band. Being ill often, Welch did not always show up for the job; consequently, he did not enjoy good control of the band. But he did manage to secure bookings, and the band held together and played regularly in Providence. "In the band when I started were two Jewish boys," recalled its pianist, "one who in later years was Eddy Duchin's manager. Also two Italian boys, one who was myself, and two Irish boys, and things looked a bit brighter." The Welch band was busy for weeks at a time, but the "brighter" outlook was its audition in Boston for May Yohe.

May Yohe, a songstress whose beauty captivated audiences of the 1890's, had given up the stage at about the turn of the century to marry Lord Francis Hope. After a long marriage which ended in divorce, Yohe returned to the stage. She was over fifty years old at the time, but she had sufficient backing and influence to promote a musical extravaganza.

The Yohe audition took place at the B. F. Keith Theater in Boston in early fall, 1920. Being theatrically perceptive, Yohe not only selected the Welch group over several others which auditioned, but also directed the management to incorporate a solo by Frankie into her act. Frankie, as well as others in the Welch band, did solos in the course of the audition.

The May Yohe show was earmarked to play the B. F. Keith circuit from Indianapolis to New York, with other theaters in between. Most engagements were for one week; some ran three days, and others were one-nighters. Yohe adjusted her itinerary to her stamina and the show was on the road from mid-September through mid-June.

It was not too far into the season when Welch dropped out because of bad health. Yohe, who had assumed control of the band in the meantime, made some changes and additions and named Frankie manager. She called the group the May Yohe Shelatone band. "Technically, I guess you could say that that really was my band," surmised the young manager.

Vaudeville with Yohe, three years of it, provided the young Providence pianist with training and experience which enhanced his talent, but Frankie cherished most the excitement of being on the same bill with great names in vaudeville. "We were billed once with Sophie Tucker," he disclosed. "Audiences sure loved her. Years later when I had the big band, Marjorie [his daughter and singer in his later big band] and I went to see her in West Virginia. Sophie loved Marjorie. Our talks went back to vaudeville days."

"Another time," he continued, "we were billed with Pat Rooney—the one I almost joined several years before when I went with Ma to Jersey. He wondered why I had never returned for rehearsal. I was embarrassed to tell him 'I was scared.' "

Frankie chuckled at this reminiscence; and as he regained consciousness after a brief reverie, he stammered, "And Olson and Johnson—they were funny. We were on with them, too, at the Palace in New York."

Probing deeply into his memory, with a frown and a squint as if trying to view a hazy screen of moving events, Frankie rose from his captain's chair to get a tiny date book from a cardboard box in his closet. "At the Colonial Theater in Erie, Pa.," he then continued, "the week of April 8, 1923"—he added positively, fingering the notation in a 1923 diary, "we were on with Ted Lorraine and Minto, an act called The Moth and the Flame, and Traps, the youngest drummer in the country. Do you know who that was," he began to ask, but blurted out the name of the drummer in the same breath—"Buddy Rich. He was only about five years old. His mother and father were there that day. I talked to them."

Many times when he was doing the Yohe show on the road, Frankie had received offers to play with dance bands. Dance bands were becoming more popular; there were more of them around now than there were when Frankie first tried getting into the business. Although Frankie enjoyed vaudeville immensely, his predilection for dance bands remained with him. But Frankie turned down all offers, primarily out of loyalty. "Yohe treated me very kindly," he said. "I was making a pretty good salary. She gave me run of the band and put solo parts in her act for me. I couldn't leave her after all she did."

Reviews of the Yohe show were generally fair. The accompaniment, however, often eclipsed the star's performance. Yohe was enough of a professional to realize that the reviewers were, at best, charitable. One review following a Kansas City engagement late in 1922 noted:

> May Yohe's voice has none of its once charming sweetness or range and while her beauty has faded with advancing years, she still possesses personality and all her stage mannerisms. The former Lady Francis Hope has a unique act. She is the attraction, but her orchestra is one of the best heard at the Towers this season. Frank Carle leads the orchestra . . .

In the third season on the road in 1923, the effects of the pace began to show in Yohe, who was approaching her fifty-fourth birthday. But, as Yohe's participation diminished, Frankie's accelerated. The show started in Portland, Maine, in September, with a jaunt into the Imperial Theater in Montreal before coming down through New England. Frankie began doing more than leading the Shelatones, often filling in for a cancelled act. At the Towers in Camden he filled in for Leo Minton, in addition to doing the Yohe show. On another occasion he played for the Warde Sisters' dancing act, and after obliging the Warde Sisters, did two solos, "Kitten on the Keys" and "Love Sends a Gift of Roses." His rendition of "Kitten on the Keys" attracted some attention.

Displaying a capability in both leading and performing, convinced management that the Shelatone band could well perform alone when the star of the show became ill. A week after the Camden show, the band went on without her for an entire week at the Globe Theater in Philadelphia. Again, when Yohe became ill, the band went on for the three-day engagement at Nixon's Grand Opera House in North Philadelphia, followed by another three-day engagement at the North Shore Theater in Gloucester, Mass., December 6-8. As a matter of fact, management only cancelled one three-day engagement because of Yohe's illness during the 1923 season. She returned for the December 9 show at Loew's State Theater in Boston, but she had informed the troupe before this time that after the remaining 1923 commitments, her theatrical career would come to an end. That left shows in Providence, Troy, and, lastly, Albany where the May Yohe show would close the week of December 23. The announcement was, in effect, notice to the troupe.

The next two shows following Loew's in Boston—the Mystical Theater in Malden, Mass., and the Broadway in South Boston—the band performed without Yohe. She returned for the one-week stand at the E. F. Albee Theater in Providence and finished the last two three-day engagements at Proctor's Theaters in Troy and in Albany, N.Y. Yohe was too exhausted to make the all-bill midnight supper on Christmas in Schenectady, which affair supposedly would have been a farewell dinner in her honor. But Yohe, emotionally spent toward the closing weeks of her career, purposely avoided a testimonial farewell. And when the curtain came down in Albany on December 29, all the troupe and the other acts, including the dance act of Walsh & Faye, individually expressed their good wishes to an appreciative May Yohe. "She was a grand lady," concluded the manager of the May Yohe Shelatone band.

III

When the Yohe show played Loew's Theater in Boston on December 9, in the audience was Jerry Cook, manager of the Edwin J. McEnelly orchestra, a Springfield, Mass.-based band doing a one-nighter. Jerry Cook remained for a second performance that night.

Edwin J. McEnelly headed an eight-piece dance band and played out of Marlboro, Mass. during the years of World War I. He organized a bigger aggregation toward the end of the war, when Jerry Cook, an energetic and enterprising agent,

May Yohe's Shelatone Orchestra. Frankie, second from right (hand on manager's shoulder) became musical director. Orchestra toured Keith circuit. Circ. 1922-23.

latched on to the 14-piece outfit and brought it to Riverside Park in Springfield.

McEnelly and Cook enjoyed financial success at Riverside. Under an aggressive Jerry Cook, McEnelly soon attracted the attention of the broadcasting networks and recording companies. Within a short two years, McEnelly became known as the "Toast of New England" and "Waltz King" (not to be confused with a later "Waltz King," Wayne King). He landed a coast-to-coast broadcast (NBC) and a Victor recording contract, his band being billed as the Edwin J. McEnelly Victor Recording Orchestra.

The public's acceptance of popular music and the consequent growing crowds at Riverside Park motivated Cook to undertake a more ambitious project, a ballroom. Riverside was a summer dance pavilion; Cook wanted a ballroom for the colder months. Cook negotiated with local banks for backing, which he secured, and leased an abandoned building on Dwight Street. Cook renovated the building. The place was exquisitely decorated, and because the reflection of the crystal lights resembled a butterfly, he named the ballroom The Butterfly.

Cook had envisioned his new ballroom as a lure for bigger name bands that at this time were gaining widespread popularity. Cook was a businessman; he knew what attracted people, and dancing promised to be one of the biggest attractions in Springfield. The McEnelly group was to be the start of a long list of bands that would play The Butterfly.

In the winter of 1923, McEnelly played Keith's Theater in Boston, a usual return-engagement for the Christmas season. Cook accompanied McEnelly to Boston, and when McEnelly proceeded to the next booking, Cook remained in town. It was at this time that Cook attended the Yohe show at the State Theater and remained for a second performance.

Cook was impressed with Frankie's individual efforts that night. Apparently, he was excited, for when he went backstage to talk with Frankie, he announced, "I like your style: did you ever think of leaving the show?" even before he identified himself or stated his purpose. Introducing himself in an afterthought, Cook explained that he managed a big band and that he was building a ballroom in Springfield. He expounded on the future of ballrooms and his hope that Frankie would join the Edwin McEnelly band. Frankie hardly uttered a word, but he did smile. The sincerity and vigor with which Cook had presented himself and his intentions effected an intuitive judgment in Frankie's mind that the man was an individual one could trust. Frankie took an immediate liking to Cook, and as the latter raved on, Frankie became interested. In more subdued tones, Cook explained that the salary would be at least $60 per week. Frankie was to understand that McEnelly already had a pianist, Frank Byrnes, who had been with McEnelly since the war years. Frankie, of course, would have to audition for McEnelly; but Cook was not so inclined to discuss the audition as he was predisposed to predict Frankie's future at the new ballroom. That future included featured spots and publicity in billing, all in due time, naturally. Cook envisioned more for Frankie than the chair of a second pianist. In the meantime, since the ballroom would not be ready until spring, Cook would arrange for Frankie to play with McEnelly in several ballroom engagements on McEnelly's itinerary.

With the Yohe show folding within a few weeks, Frankie needed little time to deliberate; he accepted the proposition.

Cook then returned to Springfield.

IV

In the summer and whenever time and distance permitted during the vaudeville season, Frankie would come home. When Frankie joined Yohe, his brother Lucio (Lucky) was born, boosting the Carlone count to nine children—Jenny, Frankie, Etta, Evelyn, Louise, Ann, Esther, Louie, and Lucky. Frankie felt a responsibility toward the family and asserted himself in family affairs whether he was home for the day or for the month. Each time he left home again, he repeatedly implored reassurance from his mother Dora that everything was "ok."

The older sisters, Jenny and Etta, were now working in the silk mills in Providence. Father Angelo seemed adjusted to his handicap and was in good spirits. His drinking had neither decreased nor increased. "Once, though," related Frankie, "Pa brought home a keg of beer one Saturday and put it in the cellar. The next day, May suggested that we have some beer with dinner." Frankie shook his head and grimaced momentarily, "Do you know there wasn't any left? Pa drank the whole keg the day before!"

Dora looked forward to Frankie's visits. She was inquisitive, but Frankie never minded obliging her. She was happy that Frankie looked good and seemed content, but she queried him about his piano playing and if what he was doing was really what he wanted to do. Frankie would generally and lightly dismiss the subject in the affirmative. With other, younger children needing constant attention, Dora had little time to worry unnecessarily about her young pianist, about whom she would boast to the neighbors. After all, he was playing the piano in all the nice places for such a big star as May Yohe.

As Jerry Cook brought the news to McEnelly, so Frankie brought the news to his family when the Yohe show played Providence the week of December 17.

The familiar aroma of garlic and olive oil permeated the Carlone house; Dora was preparing Angelo's favorite meal—spaghetti and meat balls—when Frankie came home. Frankie tolerated the aroma, but he had not partaken of the cuisine since he was a little boy. Angelo was never able to understand his son's dislike for Italian cooking and preference for chicken and hamburgers; but, after a moment of amazement, he would turn to Dora and say, "Let the boy eat what he wants." Invariably, Dora did, preparing hamburger or chicken and never minding it.

Frankie told the family the news of his prospects with the McEnelly band. The news added to the merriment of the season in the Carlone household. Jenny, the oldest of the children, and teen-age sisters Etta and Evelyn were excited to tears and smiles. The younger girls, Louise and Esther, were excited because their older sisters were excited. And the two little ones, Louie and Lucky, did not know what to think—was big brother leaving home?

Dora was happy for Frankie on more than one count. In vaudeville, Frankie's homecomings had been infrequent from September through June. Springfield was only some 70 miles from Providence. The fact of Springfield's favorable geography and the mutual enthusiasm and excitement in the family assured her that Frankie would return home often.

Angelo Carlone was happy, too, and also on several counts. Angelo understood what it meant to a young man to do "what he wants to do," and Frankie's optimism and obvious happiness assured him that Frankie was doing just that. Besides, Frankie was the first-born son and now a grown man who showed genuine concern for his family. Why, hadn't Frankie contributed willingly to the family ever since he was a young teenager? Hadn't he managed to save enough money from his numerous jobs as he was growing up to help provide his father with an artificial leg? When on the road in his work, hadn't Frankie always sent money home to help out? Angelo had never wanted his eldest son to concern himself with family needs; he would remind Frankie to take care of himself, never to deny himself anything when he was away. But Angelo was powerless when he realized how hurt Frankie would be when Angelo even intimated that the boy should not be so very considerate. He accepted his son's gestures with such expressions as "Son, you didn't have to do that," or "Frankie, now why did you do that?" Angelo recognized and secretly appreciated this quality in his young man of a son. And Angelo, too, could now look forward to his frequent homecomings; for Frankie was always good competition in a game of cards.

Angelo, who loved playing cards with a passion, particularly at the saloon with the men, had taught Frankie pinochle, rummy, poker, an Italian favorite *thrisetta,* and cribbage when Frankie was a tot in kindergarten. When Dora and Uncle Nick had talked about piano lessons for a five-year-old Frankie, Angelo's lack of encouragement was perhaps due not so much to a dislike of music as to fear of losing a card partner. The women far outnumbered the men in a growing Carlone household, and traditionally, women did not play cards.

Hence, after a festive fish dinner on the eve of Christmas Eve, Angelo pushed aside the plates and silverware, signaling only one thing—the game was on.

V

In February, 1924, with May Yohe and vaudeville behind him, Frankie went to Springfield to audition for McEnelly, as Cook suggested.

When Cook brought McEnelly the news of the discovery of a piano player, McEnelly did not seem overly enthusiastic. McEnelly did have a capable pianist in Frank Byrnes, but he also had implicit faith in Cook's judgment. If nothing else, McEnelly was at least curious.

The meeting of Frankie and Edwin McEnelly was very proper and cordial. Edwin McEnelly was a proper and cordial gentleman, and in this instance he appeared more like an elder knight of the Court receiving a 21-year old page.

Cook presided at this meeting and, typical of his business-mindedness, did most of the talking. The three men went into the studio, where Frankie proceeded with the audition. Frankie struck some 16 bars in warm-up and hesitated momentarily to adjust his seating. Then he began to play. Frankie had fingered hardly halfway through the audition when McEnelly, breaking his stern countenance with a half-smile, nodded approvingly to Cook. Nothing more needed to be said.

McEnelly's itinerary called for three more engagements—in Marlboro, Athol, and Springfield, Massachusetts. As Cook had promised, Frankie played with McEnelly at these engagements as the second pianist.

These experiences differed from vaudeville. They were strictly ballroom. The crowds were larger than those Frankie had encountered with his Syncopators. The crowds were also larger than those Colangelo's Favorites had drawn. Francis Carlone had come a long way in the eight years since Colangelo's Favorites, and Francis Carlone was yet a young man. It was just two months short of seven years since he had received his Providence Public School diploma.

Then Cook's Butterfly opened.

CHAPTER 5

The Butterfly Ballroom opened formally on April 19, 1924—the same day on which NBC's new studio for Springfield, WBZ opened, with the McEnelly broadcast that evening. Dan Harrington, manager of the ballroom and its regular master of ceremonies, emceed the program of music by the Edwin J. McEnelly Orchestra, the "Toast of New England." The opening, however, was limited to a select audience, mostly dignitaries and celebrities. The public opening of the Butterfly occurred the following Monday, April 21.

The McEnelly roster included McEnelly, violin; Ken Farnsworth, tenor and bass saxophone; Charles Diamond, saxophone; Clarence Grancey, trumpet; Fred Berman, trumpet, Homer Green, trombone; Harry Fowlkes, tuba and string bass; Louis Publicover, banjo; Waino Kuppe, trumpet; George Gallagher, drums; Frankie Marks, clarinet and saxophone; Frankie Byrnes, first piano; and Frankie Carle, second piano. McEnelly did not set a precedent by using two pianos. It is believed, but not substantiated, that Fred Waring made a similar move earlier.

Jerry Cook's dream became a reality. The Butterfly Ballroom flourished, however, not merely on the strength of the success at Riverside Park, but because of Cook's faculty of foresight and his relentless pursuit of a commercially sound venture. As the ballroom prospered, so did the bands that played there. Meeting the lease commitment was no struggle for Cook.

Besides being aware of the increasing popularity of dance bands—their growing numbers and their exposure in clubs and ballrooms and on the airwaves—Cook was also cognizant of an expanding recording industry. In addition to the earliest labels, such as Victor, Columbia, Edison, and Emerson, others as Brunswick, Gennett, Okeh, Vocalion, and Banner were pressing the sounds of big bands. By the time the Butterfly Ballroom celebrated its first anniversary, Paul Whiteman, Ted Weems, Coon-Sanders, Leo Reisman, Isham Jones, the Cotton Pickers,

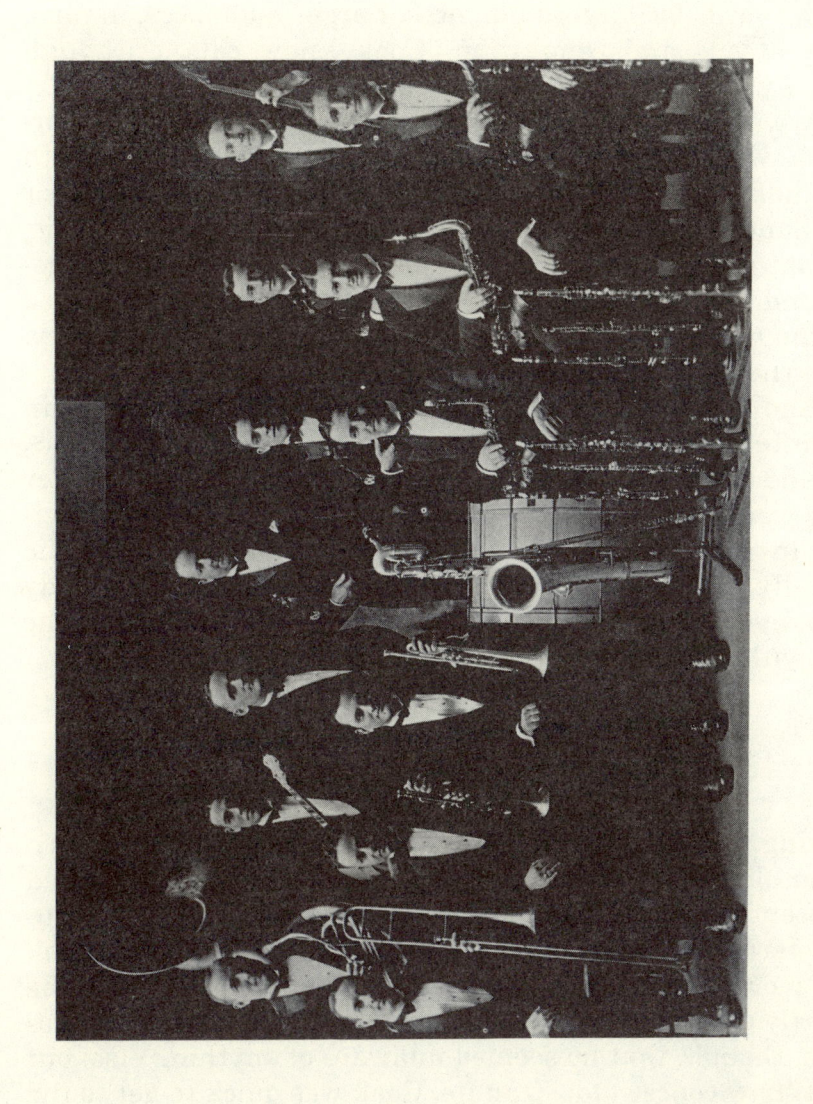

McEnelly Band, 1924. Frankie is third from right, top row.

Garber-Davis, Sam Lanin, Vincent Lopez, Abe Lyman, Ben Bernie, Fletcher Henderson, Waring's Pennsylvanians, Jean Goldkette, Fats Waller, and others had already appeared on records. And now McEnelly was on the Victor label. Bands that enjoyed exposure on records became widely known and hence drawing cards for larger audiences. Larger audiences, in turn, meant status and reputation. Cook knew this. Although McEnelly would be the "house" band at the Butterfly, McEnelly was not to be the only band there. The McEnelly orchestra was not a jazz band, i.e., "hot." It compared more with the bands of Paul Whiteman, Guy Lombardo, Ben Bernie, or Coon-Sanders. Cook intended also to bring in "hotter" music, like that of Fletcher Henderson and Fats Waller. He was determined to make the Butterfly draw big names, names linked with the music scene in New York, Chicago, and Kansas City. Before the decade was over, Cook had done just that.

McEnelly's orchestra played regularly at the Butterfly in the winter months and at Riverside in the summer months. The band traveled on occasion, but never extensively, and other bands would come into the Butterfly. McEnelly also participated in what became known as the "battle of bands." The McEnelly arrangement was a stable setup. Frankie had steady employment, and he had Sundays off—which, to be sure, he spent with his family in Providence.

I

During his first year with McEnelly, a young and taciturn 21-year old Frankie Carle, whose flirtatious broad smile belied his essentially Victorian nature, adjusted to a new environment. Jerry Cook was especially kind to Frankie; indeed, Cook acted more like a godfather than a general manager of the Butterfly enterprise. Cook was so very wrapped up in business affairs, though, that he seemed unaware of anything else; but he did show concern for Frankie. Cook was quick to get to the heart of a problem and make judicious suggestions for solving it, providing, of course, that the problem was business. In any other matter he often appeared foolish. "Once, when the band was traveling by bus to a job," recalled Frankie, "the bus driver became fidgety, muttering several times, 'there it goes again.' And when he turned to me and Cook, the driver informed us that the spark plugs were missing. Cook immediately suggested 'Well, why don't you keep the bus locked in the garage at night?' " When Frankie and the driver laughed, Cook looked at them quizzically; he thought the driver meant that someone had stolen the spark plugs!

Besides Cook, Frankie befriended many of the regular customers at the Butterfly and at Riverside, some of whom expressed their desire that he give piano instruction to their sons or daughters. He did begin to take in pupils, but was careful to budget his time so that this new activity would not interfere with his own daily practice or with his time off to go home to Providence. Other customers befriended the piano player and invited him to their homes or to dinner, even to card games. Playing cards became a habit for Frankie while he was in Springfield. Members of the Springfield Police Department were among the ballroom's customers. One of them in particular, Fred Cullen, invited Frankie to join them at cards in the station after work. Actually, the Butterfly was Cullen's beat. He was supposed to stand at the door; but he would come, in uniform, to the bandstand to watch Frankie play. Eventually, Frankie accepted his offer to play cards and became a regular pinochle player at the police station, much as Angelo Carlone had years earlier become a regular player with the boys at the saloon.

Thus, daily practice at the piano, teaching, nightly dances and mingling with the customers, card games, jaunts to Providence, constituted Frankie's routine during the first year in Springfield. The one setback he met with occurred in April, 1924, and involved Edith House. She refused Frankie's initial advances. Edith House, one of nine children, was the pretty daughter of Fred and Loretta House.

Fred and Loretta House enjoyed a better-than-average life

in Springfield. Fred had settled in that city after an assignment in the West Indies as a member of the King's Band of England, a band which traveled widely. He was a bassoon player, quartered in London for a time. In the course of his travels, he met Loretta in Nova Scotia. They were married there and then went on to the West Indies, where Bess, Fred (Jr.), Floss, Anne, and Nellie were born. Subsequently, the Houses came to Springfield, and that was where Frank, Edith, Art, and Gert came into the world. Fred, Sr., secured employment with the Spalding Company—as did most of the family at one time or another. He continued his bassoon playing with local bands in Springfield. Fred, Jr., played trombone and worked locally on and off. Mainly through his association with Spalding, young Frank House became an avid golfer and eventually a professional and club champion at the Ludlow Country Club. Brother Art followed in his footsteps. Even Edith won championships at Ludlow. As a matter of fact, Frank, Art, and some nephews hold the Ludlow record (64), "at least the last I heard," said Frankie. The Ludlow Country Club provided a social life for the Houses, but young Edith enjoyed the activity of her own age group more; she accompanied her friends to the dances at the Butterfly and at Riverside Park.

With dancing becoming a favorite pastime around the country, the popularity of dance contests flourished. Edith and her sister Floss were exceptionally good dancers, particularly Floss—who went on to dance professionally with Ted Healy and the Three Stooges. Such incentives as dance contests did not escape the notice of Jerry Cook, who immediately inaugurated the practice at the Butterfly and at Riverside, and it was upon such an occasion that Frankie met Edith for the first time.

Edith won a dance contest at the Butterfly. McEnelly selected his second pianist for the task of presenting trophies to the contest winners. Why McEnelly selected Frankie to do the honors will never be known, for Frankie, growing up in an environment where broken English prevailed, was the least qualified at elocution. Besides, Frankie's broad smile was the facade of a most bashful and proper young man. As Jerry Cook was naive in most things other than business, so Frankie was naive in most things other than music. Because of his lack of experience in coping with more mundane situations—very unlike the dashing Rough Rider Angelo Carlone—Frankie approached Edith on his own after the presenation ceremony. The moment was very trying and he was naturally awkward as he asked to see her home after the dance. A beaming Edith—elated not at Frankie's invitation but rather at winning the trophy—rejected the offer with the attitude that her winning the trophy did not presuppose escort of trophy and recipient safely home, particularly if the recipient had been escorted to the occasion by husband, fiancee, or friend.

As a blushing Frankie returned to his piano after the brief presentation and encounter, his thoughts were foggy; for, one Edith House had stimulated some strong emotions in the young piano player.

Edith continued coming to the dances, but Frankie did not succeed in escorting her home until one month later. His approach this time was as awkward and unromantic as usual; but Edith, feeling her friendly acquaintance with him had been sufficiently noted by her peers to be considered adequately established, consented—not, however, without chaperon. The courtship, nevertheless, began that May, and, as Frankie noted in his diary: "May, June, July, August, September—didn't hardly buy her a box of chocolates."

It was understood that if Frankie was to keep company with Edith, he would have to meet her family. And this event occurred shortly after the piano player had acquired a tenuous hold on the affections of the pretty lass.

Although the menu that night did not depart from the usual, Loretta House set the table a bit more elaborately the evening Frankie came to dinner. Most of the family members were present; some of the married ones did not make it. Frankie felt uneasy, but he remained calm during the conversation before, during, and after dinner. "They were a bit skeptical of me at first," remembered Frankie, "but then they got to like me."

Fred House, in precise British articulation, interrogated Edith's beau diplomatically, only intimating approval of Frankie's seeing her. Mr. House was not overly worried, for he knew that because of the piano player's working hours the courtship at best could be only sporadic.

Riverside Park was the principal summer amusement in Springfield. Under the existing "blue laws," there was no dancing on Sunday, and when Frankie did not go to Providence for that day off, he and Edith would spend their time at the park. For the rest, he played from 8 P.M. to 11 P.M. nightly, and for an extra 30 minutes on Saturday. Thus he would see Edith during the day or in the evening when she came to the ballroom. During the winter months, they would go out to dine occasionally—extremely occasionally, for Frankie, being in the habit of sending money home and not having considered the probability of his having a girlfriend, had never established a savings account. As it had been understood that Frankie must meet the Houses, so Edith had to meet the Carlones. That introduction occurred on a bright and sunny Sunday, the winter after they met.

Dora and Angelo and the others were on hand to greet Frankie and Edith when they arrived in Providence. Frankie engaged in the usual family kisses and caresses, but they were of shorter duration this time so that he could get on with the business of introducing Edith to all the family. The Carlones were exceptionally hospitable and congenial, even though somewhat astonished that Frankie had brought home a girl!

What went on in Dora's mind in the course of Dora's becoming acquainted with Edith could only be conjectured. But total acceptance of Edith meant that Dora had every confidence in her son's taste. If she at any time seemed reserved or uncertain about the girl, it was only because Dora was a mother who clung secretly to a notion that this was her "little" Frankie, and the reality of his being a grown man had not fully occurred to her. Or could it have been that Edith was not Catholic? All the Carlones were devout Catholics. Dora attended Mass daily. Even Angelo was a churchgoer; he belonged to the Society of

St. Anne's. Frankie, as mentioned earlier, used to be an altar boy there when he attended grammar school. Angelo, on the other hand, thought as he had always thought: "If that's what Frankie wants, that's fine." But Dora and Angelo liked Edith as a person immediately, and the relationship remained a loving one.

Typical of an Italian mother, Dora lost no time in insisting that Frankie and Edith have something to eat. But Edith's first encounter with Italian cooking was more than that young lady could take.

The aroma of olive oil and garlic that arose as Dora prepared the sauce for spaghetti and meat balls, Angelo's favorite Sunday dish, moved Edith to confer with Frankie. Fortuntely, the latter—himself accustomed to it—was able to understand how others not used to the aroma might find it overwhelming. Frankie made excuses: that Dora shouldn't worry about their being hungry; that he and Edith didn't feel like eating; that Edith, like himself, had no particular liking for spaghetti; that both of them wanted to see the town. Dora was willing to cook chicken or anything else Edith and Frankie might like, for she was long since used to cooking—as Angelo had directed long before—"whatever the boy wants," and she now unconsciously extended this habit to include Frankie's girl. Nevertheless, despite Dora's persistence, Frankie won out. His mother conceded that Frankie was in love and that he was anxious to show off Edith around Providence and that they did, indeed, have very little time.

Thus, Edith's first visit an accomplished fact, she and Frankie went downtown to a Providence diner for what they both enjoyed—hamburgers.

That was the one and only time Frankie and his girl went to Providence, not, however, because of the pungent aroma of oil and garlic, but because the next time, in the spring, they went there as husband and wife.

Almost a year to the day after Frankie joined McEnelly, the 22-year-old pianist proposed marriage. "I just decided to get married and told Ede, 'Let's get married,'" related Frankie, chuckling at the recollection 54 years later. Edith's response was affirmative, even if her only remark was a stunned "Really!" She knew, though, that Frankie's locution, a poor substitute for a romantic proposal of marriage, was about as fancy a proposal as the piano player was capable of conjuring up.

Frankie telephoned Providence to announce the marriage—the marriage that was to occur the very next day. The surprised Carlones—surprised not that Frankie would marry Edith, but that the event was so close at hand—were pleased; so they insisted. But how could Angelo and Dora get away on such short notice?

The Carlones' involvement at St. Anne's and Frankie's marrying out of the Church seemingly would have caused some disappointment. Was that the reason why Angelo and Dora could not make the wedding? "No, not really," assured Frankie. "It happened quickly. I didn't want to bother the folks. It was hard."

Angelo was usually liberal in his thinking on Canon Law. In his day everybody got married first by the judge and later in Church. Dora, perhaps not wanting to cause any guilty feelings in Frankie and Edith, had never made an issue of their marriage by a minister. Yet, when a Catholic priest remarried Frankie and Edith ten years later, the priest remarked, "It was more satisfying for everyone concerned," apparently sensing satisfaction by all who were involved.

Frankie assured his parents that their not making the wedding was all right; the wedding was not going to be anything big. He even had to go to work the same day. He promised Dora that he and Edith would come to Providence as soon as possible after the wedding.

Frankie and Edith hurriedly informed the Houses and, with so much to do in a very short time, set a 24-hour whirlwind in motion. Frankie immediately borrowed two dollars for a marriage license from Edith's brother Art. Ede arranged for the minister.

Thus it was that on April 20, 1925, several days short of his

Miss Edith House—Mrs. Frankie Carle. She and Frankie met at the Butterfly and have been together ever since.

first anniversary with the McEnelly band, Frankie Carle married Edith House, in the singular company of the Fred and Loretta House family and one minister. To pay the minister, Frankie again borrowed two dollars from Art. The House family and Mr. and Mrs. Frankie Carle enjoyed a matrimonial celebration—nothing particularly special—and when the clock struck seven o'clock, Frankie Carle prepared to go to his job at the Butterfly. But he would return after work to the House's, where a permanent room had been prepared for the newlyweds.

When Frankie finished work that evening, he did not go to the Police Station to play pinochle.

Two weeks later, McEnelly and the crew set out on a five-day tour of the Boston area, and Edith went along. That was the extent of the Carle honeymoon, but Frankie's routine in Springfield was complete.

II

With McEnelly, Frankie blossomed into a virtuoso of popular piano. Having assumed a more serious attitude about music with his own groups, with Welch, and in vaudeville, Frankie became very exacting as to the tone quality of each piano he played and extremely conscientious about his technique. He possessed an uncanny ear for music. Vivid impressions of the virtuosity of Rubinstein and Rachmaninoff, coupled with obedience to earlier demands of Dora Carlone and his eventual realization that he really enjoyed the piano, nurtured a natural faculty for distinguishing tone quality. He had developed such a keen sense of tone that he began, unconsciously, the practice of tuning each and every piano he was to play. Even if he inadvertently ran his fingers over a keyboard because he was passing one, he would analyze its tone quality and, on occasion, tune the piano. (Frankie always carried his tuning kit with him.) "I do remember," writes Butch Gillman, "Frankie had perfect pitch. On a number of occasions, even when a church bell would ring, for instance, he could tell you whether it was

A or A# or whatever. Invariably, he was right." Hack O'Brien made a similar observation. "He (Frankie) has a perfect ear," writes O'Brien. "I know because he'd keep us rehearsing until he had cleared away bad notes, dissonances that weren't acceptable to his ear."

Vincent Gamelli, who was known as Jimmy James in vaudeville in and around Boston, where he did a banjo-comedian act, and who joined Frankie in the mid-1930's, discloses a rather humorous and pertinent incident:

> No matter how late we got through Saturday night at the club in Albany, he [Frankie] was in church Sunday morning. The next Sunday I was in church with him. I found out then and there that he was truly a great musician. The organist was playing—Frankie had his prayer beads and he would finger the beads from one to the next and pray. The organist played, Frankie would hesitate and flinch a bit, and then continue to pray—roll his finger from one bead to another—pray—flinch—pray—flinch. Finally I heard him mutter something that wasn't a part of a prayer. It was, "I wish they'd tune that damned organ!"

As Frankie proceeded with McEnelly, he was refining his technique. His daily schedule included many hours of practice, and because of his remarkable proficiency in reading, he played any music he could get his hands on—waltzes, jazz, honky-tonk, classical. He challenged his fingers to react precisely to what he read. Gillman recalls how Frankie "would always have a soft rubber ball which he kept manipulating, or rather squeezing, to keep his fingers limber."

Frankie's time to be featured at the Butterfly had not come immediately. As a matter of fact, Frankie actually effected solos under McEnelly, not of his own doing, however, but at the behest of the customers. Frankie performed his job to the utmost of his capability, and before long, Frankie Carle, pianist, began attracting the attention of spectators, of sidemen, and of leaders alike.

Mac J. Benoit, a Yale music major who engineered at Muzak and then went on to supervise music production at BMI before joining WOR New York, was atop the music scene in the 1920's. Benoit remembers the Butterfly days well and writes:

> The Bandstand at the Butterfly Ballroom was a half circle with a two-foot railing around the back half of the stand. Not only the dancers would stop to listen and watch, but also many people who did not dance, and would just stand there just to hear him [Frankie], and believe me, each night was a new surprise in performance.

Thus it was, there at the Butterfly, that Frankie Carle began "stopping the show," as he would continue to do in later years with his own band. Maria Benoit, Mac's wife, remembers: "I heard him at the old Pennsylvania Hotel in New York, and there, too, the dancers stopped and clustered around the bandstand to watch." Mac Benoit, himself a piano player and arranger, contends, "Without Frankie, there wouldn't have been any McEnelly."

Fred Wade, vocalist who joined McEnelly in 1927, tells of one Carle fan in the Butterfly days, Leo Durocher, a young ball player at the time, who "never partook of the dancing much, but spent his time leaning on the railing near the bandstand and watching Frankie doing his stuff at the piano." Durocher remained a Carle fan throughout the piano player's career. (Wade left McEnelly to join WTIC Hartford, where he sang, announced, produced, and acted, and became one of the Norman Cloutier's Merry Madcaps.)

Frankie earned the respect of his peers; they were awestruck at his talent. "The first job I played with him," asserts Gillman, "filled me with awe and inspiration, and that has multiplied over the years." Even earlier than McEnelly's time, other musicians felt that same kind of inspiration. Henry Jacobson admits, "When Frankie left town [Providence], I lost interest in playing."

Leaders, too, were to note the growing attraction of a convincing pianist. McEnelly was polite, but not overly complimentary about any individual's performance; he showed little emotion as Frankie's popularity grew. However, on one occasion Frankie's performance generated enough excitement to cause even McEnelly to react. It was during a "battle of bands."

The "battle of bands" had become a popular practice, and the McEnelly orchestra had been participating, encountering such bands as those of Earl Hines, Isham Jones, Red McKenzie, Fletcher Henderson, Emerson Gil, and Mal Hallett. The incident in question occurred at Mechanics Hall in Worcester, Massachusetts, with McEnelly and Hallett the principals.

Hallett's group was scheduled to perform first, but the group was not quite all together. McEnelly's boys, being more regimented, were already set up, so McEnelly agreed to start. In one of the numbers, Frankie had a long solo in a fast tempo, and as he fingered the keys, dancers gathered in front of the bandstand. Hallett, who was overseeing his band's readiness, watched momentarily; he then moved hurriedly to one of the spotlights and turned it on Frankie. When Frankie finished, the audience responded enthusiastically. Hallett was either very impressed with Frankie's performance or moved by the audience's reaction, for that very night he made Frankie an attractive offer. Laughingly, as he walked past Cook, Frankie remarked, "Hah, I just got a raise."

But Frankie, enjoying the McEnelly association, especially his friendship with Jerry Cook, and the new life that he was etching in Springfield, turned down Hallett's offer, as he had previously turned down other offers, notably one to join Sam Lanin and another to play in the pit at the Paramount on Broadway. Hallett's manager, Charlie Shribman, who befriended the young piano player, would often remind Frankie when their paths crossed, "If anything goes wrong, Frankie, you always got a job with me." Leaders, too, began to take notice of a young Frankie Carle.

When McEnelly learned of the Hallett offer, an offer which did not surprise him inasmuch as he himself had witnessed Hallett's enthusiasm, he raised Frankie's salary from $60 per week to $125. After better than five years with McEnelly,

Frankie thus finally got a raise, an exceptionally good one. The raise was good news for Frankie to bring home to his family—Edith and a four-year old daugher, Marjorie.

III

The popularity of the "smiling" pianist with Edwin J. McEnelly grew steadily, however, not entirely on the merit of The Butterfly alone. In 1925 Frankie landed a featured-soloist spot, his first in radio, on station WBZ (NBC) Springfield in a special series program. "Being featured at The Butterfly finally—Mac was interested in a team-band, not solos—I suppose had a lot to do with it," reflected Frankie. Then, squinting his eyes as in a moment of deep concentration, he added, "Cook probably pushed for it."

Station WBZ aired McEnelly concerts weekly from The Butterfly since the ballroom opened. Both the Springfield papers, the *Daily News* and the *Union,* carried notices routinely. Early in 1925, the *Union* purported that "since their first concert program, the orchestra has received much favorable comment throughout the country." The article concluded, simply, "As another added feature, Frank Carle, the popular pianist of the orchestra, will present B-Minor Concerto."

By mid-year, WBZ approached Frankie to do a spot in its special series, which series WBZ had been doing all along with other single artists and other bands, notably the bands of Leo Reisman and George Olsen. Frankie, of course, accepted. The *Union* carried the announcement, with Frankie's picture, in a headlined article: FRANK CARLE, NOVELTY PIANIST, ON RADIO TONIGHT

> Francis Carle, whose piano work with the McEnelly Singing Orchestra is one of its a outstanding features, will be heard in a recital at the local studio. Mr. Carle was formerly leader of an orchestra that played on the Keith circuit.

The program, originating from the station's Kimball Hotel studio, became popular, and as it did, so did the name of Frankie Carle; and conversely, as the reputation of Frankie Carle was enhanced, so was the program's. Although Frankie had begun to compose by this time and the local papers had mentioned this fact, his technique at the keyboard remained at the forefront of his growing reputation. By December 1925, the *Union* had expanded its description of The Butterfly's pianist, dropped the term "novelty" in favor of "popular," and publicized Frankie's first song which, unbeknownst to him, had been recorded:

> Frank Carle, who will present a program of popular piano selections, is a member of McEnelly's Singing Orchestra. He was formerly leader and manager of an orchestra which toured with May Yohe, formerly Lady Francis Hope, on the Keith vaudeville circuit. Listeners will recall one of Mr. Carle's numbers entitled "My Big Best Black" which has been played by McEnelly's orchestra, and which was recorded by the Mound City Blue Blowers for the Brunswick company.

Frankie corrected the song title, which should have been "My Best Gal."

The point, however, is not the composition, which is treated later, but the time element. The time of the article is six months after the initial recital, which, being a trial run, would only be continued if listeners responded favorably. Listeners did respond. Thus, in 1925, Frankie Carle had arrived as a featured soloist in radio. And notices of his talent became more frequent and complimentary.

In the early months of 1926, the *Union* referred to Frankie as the "foremost pianist throughout this vicinity." By mid-1926, the reference became, "Frankie Carle, who has been acclaimed as one of the finest pianists in this section of the country." By the end of the year, the *Springfield Daily News* (December 3) carried an 18-point headline, CARLE SEEKS NAME FOR COMPOSITION, with picture and exclusive ar-

Mound City Blue Blue Blowers. William "Red" McKenzie, seated, originally recorded Frankie's first song (1925) "My Best Gal." It was not known that Frankie was the composer of the song which was called "Georgiana" published by Shapiro, Bernstein in 1937.

ticle referring to his performance as a "much anticipated program" and to Frankie himself as "a piano soloist extraordinary," both plaudits exceeding the boundary of Springfield:

> To Springfieldites, Frankie's name is usually associated with McEnelly's orchestra, as he serves in the capacity of pianist for that group, but to outsiders the name of Frank Carle means a piano soloist extraordinary, for his work as a composer has won nationwide recognition. In the program tonight he will include his latest composition, that he has not yet named. It is his intention to ask his listeners to send suggestions for an appropriate name.
>
> Still another feature on his program will be the playing of a selection recently composed by Edward J. McEnelly entitled "Enchantress." While most often heard playing the most popular melodies, Frank Carle is acknowledged master of the classics as well, and when not arranging or writing numbers, spends his time teaching.

Although the article exaggerated Frankie's reputation as a composer, it did ascertain: (1) a young Frankie Carle did in fact gain prominence in radio entertainment; (2) he did, perhaps, earn some notice as a composer, but not to the degree reported; (3) he did display showmanship of a sort in personalizing his contact with an audience and in so doing, ushered in a new concept of audience involvement; and (4) he did introduce without hesitation or envy, a number by another composer or anyone else, a practice he was to maintain throughout his long career.

Previous to the article quoted above, a report stated that "request from radio fans in all parts of the United States has resulted in the arrangement of a three-part special program to be offered as a supper hour feature by Edward J. McEnelly and his orchestra." When the *Daily News* (December 3) referred to "outsiders," it was quite possible that the locution alluded to "fans in all parts of the United States." WBZ did effect the "three-part special" and the "solos" segment named Frankie Carle, along with other sidemen Carrol Bates, Frank Marks, Ken Farnsworth, and George Gallagher. Solos, though not indigenous to McEnelly's method, to some degree infiltrated the orchestra by popular demand.

In December 1927, station WBS aired a Springfield Hour concert, featuring tenor Frederick L. Wade, Victor artist recently joining McEnelly, in a program which included the works of Beethoven, Rachmaninoff, Pierné, Salisbury, and Suppé. Frankie Carle performed as accompanist and as soloist. Reported the *Boston Post* (December 4, 1927):

> The Springfield Hour, WBZ, rested its evening last night on the doings of Edward F. MacEnelly's Orchestra and Frederick L. Wade, soloist. During the pauses the pianist in the orchestra emerged with a solo. And pianists who emerge with solos invariably pounce upon Rachmaninoff's "Prelude in C Sharp Minor," which is so vulnerable and so inviting to strong and able fingers. The fingers of Mr. MacEnelly's pianist are very strong and aimed, we judge, from on high, for those opening chords strike the keys with the unerring marksmanship of a pianistic Annie Oakley.

Interestingly enough, the reviewer either did not know or would not say the name of the pianist, despite Frankie's reputation in New England and his numerous appearances in Boston. And, incidentally, Frankie's arrangement of Rachmaninoff in that program was the very same he was to record for Columbia many years later.

Nevertheless, when WBZ in that same month had hosted the Fourth Annual Radio Ball at The Butterfly, where fifteen acts and seven bands were billed (McEnelly, Jerry Falvey, Bert Dolan, Dick Newcomb, Bancroft Hotel Orchestra, Brinkman's Society Orchestra, and Bill Tasillo), two McEnelly representatives shared the spotlight in that seven-hour program—vocalist Fred Wade and pianist Frankie Carle.

Throughout the late 1920's and early 1930's, reviewers in New England acclaimed the artistry of Frankie Carle. The *Springfield Daily News* reported (May 12, 1929), "Frankie Carle, whose 'unbelievably supple fingers' won him a wide circle of radio enthusiasts, has been booked for an additional series on WBZ." A review of a McEnelly State Armory engagement in Norwich, Conn., (May 30, 1928), alluded to the "marvelous little pianist," and later, another review in Norwich (January 15, 1930) contended "this young genius is regarded by all authorities throughout the country as the greatest pianist of them all. He has been sought by none others than Paul Whiteman, Vincent Lopez, and Rudy Vallee."

Frankie denied the offers mentioned by the reviewer, but there were offers; some have already been mentioned. Bob Baker, formerly saxophonist with McEnelly, who had gone with Henry Busse, wired Frankie from Cincinnati (June 7, 1930): WOULD YOU BE INTERESTED IN GOOD PROPOSITION WITH BUSSE WIRE ME YES OR NO IMMEDIATELY AND WILL SEND DETAILS.

In 1930 Mills Music published "Piano Stylings by Frankie Carle."

Two Big Holiday Dances At The RITZ BRIDGEPORT TONIGHT
M'ENELLY'S GREATER VICTOR ORCHESTRA
with Frankie Carle, Pianist Wizard & Ray Barlow, Soloist
ADMISSION 40c

ATTEND CONNECTICUT'S LARGEST
NEW YEAR'S EVE CELEBRATION
MAMMOTH MARDI GRAS CARNIVAL
Souvenirs ... Favors
Continuous Dancing To 2:00 A. M. With
CASA RITZ ORCHESTRA
Buffet Lunch Served Free At Midnight
Admission for this Stupendous Attraction $1.00

PROSPERITY DANCE — THURSDAY, JANUARY 3 — ADM. 25c

SAT., JAN. 12 — NIGHT CLUB NIGHT AT THE RITZ
Dine and Dance .... Floor Show Revue .... Admittance — 75c

Typical Billing with McEnelly

IV

Frankie Carle did not attract nearly so much attention on records in the 1920's as he did in radio. But there was good reason for that.

Frankie first appeared on records when McEnelly recorded five songs on Victor records in 1925. Although McEnelly had never attained the reputation of a Paul Whiteman or the stature of a Fletcher Henderson, the band possessed the potentiality. Conservative McEnelly pursued music commercially; he did not pursue instrumental solos *per se,* except in situations already noted. His recordings, though, definitely foreshadowed elements of the later "swing" music that was to sweep the country ten years later.

In March 1925, McEnelly pressed "Desert Isle" (19617-A) and "I Like Pie, I Like Cake, But I Like You Best of All" (19617-B), with vocal by Billy Murray and Franklin Burr on the latter. In November of that year, McEnelly recorded "Normandy" (19841-A), with vocals by Lewis James and Elliot Shaw; "What a Blue-eyed Baby You Are" (19841-B), with vocal by Billy Murray; and "Spanish Shawl" (19851-B). Frankie, though not featured, played in all of these recordings.

In March 1926, McEnelly cut a pair: "Moonlight in Mandalay" (19988-A), with vocal by Lewis James, and "In the Middle of the Night" (20018-B). In October: "That Night in Araby" (20259-B) and "Blame It on the Waltz" (20370-B), both with vocals by Henry Burr; and "Tuck in Kentucky and Smile" (20379-B). (For some unknown reason, all McEnelly's recordings occurred either in February-April or in October-November, never between May—September.)

It was not until the first recording date in 1927 that McEnelly gave Frankie a solo, his first, in "My Sunday Girl" (20589-B), with vocal by Fred Wade; it was Frankie's only solo that year. Other recordings in 1927 included: "I'll Take Care of Your Cares" (20597-B); "Just Across the River from Queens" (20601-B), with vocal by Fred Wade; "A Siren Dream" (21011-B); and "What Are We Waiting For?" (21154-A) with vocal by Johnny Marvin.

McEnelly poster. Circ. 1925.

DANCING
One Night Only Thursday, Sept. 12
STATE ARMORY, RUTLAND
McENELLY'S VICTOR RECORDING ORCHESTRA

SPRINGFIELD, MASS., NEWS SAYS:

It is useless and unnecessary for us to say anything regarding the excellency of this band. Many dancers have heard them and know that they are one of the nation's best. Their dance music is the last word, regardless of how you like it for they have a brand of music and a style that pleases all. Their singing and entertainment is of the very highest grade and it is worth the price of admission to hear their piano player play alone.

E. J. McEnelly

MANCHESTER, N. H., NEWS SAYS:

The appearance of the McEnelly orchestra at The Arcadia Wednesday evening has awakened lively interest among the lovers of dancing in this community as well as among the masses of people who enjoy hearing modern syncopated melodies given by a first class orchestra. The work of this band is not confined to dance music, but includes vocal solos and choruses of musical hits, which are presented in a distinctive manner. McEnelly's orchestra is well known throughout the country as celebrated recording artists for the Victor phonograph company, and its dance records have been played in thousands of homes. Vast audiences also have been entertained by these musicians over the radio, the orchestra being featured by Station WBZ.

In presenting this popular attraction it has been the purpose of the management to provide an entertainment of such variety and excellence that those who come to hear or dance to their music will be well repaid.

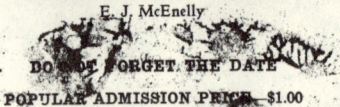

DON'T FORGET THE DATE
POPULAR ADMISSION PRICE—$1.00

JUNE 28, 1927 (Union)

TUESDAY CLUB IN RADIO CONCERT
Younger Musicians of Community Open Series From WBZ Tonight — Frank Carle, Pianist, and a Boston Quartet on Earlier

Another feature attraction is the program arranged by Frank Carle, who has been acclaimed as one of the finest pianists in this section of the country, and the many piano solos he has written have brought him nation-wide fame. His latest work he will include in his program at 7.30 tonight. As yet it is unnamed, and it is his plan to ask the radio audience for a suitable title. Another feature of his little act tonight will be the playing of a number recently composed by Mr McEnelly.

Farnk Carl Novelty Pianist at WBZ Tonight

FRANK CARLE BACK ON THE AIR
Pianist of Merit Will Give Novelty Numbers at WBZ Tonight —The Testers on at 10 o'Clock

Frank Carle, the popular pianist of the McEnelly orchestra will present several novelty piano numbers tonight at 7.03, from radio station WBZ. After an absence of several months from the air, the radio fans will more than welcome this musician back, as he has many admirers, both over the air and among the musicians. Mr Carle is considered one of the finest pianists in New England appearing with a dance orchestra, and is one of the leading soloists with McEnelly. He has composed many piano solos, besides arranging music for the orchestra.

Frankie Carle recognition

RITZ-CHARLTON TONIGHT

Pottsville, Pa. Nov. 18-29

W. J. COOK PRESENTS

McENELLY'S VICTOR RECORDING ORCHESTRA

BELIEVE IT OR NOT

McEnelly has played for over ten million dancers. The organization is 22 years old but gets younger every day. They have recorded for Victor for more than 10 years. Who else has? His pianist is acknowledged the world's best. He will have a special program for you.

The Master of Them All
"NEW ENGLAND'S WALTZ KING"

McENELLY'S

VICTOR RECORD AND RADIO ARTISTS

Featuring

FRANK CARLE

Pianist Extraordinary

A Record Crowd Is Expected at This Low Price

NORTH ADAMS - MASS.

TUESDAY OCT. 25
LOOK! NEW PRICES!
50¢ Plus Tax
A BARGAIN
DANCE 12:30

WESTERN UNION

PATRONS ARE REQUESTED TO FAVOR THE COMPANY BY CRITICISM AND SUGGESTION CONCERNING ITS SERVICE

1201 8

CLASS OF SERVICE
This is a full-rate Telegram or Cablegram unless its deferred character is indicated by a suitable sign above or preceding the address.

SIGNS
DL = Day Letter
NM = Night Message
NL = Night Letter
LCO = Deferred Cable
NLT = Cable Letter
WLT = Week-End Letter

NEWCOMB CARLTON, PRESIDENT   J. C. WILLEVER, FIRST VICE-PRESIDENT

The filing time as shown in the date line on full-rate telegrams and day letters, and the time of receipt at destination as shown on all messages, is STANDARD TIME.

Received at 180 Worthington Street, Springfield, Mass. ALWAYS OPEN

BB626 21 2 EXTRA=CINCINNATI OHIO 7 NFT   1930 JUN 7 PM 8 41

FRANK CARLE=

  CARE MCENELLYS ORCH RIVERSIDE PARK SPRINGFIELD MASS=

WOULD YOU BE INTERESTED IN GOOD PROPOSITION WITH BUSSE WIRE ME YES OR NO IMMEDIATELY AND WILL SEND DETAILS=

  BOB BAKER   BROADWAY HOTEL.

THE QUICKEST, SUREST AND SAFEST WAY TO SEND MONEY IS BY TELEGRAPH OR CABLE

WANTED

1,000 People

To Buy Frankie Carle's New Song

"Deep in Your Eyes"

Come in and hear him Saturday, April 16th from 3 to 5 P. M., only.

JOHN T. ROY CO.
326 HIGH ST.

RITZ BALLROOM
BRIDGEPORT, CONN.

Announces the Biggest Attraction of the Season

Sunday, January 15, 1933
PRESENTING

Edward J. McENELLY
and His Orchestra

18 Musicians and Soloists **18**

Smiling Frankie Carle, Piano Soloist Extraordinary
Ray Barlow, Tenor Vocalist Soloist
Butler Gilman, Xylophone Virtuoso
Master Bernie Buscemi, Boy Wonder Tenor
Paul Noffke, World Renowned Magician

55c. ADMISSION (Including Tax) 55c.

THURSDAY——PROSPERITY NIGHT
Saturday Is Always A Ritz Night

Coming Sunday, February 5th
Al Katz and His Kittens
Columbia Recording Orchestra

Join Our Tango Class Every Monday Evening

EDWARD J. McENELLY

The only other solo Frankie performed on a McEnelly recording occurred in October 1928, in "Take Your Tomorrow" (21773-B), which also included a duet by Jim Miller and Charles Farrell. Other recordings at that time were "Jo-Anne" (21732-A), with vocal by Elliot Shaw; "All of the Time" (21732-B), with vocal by Jim Miller and Charles Farrell; and a Frankie Carle-arranged "Sleep Baby Sleep" (21786), with vocal by Elliot Shaw and yodeling by Edwin McEnelly.

McEnelly recorded only two numbers—the last of the released McEnelly numbers—in February 1929: "Dear, When I Met You" (21910-A) and "Raquel" (21910-B), both with vocal by Frank Munn.

It would be unfair to presume that McEnelly purposely minimized solo instrumental work, but it would be fair to surmise that he did not use the talent in the band to advantage, i.e., to attain the stature of a Whiteman or Henderson. No one, perhaps, used more vocals than McEnelly in recordings. From 1925 through 1929 he used ten male vocalists, all tenors (Billy Murray, Franklin Burr, Lewis James, Elliot Shaw, Fred Wade, Henry Burr, Johnny Marvin, Jim Miller, Charles Farrell, and Frank Munn) on fifteen of the twenty-one recordings. And the trend after, say 1920-1921, was for the fuller instrumental sound with fewer vocals!

McEnelly was certainly aware of the numerous requests Frankie was receiving on his radio broadcasts; the announcer always mentioned when a number was requested. "The most frequent requests," remembered Frankie, "were 'Canadian Capers,' 'I Got Rhythm,' 'Nola,' 'Kitten on the Keys,' 'Spring Fever,' and 'Doll Dance.' " McEnelly never approached Frankie relative to recording any of them. McEnelly did not promote the Carle piano.

McEnelly had a gifted trumpeter in Clarence Grancey who smacks of Clyde McCoy on "I Like Pie," and who stands out beautifully in "Spanish Shawl." The crisp piano in "Spanish Shawl," plus Grancey's trumpet, makes the record near "swing." And toward the end of "I Like Pie," the band approaches "jazz," as it nearly approaches "bop" in "Desert Isle" twenty years before "bop" was heard of. In "Tuck in Kentucky and Smile," there is a conglomeration of stock sounds from railroad engines to hillbilly fiddle, but what stands out is Louis Publicover on banjo. Exceptional saxophone is evident in "All of the Time," with plain "jazz" at the end, and in "Take Your Tomorrow," the great piano and outstanding trombone cannot be overlooked.

No, McEnelly did not feature his talented performers; he persisted in typical McEnelly, as represented by the regularity and monotony of "I'll Take Care of Your Cares." There was good reason why McEnelly, when not billed as the "Victor Recording" crew, was billed as the "Singing Orchestra." That was commercial; and that was "packing them in" at The Butterfly and other ballrooms; and that was why McEnelly records were not selling coast-to-coast as were recordings of such other bands as those of Guy Lombardo, Jan Garber, Duke Ellington, King Oliver, Red Nichols, Louis Armstrong, the Dorsey Brothers, Ben Pollack, Earl Hines, and Pinetop Smith, and others, who were sounding a new era in recorded music.

V

Springfield remained the hub of Frankie's life and work from the time the new twenty-one-year old novice joined McEnelly in 1924 until the time the thirty-year old virtuoso left McEnelly in 1933. Were it necessary to designate a milestone year in the talent and person of Frankie Carle, the year would be 1925. The now 76-year old talent who earned respect and admiration in the field of popular music in America achieved recognition at a regional level 51 years earlier, when he emerged as a "star" with the McEnelly crew; the talent who composed some 150 songs composed his first in 1925; the talent who contracted to record in 1976* recorded for the first time in 1925; the talent who was heard over every radio frequency in America for a

*For *Readers' Digest*

period of 54 years (to now, 1979) performed for the first time in that medium in 1925; the person who celebrated his 54th wedding anniversary in 1979 exchanged "vows" in 1925; and the person in whose life "the family" was the focal point began a family of his own with the birth of Marjorie in 1925.

But no one year makes the talent, nor the person. A natural talent needs only growing up; a basically good individual needs only maturation.

Hence, in contrast to the steadily growing talent of the McEnelly pianist in his almost ten years with that band, Frankie's life—his habits, his demeanor, his motivations—remained virtually unchanged from the routine he adopted during the first year in Springfield. Whatever he did, he did happily. He had disciplined his life in a manner so that all else seemed to fall in place. His provocations were few as a consequence. No one in Springfield, perhaps, was as easily befriended.

Frankie practiced every morning. Everything else followed. He gave piano instruction enthusiastically and, at one point, had thirty pupils. When he was not giving lessons, he would either work on an arrangement or go out with Edith and little Marjorie for a ride or for a visit to the Houses, with whom he lived until after Marjorie was born. (Marjorie was prematurely born as a consequence of Edith's tripping and falling down a flight of stairs.) Frankie accompanied little Marjorie to the Ringling Brothers circus when it came to Springfield. That was the one and only time he had ever seen a circus. Sometimes, he and Marjorie would ride in the park or in the country, when Edith went for golf lessons or competed in the Women's Club tourneys at the Ludlow Country Club. Edith won championships there twice.

Frankie also took eagerly to golf. Edith's brother Art was the teaching professional at Ludlow. Art was assistant to his older brother Frank. When Frank died, Art took over and remained teaching pro for forty years. Frankie and Art got along splendidly, even if Art found his pupil difficult on the links. They saw each other often. They would frequently toy with a crystal set for hours. "We'd get WLW Cincinnati, Little Jack

Little," remembered Frankie. "We'd monkey with the set for hours, nibbling on sardines and onions."

Springfield's band concerts at the park and picnics in the summer and ice skating in the winter were other diversions available to the Carles. "Sometimes we'd make the dog races in West Springfield," added Frankie, "or the matinee at the Poli Theater."

But the one activity most consistently followed in the routine was the weekly visit to Providence. "We would go to Providence every Sunday morning—Saturday night after the job when Marjorie got a little older," disclosed Frankie, emphasizing "every."

Primarily, these weekly visits were family get-togethers. Frankie sometimes made brief visits to friends. One friend whom he would see often was Arthur Addeo, the violinist chum of the earlier days. Addeo had eventually worked his band into the Biltmore Hotel where Frankie would see him. Addeo would tease Frankie, "Wanna work for me?", of course referring to the time that Addeo would not give Frankie a spot in the young Addeo band.

Almost always, the family get-togethers were happy and festive affairs. Frankie added quickly, "I looked forward to going home."

Sunday started typically with Mass at St. Anne's for the Carlones. "There always seemed so much to do and talk about on these Sundays," reflected Frankie, "that the day went fast." He added, "too fast," and putting down his pipe, caught a glimpse of the afternoon sky; he stared into space momentarily, as if searching the universe. "Yep, too fast."

Frankie would give impromptu piano instruction to Louise or Ann or Esther. Aunt Daisy would challenge Frankie's playing when she was home. Uncle Nick was not often there, but when he was, he commented authoritatively on the merits or demerits of some original work his star pupil demonstrated. Sometimes Etta and Evelyn, who were married now, would come in from Union City. Jenny, too, was married; she lived in Providence. Angelo would get out the playing cards, and

Dora was forever providing snacks and treats, despite the enormous Sunday dinner which by now regularly included chicken or other dishes to accompany the usual spaghetti and meat balls.

Little Marjorie was the only grandchild at this time. Dora and Angelo would pamper their grandchild, as grandparents do. As far as "grandma" and "grandpa" and all the Carlones were concerned, there was no one in the whole world as beautiful, as talented, as cute, as precious, as precocious, as intelligent, as independent, as clever, or as fascinating as little Marjorie.

With so very much love and enjoyment for one another at the Carlone get-together, it was no wonder that the 76-year old pianist sighed, "Yep, too fast." The Providence visits were an ingredient of contentment. Frankie really was—as Dora always reminded him—"thankful to God that things turned out well."

Another activity in which Frankie participated regularly in the Springfield years was his playing pinochle at the Police Station. "It was a good way to relax after the job," commented the local celebrity. Before he owned an automobile, Frankie often hitched a ride home in a police car. "Sometimes I'd go with the boys on a call. This one time," he continued, "a call came in to investigate a report of a burglary suspect. I went along—and by God, we pulled up to my own apartment! Ede made the call because she heard a prowler."

One of the virtuoso's most cherished mementoes is a badge from the Springfield Police Department designating Frankie Carle Honorary Chief of Police.

Only some illness or other urgency at home or some particularly exciting event at the ballroom kept Frankie from his card-playing ritual. One such occasion was the appearance of Fats Waller in a battle of bands at The Butterfly. "I think it was '28," recollected Frankie. "I spent all night there with Fats after the job. He said, 'You play great commercial piano,' and that started us off." What Frankie meant was that the two had their private battle of pianos. He'd play something—Fats would play—then Frankie again—then Fats again. Frankie had never arrived home later than he did that night. "We drank and played—Fats never played without his whiskey; he brought it with him—there was none at The Butterfly.* He was really great—what I call one of the very few stylists."

Another occasion on which Frankie skipped the pinochle happened when Paul Whiteman and McEnelly did a battle of music at Riverside. "Around '26 or so," thought Frankie. The name of Paul Whiteman dominated the world of popular music at that time. "I was about twenty-three or so—wasn't married too long—and the idea of playing with the great Whiteman enticed me to ask him for a job. He said he thought the world of my work but he was pleased with his pianist." Frankie remembered that Whiteman played "Rhapsody in Blue" that night.** "He was nice enough to talk to me, anyhow. We talked for quite a while."

That was the one and only time Frankie had ever seriously thought of leaving McEnelly. Many years later, when Whiteman became music director at ABC in New York and Frankie made a guest appearance, the two talked about that Riverside meeting.

Thus the life of the Carles in Springfield was not overly exciting, Frankie's hours precluding many other opportunities. Springfield being a thriving city, with such industries as the Spalding Company, Westinghouse, Indian Motorcycle, a toy factory, and others, nurtured recreational enterprises. Springfield was also the home of the famous Springfield Armory, located practically across the street from where Frankie and Edith took an apartment, or rather a "flat" as it was called then. "I remember being awakened by their shooting off a cannon in the morning," recollected Frankie, apparently the ritual of revelry at the Armory.

Fortunately, Edith had family in Springfield. She had company when Frankie was on the road. Frankie and Edith were

*The Butterfly maintained a soft drink bar only.
**Whiteman recorded "Rhapsody in Blue" for Victor Records (35822), with George Gershwin playing the piano.

happy with each other and enjoyed whatever diversion they availed themselves of during the fifteen years' residency in Springfield. Edith understood and accepted Frankie on the terms of his work; she never resented the demands of that work as he pursued it.

VI

With the publication in 1930 of "Estelle" and "Piano Stylings by Frankie Carle," both by Mills Music, a twenty-seven-year old Frankie had achieved some professional mention. The smiling pianist had earned top billing as "pianist extraordinary" with the McEnelly band wherever it played; he had gained popularity as a radio personality, with a "much anticipated program;" he had emerged a piano stylist, according to the judgment of a music publisher; and he had established what reviewers heretofore intimated, a reputation as a composer. Reported the *Springfield Union* (December 8, 1930) prophetically:

> His first composition, "Estelle," is already enjoying a big sale throughout the country. This number has only been out about three weeks.
> It is expected that many compositions will emerge from the pen of Carle, now that his first number has proved popular.

It was not his first composition. However, the individual achievements of the piano player were sufficiently credentialed at this time to permit him to pursue any course he wished. But Frankie, out of loyalty to Cook and McEnelly—much like the loyalty to Yohe years earlier—decided to forego his opportunities and remain in Springfield, despite the economic condition that had begun to affect the Cook enterprise. Besides the Busse offer and others, Frankie had refused an offer to play in the pit at the Paramount in New York. Cook, of course, knew of the offers. He confided in Frankie, as Frankie did in him. Both knew that the Cook enterprise was beginning to feel the effects of the Depression. "Early in '31," remembered Frankie, "Cook told me he was worried that he might not be able to get the lease renewed." Cook queried Frankie about what he might do; he did not want to hold Frankie back. "I told him I'd stick it out as long as I could—but I saw it coming," said Frankie.

"It" simply meant that it was the beginning of the end for the Springfield heyday.

McEnelly no longer recorded. Early in 1929, Victor released his last two records. (According to a McEnelly collector in Boston, magician Bob Switzer, three more records were made but not released: "Alabamy Bound," "Butterfly Waltz," and "Lonely and Blue.") There was no new contract. Victor instead pressed the bigger attractions, like Ben Pollack, George Jessel, Helen Morgan, and Earl Hines. In 1930 and 1931, Hoagy Carmichael, Henry Busse, Ray Noble, Cab Calloway, and Russ Columbo were occupying Victor's attention. By 1932, McEnelly was forgotten. Frank Munn, who did the last two numbers for McEnelly in February 1929, was by the end of the year recording for Columbia, joining there Bing Crosby and Ethel Waters. Columbia, too, was pressing music comparable to McEnelly's, but the leaders were Guy Lombardo and Jan Garber (who had recorded as Garber-Davis earlier, on Victor). Hal Kemp, another in the style of McEnelly, appeared on Brunswick. Thus, though the Depression may have had some effect on Victor's dropping the McEnelly orchestra, comparable bands continued recording; McEnelly did not. His not recording was only one phase of the decline.

More importantly, attendance at The Butterfly and at Riverside fell off. Even the usual one-nighters at other places which the McEnelly crew played since 1923 diminished noticeably. (Cook may well have been the pioneer for the practice of one-nighters.) "I remember we stayed in Springfield quite a bit more in '31 and '32," commented Frankie.

Cook tried everything to rekindle the excitement and the business once generated by McEnelly engagements. He even proposed a renovation program, hoping that modernization of

The Butterfly might recapture the customers. To offset the dwindling numbers, Cook accepted more special occasion dances, like the dance of the Girls' City Club of Keene, N.H., and Jewett City Fire Department dance in January 1933. Cook further negotiated for a weekly Wednesday-night dance at Buckingham Hall in Waterbury, Conn. He even had designated special nights at The Butterfly to draw the high school set or the old-timers and arranged with city officials to make available special runs of the Springfield trolley service on these nights.

Cook was doing much the same as promoters elsewhere were doing to stimulate business. Promotion billboards added a new dimension in advertising an engagement. Along with the usual lures—credits, features, acts—the billing included an outright appeal for support, as illustrated in the following McEnelly billing at Schuylkill Park around 1930-1931.

Some promoters were more successful than others, depending upon the talent they were promoting—which had become more selective—and the places they were booking—which had offered the widest exposure to the greatest number, e.g, the Roseland in New York, not the Roseland in Taunton, Mass.; the Meadowbrook in New Jersey, not the Meadow Brook in North Adams; or the Commodore in New York, not the Commodore in Lowell. Unfortunately, not The Butterfly, either.

When Frankie received a second offer from Busse in December 1932, he hesitated, but he did not accept. His home was Springfield; he had found contentment there. He, Edith, and little Marjorie lived a pleasurable routine. And Frankie was composing more. He composed eleven songs in 1931. "I had plenty of time in '31," he quipped, referring to the lack of McEnelly engagements on the road. (Although Frankie was a prolific composer that year, as the *Union* predicted, Mills published only one song, "Deep in Your Eyes," that December.) Though as a composer he was doing more, as a performer he was doing less. Hence, when Frankie received that second Busse offer, he hesitated; when he thought of Shribman's reminders, he hesitated. Had the time come?

Schuylkill Park

Pottsville, Pa

::TONIGHT::

McENELLY'S Victor Recording ORCHESTRA

It is useless and unnecessary for us to say anything regarding the excellency of this band. Many dancers have heard them and know that they are one of the nation's best. Their dance music is the last word, regardless of how you like it for they have a brand of music and a style that pleases all. Their singing and entertainment is of the very highest grade and it is worth the price of admission to hear their piano player play alone.

Adm.: Ladies, 50c; Gents, $1.00

E. J. McENELLY

JUST A WORD ABOUT OUR MONDAY NIGHT DANCES

For three years we have been building up a dance catering to the best among the young people who dance for pleasurable and healthful exercise. We have spent thousands of dollars for the best music the world can provide and we have conducted the dance in a manner that has brought us much commendation. We have kept the prices down to a popular level even for bands that cost us $500.00 and more and we ask your support for the greatest musical program that has ever been staged at this, or any other park.

OUR PROGRAM FOR THE NEXT THREE WEEKS
WILL COST US OVER $2500.00 FOR MONDAYS ALONE AND INCLUDES
EDWARD McENELLY --- GEORGE OLSEN -- MAL HALLETT

Innovative billing in a depression year

"I think it was January or February in '33 that I talked to Shribman," Frankie disclosed. He meant Charlie Shribman, who had managed Hallett's earlier band, the one that vied with McEnelly in a battle of bands in Worcester years before. Hallett had been inactive for more than a year. Some newspapers reported that Hallett had gone to Arizona for his health; others stated that he had broken some bones in a fall and left the business. "I don't know about the Arizona thing," offered Frankie, "but here's what he told me: he was drunk one day, fell in a car-pit at a garage and broke his arm." At any rate, Hallett was coming back. Shribman was recruiting the sidemen for a bigger Hallett band and, indeed, Shribman did have a spot for Frankie. And indeed, Shribman had always been a successful promoter.

Frankie went to Cook. "Sometime in February," thought Frankie. Both agreed that the Hallett deal promised to be a good one, at least musically if not financially, for Frankie would be taking a cut in salary. Cook understood; he felt a sadness, but confided, "I'd rather see you go with Hallett than anyone else."

At the end of February, Cook, McEnelly, and Frankie Carle met unceremoniously in a small studio at The Butterfly—as they had done almost ten years before—to bid farewell. The once young page, now a full-fledged knight, took leave of McEnelly's court, thus ending the saga of Springfield.

The *Springfield Daily News* (March 1, 1933) reported:

> "Smiling Frankie" Carle, for 10 years pianist in E. J. McEnelly's orchestra, and frequently leader of that organization on tour, has severed his connection with that widely known band and will leave shortly for New York City, for an audition with the National Broadcasting Company. He will continue his orchestra work and within a few months plans to organize a band of his own.

There was no NBC audition, and there were no plans to organize a band of his own. But there was, less than a month later, a featured pianist, Smiling Frankie Carle, with the new Mal Hallett orchestra.

CHAPTER 6

The new, "swinging" aggregation of Mal Hallett in 1933, once he got it all together, can be compared with any of the later swing bands of the big band era. Hallett and Shribman assembled an arsenal of instrumentalists which very well could have been a Larry Clinton, a Glen Gray, a Harry James, or any of a host of other bands. "There were some great musicians in that orchestra," appraised its featured pianist. Great they were, and Hallett was the "jump-off" band, for most of them became famous with their own bands or joined such leaders as Benny Goodman, Glenn Miller, and Glen Gray.

"It was not only a swinging band," continued Frankie, "but the men, the jobs—all was a new experience for me. And talk about one-nighters, boy, Hallett was 'king'!"

In leadership, personnel, style, and itinerary, the Hallett experience, to be sure, was the antithesis of the McEnelly experience.

Hallett was a tall, skinny individual, a violin player*—"Well, he carried a violin," joked Spud Murphy, emphasizing "carried," in a telephone conversation with me from his Los Angeles office. Hallett had a keen sense of musicianship and showmanship, using both to advantage, whereas McEnelly, a grand musician himself, remained basically a conductor. Hallett was usually restless and nervous; McEnelly, relaxed. McEnelly was soft spoken; Hallett, hardly ever. McEnelly was always sober; Hallett was not. Quick-tempered Hallett was not amenable to suggestion, would not give anyone the benefit of discussion. "That's how he lost Krupa," explained Frankie. "Gene wanted a $5 raise—he really had one coming, I thought—but Hallet wouldn't hear of it. It's not that Hallett said 'no,' but the way he talked, rather yelled, at Gene. Gene quit, and Hallett didn't care." McEnelly did not have to face problems of that kind. There were hardly any suggestions and no one requested raises.

*Guy Lombardo is, perhaps, the most famous of the bandleaders who "carried" a violin.

1933: (Left to right) Joe Carbonero, Vic Mondello, Mickey McMickle, Gene Krupa, Pete Johns, Cliff Wetterau (Weston), Toots Mondello (front), Frank Ryerson, Frankie Carle, Ollie Ahern, Jack Jenney, Spud Murphy, Dick Dixon, Mal Hallett.

Hallett showed favoritism for Frankie from the start. Hallett liked Frankie not only as a pianist but also as a person and came to rely on him, as Murphy commented earlier, as a performer "on whom you can always rely to fulfill his musical obligation." Hallett soon made Frankie assistant leader, replacing Toots Mondello, a move that did not exactly please Mondello, particularly since no reason for the change was given; but that is the way Hallett did things.

"Hallett always managed to pick on someone," related Frankie. "Mondello was a great guy. He didn't drink or smoke." After a brief pause, the Hallett pianist quipped, "He was a mama's boy—just like me!"

Mondello gave notice.

The personnel in the Hallett organization were outstanding musicians, but the one drawback of the Hallett team was its vituperative and unbridled demeanor. Hallett's sidemen, almost to the man, were less inhibited than McEnelly's. The contrast of disciplines in the two orchestras was obvious. Frankie sensed this difference immediately. He found it difficult to accept anything less than propriety in every occasion. He was often appalled at vulgarity or "horse play" or excessive drinking and "pot" smoking, habits in which some of the Hallettmen indulged.

So long as the sidemen performed and pleased the crowd, Hallett let them play their hearts out, notwithstanding their foibles. But Hallett's temperament often clashed with the temperament of his men, especially when he himself had been drinking rather heavily. The consequences were costly.

"On a job in New Hampshire that first winter," related Frankie, "we were playing "Hiawatha's Melody," a number which Jack Jenney improvised beautifully. But Hal stopped the music!" Frankie grimaced, searching for exact words to relate the incident. Imitating Hallett, Frankie dramatized the end of Jack Jenney with Mal Hallett:

"I don't like the way you're playing," shouted Hallett in an irate tone.

"Well, what . . ." Jenney hardly got out.

"Don't argue with me," interrupted Hallett.

"I always play like that," defended Jenney.

"Don't argue with me," repeated Hallett very excitedly. "This is my band. You're through."

"You're firing the wrong man," intervened Teagarden, who found absolutely no fault with Jenney's trombone.

"Don't you interfere," began Hallett, emphasizing YOU, but before he proceeded further, Teagarden, very coolly and emphatically, informed Hallett, "If Jack goes, you got my notice."

It was a very short time afterward that George Troup was occupying Jenney's chair. Alas, even Troup—not exactly a teetotaler—engaged Hallett in a battle of invectives a few months later. "Hallett hit him with a trombone," laughed Frankie, extending his arm in gesture.

That same winter, Teagarden left, as he promised, having served a short five-month tenure with the Mal Hallett orchestra. By the time Hallett landed an extended engagement at the Hotel Kentucky in Louisville in early 1934, Mondello, Jenney, and Teagarden were gone, and it was at the Kentucky that the Krupa-Hallett hassle took place over the raise in salary. Ernie Link, whom Krupa had replaced, now replaced Krupa.

Frankie's 1934 Diary noted:

January 18:	George Green through.
January 23:	Krupa through. Replaced by Link.
February 4:	George Troup through.
February 22:	Teddy Grace joined.
	Jim Johnson, trombone, in.
April 1:	Frank Jordan replaced Dixon.
	Gus Benvenuti replaced Linton.
April 3:	Ann Graham joined.
April 8:	Sunny Blake replaced Link.
May 19:	Clark Yokum, guitar, replaced Jordan

In the McEnelly experience, sidemen remained forever, seemingly; in the Hallett experience, sidemen would come and go. Frankie could not understand the flare of tempers, the "up tight" feelings, and above all, the failure on the part of all the musicians in the Hallett band to feel that they were part of a great "swinging" group. The Claude Hopkins battle was proof of that.

When Frankie first joined Hallett in March, the band consisted of Joe Carbonero, bass, formerly with the old Hallett band; Ernie Link, drums; Lyle "Spud" Murphy from Jan Garber, Pete Johns from Phil Spitalny, and Toots Mondello from Irving Aaronson, saxophones; Cliff Wetterau (Weston) from Bert Lown and Chet Gonier from McEnelly, trumpets; Vic Mondello, an uncle of Toots, guitar; Dick Dixon, trombone; and Olie Ahern, a baton twirler and band boy formerly with the old Hallett band.

Shribman and Hallett were still recruiting. Shribman arranged a road trip to give the new group some experience in playing as a team before he brought it into New York. "About three months later—about the time Krupa joined us—" related Frankie, "he brought it into the Roseland to battle Claude Hopkins." After a brief reflection, he added, "we were humiliated!"

A yet-developing Hallett aggregation was no match for the multi-talented, swinging Hopkins team. The audience reacted with some heckling, some downright impoliteness, and some seemingly joking *innuendo* to the effect that the Hallett band ought to "get lost." The Hallettmen accepted the embarrassment, "but we were damned determined to get 'em at another time," disclosed the embarrassed piano player. "The crowd would yell 'Give us Claude. Give us Claude'!"

"About three or four months later, though," continued Frankie, "we went back to the Roseland. Against Hopkins again. It was different this time. That's when we had Krupa, Teagarden, Mondello, and all the others, and we had played together a bit. Murphy did our arranging."

In the interim between the two battles, Stuart Anderson joined the saxophone section of Mondello, Murphy, and Johns. Chet Gonier left, but trumpeter Frank Ryerson from Art Landry came in. Weston left; then Bob Alexy and Mick McMickle from Cal Logan came. Hallett then picked up trombonist Jack Jenney from Isham Jones and Jack Teagarden, who not only attracted attention with Ben Pollack, but also pressed some records for Columbia with his own group.

Hallett added singer Jim White from Larry Funk; but Irene Taylor, a blues singer from Paul Whiteman, replaced White shortly. Another singer, Teddy Grace, joined the organization that winter, replacing Taylor.

"The band never sounded so good as it did that second time at Roseland against Hopkins," appraised Frankie. "The crowd couldn't get enough. This time they shouted 'Give us Hal. Give us Hal'!"

It was a night of sweet revenge for the Hallettmen. But it was a night to remember for other reasons also. Benny Goodman was there; he smiled approvingly at the Hallett swing.

"Hal introduced Goodman. Benny led us in a number at the end of the evening. We were really swinging," offered Frankie, "and never again afterwards had the band played so darn good."

"Another thing," added Frankie, "that's the night we had to carry Teagarden home. By the last number he had drunk more than a fifth. Krupa, too, was pretty high. He and Stuart (Anderson) used to smoke pot."

In the brief period of time that Hallett enjoyed the likes of Teagarden, Jenney, Mondello, Krupa, McMickle, Murphy, Johns, and Frankie, there were no recordings, unfortunately, for the Mal Hallett orchestra.

Joe Carbonero, the "funny man," along with Frankie, Jenney, Teagarden, and Krupa, were featured regularly in shows. In the shows they "jazzed." "Krupa, Teagarden, and I loved doing some up-beats—'Old Fashioned Love' and 'I Got Rhythm' were two I remember," said Frankie. "Jack used to love 'Basin Street Blues,' his favorite; he used to sing it," he explained. "Of course, we did sweet, too, not up-beats all the time. Jack (Jenney) did sweet solos in the band, but not in the shows."

Among the titles the Hallett pianist offered as favorites were the Glen Gray numbers "Memories of You," "Smoke Rings,"

"For You," "White Jazz," "Little Man You've Had a Busy Day," and "Casa Loma Stomp."

Showman Hallett, in addition to featuring Frankie in every show, began using him in a novelty number, one in which Frankie played with his hands behind his back, with his back facing the piano. The act came about accidentally, not too long after Hallett had made Frankie his assistant.

"We were playing Clemson College," began Frankie, putting down his pipe and slapping his lap, his signal that a narration was to follow.

"Mal hadn't showed up yet. So I started the job. We were playing for almost an hour, when some guy gave us a bottle of 'moonshine' after a number—real 'moonshine'!"

Frankie was not a drinking man, but some of the boys who were sipping the spirits, including Krupa, coaxed Frankie into taking some. He did. There remained yet some time before the next set, and sufficient time for the boys to consume the contents of the bottle. The drinkers were far from inebriated, but were "loose." They began playing the next set and during one number, Krupa yelled to Frankie, "Come on, Frank, let's liven things up—do some stuff."

Little encouragement was needed for a "loosened" piano player to show off a little, and for some unexplained reason, Frankie went to the piano, started to play, and then stood up, turned his back to the piano, extended his hands, and played backwards. The crowd gathered in front of the stand and demonstrated approval. As this spectacle proceeded, Hallett was making his way toward the bandstand. When the number concluded, the audience showed its satisfaction with "hoops" and whistles. With a faint grin on his face, Hallett said nothing, assuming his place to go on with the next number.

"No, Hallett didn't say say anything," grimaced the assistant leader, "but from then on, he'd have me do it more. One thing about Mal, he'd give the customers a show."

If that were McEnelly? "I wouldn't have dared!" Frankie blurted out.

Thus Hallett the showman added a novelty piano act to his

repertoire of comedy, impersonations, a variety of singers, much swing, and plenty of solos, more than most bands in 1933 featured, an observation already noted by George Simon.

Hallett's itinerary criss-crossed New England and points south and west. This part of the Hallett experience was difficult for Frankie. "I didn't get home much," lamented the family man who had maintained his residency in Springfield. "One night it would be the Ritz in Bridgeport," he explained, "and then we'd shoot up to Dreamwood at Bar Harbor. We (Ede and Frankie) didn't visit my folks like we used to."

Hallett played them all—The Elk's in Williamsport, Pa.; the Commodore Ballroom in Lowell, Mass.; the George F. Pavilion in Binghamton, N.Y.; the Ritz in Pottsville, Pa.; Bayside in Burlington, Vt.; Tantilla Gardens in Richmond, Va.; and dozens of others.

On June 17, 1933, Hallett played Springfield's Riverside Park for the first time since Frankie's joining him some three months earlier. A Springfield paper headlined FRANKIE CARLE HERE WITH HALLETT BAND, with the usual "local boy" story. "It felt good playing in Springfield again, coming back, but I remember I disappointed Marjorie." What Frankie meant was that little Marjorie, seven years old at this time, was to give her piano recital the next week, and "daddy" would not be home for it. "Yeah, sometimes it was hard being on the road," he said.

"The only time we'd stay put would be the Commodore in Lowell [when Frankie did his second stretch with Hallett] or the Hotel Kentucky." After a pause, he added, "Then Ede would come up."

Hallett opened at the Kentucky Hotel in Louisville on January 10, 1934, and remained until February 18, the longest engagement the band had played up to that time. It was not until July of that year that the band stayed a week at Atlantic City, and again, in August, a week at Enna Jettick Park in Auburn, N.Y. Then, the Steel Pier in Atlantic City the first week in September, followed by an Albee Theater engagement in Brooklyn, September 21-27, and the Palace Theater in New

York, September 28-October 4, constituted the longer-than-one-nighters that the Hallett orchestra enjoyed.

The flare-ups between Hallett and the sidemen and the endless one-nighers were somewhat inimical to Frankie's nature. On occasions, even Frankie entertained the notion of giving it up. At the Hotel Kentucky, Hallett featured Frankie and Krupa in nightly broadcasts over station WHAS, that is, until the night Krupa and Hallett had words over the raise in salary. About a week after Krupa left, Hallett found fault with George Troup. After a very brief exchange of invective, Troup was out. "What, again?" was Frankie's reaction.

Several days later, Ted Lewis contacted Frankie. Lewis invited him to dinner and offered Frankie a spot with him. Frankie hesitated. The very next night, Lewis again invited Frankie to dine and discuss the possibility of Frankie's joining him. But, the Kentucky engagement being what it was—in one place—plus Ede's being with Frankie, plus Frankie's performing solos on WHAS broadcasts (he did on all 36 broadcasts), Frankie decided against the offer.

After Hallett closed at Louisville, he resumed the one-nighters and sustained a hectic five months on the road, finally ending up with that week at Atlantic City in July. One night the orchestra would play a date at Pottsville, then a dance at Temple University, on to Bridgeport, to Boston, to Waterbury, to Holyoke, back to Bridgeport, etc., and then start all over again. Sometimes Hallett played two-nighters, usually at Tantilla Gardens in Richmond, but they were few. The band continued, from Raleigh, N.C. to Wilmington, to the University of Georgia, back up to Carbondale, Pa., Dover, N.H., on and on! Frankie wondered what it might have been like had he gone with Lewis. "Yep, Hallett was sure the King of one-nighters," appraised his pianist, "and it got to me."

The pace began to affect Frankie. He became irritated more easily; he often felt tired, less enthusiastic. The "smiling" Frankie Carle was not smiling so frequently.

Hallett's crew traveled in cars, and often in the worst conditions. More often than not, the musicians froze. "We would wrap our feet in newspapers," Frankie explained, "and then cover them with bricks. Seventy or eighty miles in snow, ice, and cold—we were crazy!"

Frankie would ride in Frank Ryerson's car. On one occasion, both he and Ryerson were almost killed. Ryerson was descending a mountain road when he hit an icy spot, semi-spinning the car from side to side. The car slid almost broadside into the mountain-side, luckily, and the impact shook up both occupants. Frankie passed out, but Ryerson managed to get help. "I was taken to the hospital, but I only had a couple of ribs broken," narrated Frankie. "I couldn't breathe; it scared me."

The pianist shook his head in this recollection. There had to be a better way. Would the Lewis job have kept Frankie in one spot for longer periods?

"You should have seen me play that night," laughed Frankie. "Oh, yeah, I played. I sat there stiff, just my hands moving, the rest of me stiff, and it hurt."

Despite the disadvantages of one-nighers and the volatile nature of the Hallett organization, Frankie the musician enjoyed the kind of music the Halletmen dished out. He enjoyed meeting others in the business, like Ted Lewis, Henderson, Lunceford and others just breaking into the business. He visited with Hal Kemp when Hallett did Pottstown. Frankie especially liked doing the battle of bands.

"I first heard Vaughn Monroe when we were doing Scranton, Pa.," he remembered. "Vaughn was singing with Larry Funk, the Band of a Thousand Melodies. Jim White used to sing with Funk." But that was all he narrated.

"Oh, yeah. We were in Bridgeport. We were doing a battle against Fletch Henderson," he proceeded.

A young man in the audience that night wanted to sing a number with the band. Hallett ignored the request. When Frankie learned of it, he coaxed Hallett. If anyone could ask Hallett for anything, Frankie could.

"Let the kid sing, Mal," he said.

"Ah, you do it," conceded Hallett, as he went for a cigarette. The young fellow, around 20, did sing. His style was unique.

Henderson and Frankie enjoyed the number, "even Hallett," added Frankie. The young singer drew an enthusiastic response from the crowd. However, that is as far as it went. Henderson could not use the singer, and Hallett was not interested. The young singer was Frankie Laine.

That incident was the one and only time that the careers of Frankie Laine and Frankie Carle were to cross. Even so, Laine remembered the incident and the piano player who "went to bat" for him. Wrote Laine, "The only contact with Frankie that I remember was when I sang for the band that time," and, he added, "Frankie is a great artist and grand guy."

Frankie enjoyed the challenge in the battle of bands. After the second battle against Claude Hopkins, the Hallett orchestra felt it could beat all comers. However, the cloud of confidence burst when the likes of Mondello, Teagarden, and Krupa left. Nevertheless, battles continued, and if the Hallett crew did not outdo the opponent, it at least put up a good battle.

In April 1934, Hallett waged a musical war against Ozzie Nelson in Berwick, Pa., and then Fletcher Henderson in Troy, N.Y. The next month, Hallett battled Felix Ferdinando in Waterbury, Ozzie Nelson again in Bridgeport, and then Larry Funk in Swampscott, Mass. It was Jimmy Lunceford's turn in June in Waltham, Mass., Hallett's favorite ballroom. The last two battles Frankie was to do with Hallett were both against Ozzie Nelson, one in Waltham in July and another at the Steel Pier early in September, where Hallett was doing one of his few "more than one night" engagements.

Frankie enjoyed the radio broadcasts. The nightly broadcasts over station WHAS Louisville were the longest sustained broadcast of the Hallett orchestra. Station WABC carried nightly shows on both occasions that Hallett played the Steel Pier. Otherwise, radio broadcasts were generally sporadic.

"Nola," "Doll Dance," and "I Got Rhythm" were among the favorite solos Frankie did over radio. In one of the Steel Pier shows, he did his own "Estelle." These numbers were repeated, too, in the week-long theater shows Hallett did at the Albee in Brooklyn and at the Palace Theater in New York.

The grueling pace began to show in a 31-year-old Frankie Carle when Hallett played the Palace (September 28-October 4). Frankie finished the engagement, but during that week he was not quite himself. He would feel nervous and tired, often becoming easily irritated. And Mills' rejection of Frankie's latest song, "Blue Fantasy," compounded his uneasiness. He worried about his performance. He lacked drive, and only he knew it. When Frankie finished at the Palace that October 4, 1934, he went to Hallett. He explained to Hallett that all was not well and he just had to take some time off. Hallett left it that way. Frankie would take time, and when he felt fit again, he would return.

When Frankie returned to Springfield on October 5, he collapsed. The doctors diagnosed exhaustion; they prescribed complete rest. Frankie Carle lay in bed for three solid weeks before he felt strong enough to get up.

During Frankie's convalescence, Jerry Cook was a constant visitor. Jerry Cook wanted Frankie to come back.

Billings with Mal Hallett. Frankie was always featured. Circ. 1933-34. Others going on to better things were also featured.

Mal Hallett's Kentucky Hotel Orchestra

Hallett's orchestra, early 1934, picture at the left, sustained a string of one-nighters of record proportion. This picture was taken at the gig where Gene Krupa, second from right and on Frankie's left, quit because of a flare-up over a raise.

CHAPTER 7

Having secured a lease renewal on the Butterfly property, Jerry Cook proceeded with his plans to modernize the ballroom in 1934. Cook had weathered the difficult times of the early 1930's, remaining optimistic that the Butterfly would again be the dancing scene of New England. He was excited when Frankie agreed to rejoin the association, even if Frankie's participation was going to be temporary. Frankie entertained the notion of his own band.

Cook agreed to manage Frankie's own orchestra whenever Frankie was ready to put one together. In the meantime, Frankie would be guest conductor of the McEnelly band and would use the Butterfly facility to audition and rehearse musicians. The *Springfield Times* (November 9, 1934) in carrying the story of Frankie's return, reported: "In this appearance at the Butterfly he will play piano solos and conduct the orchestra in the absence of Mr. McEnelly. He is now formulating plans for the organization of his own dance band."

The formal opening of the New Butterfly was to occur over a long Armistice weekend, November 10, 11, 12, with Frankie Carle, guest conductor. Cook geared for capacity crowds; he felt certain that with Frankie's return many who would not otherwise be present would attend. The formal opening at that time was appropriate, too, because Frankie was present at the first opening of the Butterfly almost eleven years earlier.

As predicted by Cook, a very large crowd attended the three-day affair, including the dance on the night of November 11 which began at midnight! Frankie, however, did not play that November 11 date, for he had gone to see Hallett and had played with Hallett that night in Bridgeport.

During December of that year and the early months of 1935 Frankie devoted most of his time teaching piano and substituting for McEnelly. Needing additional money, he would also play jobs elswhere. He was getting $60 a week from Cook, substantially less than what Hallett paid him. Organizing a

Sphere and Stratosphere
By E. CHRISTY ERK

AMONG LIFE'S SOUVENIRS.

1934

There are letters, many letters,
  That have come the way of years,
Some have had a touch of sadness,
  In this vale of smiles and tears,
But there's one, I'll always treasure,
  As I make the stumble through,
Three words, on a faded letter,
  With the legend, "I love you."

Catch it.... 6:15 to 6:30, W1XBS presents in a studio broadcast, "Smiling" Frankie Carle, pianist with McEnelly's Victor Recording ork.... Carle is the top.... Played Mal Hallett and Joe Haymes.... Opens tonight with "Medley" comprising "Estelle," "Doll Dance," and "Nola." Then swings to "I've Got Rhythm," "Looking Out the Window," and "Humoresque".... "Looking Out the Window" is his own composition.... If you want to hear a piano going to town, tune in on Frankie.

CARLE

Chatterbox.... Something diff. Co-Ed Valentine dance, Central Y, next Tuesday, 200 gals, easy-on-the-eyesers, invite 200 boy friends to dunk hearts in valentine sweetie-sweet bowl. It's the dance you should attend if you're out valentine-ing this year. Bill Briggs' genius responsible. Thanks for invite Bill. I'll B-seein' you....

W1XBS.... 6:45, Dr. Walker, new pastor, Second church, speaks in weekly radio forum.... 7:15, Thurman Lamb, bary.... 8, Gypsy Wanderer.... 8:15, Major Charles Shons.... 8:30, McEnelly's Victor Recording orchestra from Hamilpark.... 9:45, Skit Simpson's Hill Billies. (All studio programs).... 11:05, Harlem Amateur night, 12, Cab Calloway.

Dec. 10 -34

ROSELAND BALLROOM
Taunton, Mass.

TONITE
McENELLY'S ORCH.
Featuring FRANKIE CARLE
As Guest Conductor
Piano Solo and Songs
Adm. 40c

FRANK CARLE TO VISIT LOCAL BALLROOM TONIGHT

Former Pianist for McEnelly's Will Be Guest at the Butterfly

1-26-34

"Smiling" Frankie Carle, for many years pianist for McEnelly's orchestra of this city, will be a guest of the local orchestra and Butterfly ballroom management here tonight. Carle has just returned to the city for a short visit following an extended stay in the South where he went with Mal Hallett's orchestra. Although he has been connected with the Boston dance band for some time past, Frankie still maintains his home in the immediate vicinity and misses no opportunity to revisit the local ballroom where he made a number of friends and attracted the attention of prominent members of musical circles throughout the East. It was while in Springfield that Frankie wrote a few piano numbers which have been used frequently by dance orchestras.

New BUTTERFLY BALLROOM
Tonight! Dan Murphy and His 12 Musical Skippers
Band Attired in All-White
C. P. O. Naval Uniforms
Featuring Tubby Randall, Vocalist
ADM. 40c

Monday, Nov. 5
Night Before Election Dance
with Merry Widow Prize Waltz
Featuring Smiling Frankie Carle
in Piano Solos and Songs and as Guest Conductor
The Merry Widow Waltz Contest
The Winning Couple
Will Be Presented with a
SILVER LOVING CUP
from Maurice Chevalier and Jeanette MacDonald, Stars of "The Merry Widow," Now Playing
Poli Theater

Nov. 5-34

Frankie's return to Springfield

band would take money, and Frankie was sinking all of his savings into the venture. Edith encouraged Frankie to go ahead with his plan. Whatever additional money Frankie could earn, he did. The Elliot Radio School ran the following advertisement in March:

> **The Elliot Radio School**
> 12 Harrison Ave.
> A new instructor has been added to our staff
> **"Smiling" Frankie Carle**
> Teacher of MODERN PIANO
> Free auditions testing radio ability for Adults and Children
> Voice Drama-Announcing
> Classical Piano-Elocution
> **PHONE 3-9578**
> Auditions by Appointment

The excitement, the anticipation, and the anxiety accompanying the organization of a band were omnipresent. Frankie was thirty-two years old now, not fifteen; this was the "big time" now, not a neighborhood combo. Frankie sought musicians; others came to him. In his traveling with Hallett, Frankie had established a reputation among musicians. "I was doing some vaudeville," writes Vincent Gamelli, "comedy with a banjo. I appeared in and around Boston as Jimmy James. I got word that Frankie Carle was auditioning musicians in Springfield so I hopped a train and headed for the Butterfly."

About the latter part of April, 1935, Frankie garnered a full complement. He and Cook recruited Andy Methot, trombone, formerly with the Al Katz orchestra; Frankie Granato, bass and violin, formerly with the Albany symphony and Bill Sokol; Paul Robillard, trumpet and singer, from Barney Rapp and the Silvertown Cord band; Herbert Renth, drummer, who was performing with Ernie Andrews at Tantilla Gardens, Richmond,

L-R: Slim Overman, Gus Benvenuti, Herb Renth, Bernie Barton, Frank Granato, Frankie, Paul Robillard, Jimmy James, Andy Methot, Doc Dibert, Joe Duren. Frankie's 1935 Band. Opened at the Butterfly, May 24, 1935.

when Hallett played there; Augustus Benvenuti, first saxophone, flute, clarinet, and singer, from Hallett; Joseph Duren, saxophone, bass clarinet, and flute, from Jean Goldkette; Ralph "Slim" Overman, tenor saxophone, a featured soloist with Henry Their; Doc Dibert, trumpet, from Tal Henry; and William Mazur, trumpet, formerly with the Bay State Aces.

On May 24, 1935, the "Smiling" Frankie Carle orchestra opened at the Butterfly Ballroom.

However, the success of the band would not be appraised at the Butterfly. Frankie knew too many people in Springfield. Would they come and come again because of him and his piano or because of his orchestra? The test, of course, would be on the ballroom circuit, that is, what was left of the ballroom circuit after the depression years. Bands had come into their own in 1935, and if bands were to succeed, they would have to make it on their merits to attract and sustain the gate. Customers were more sophisticated in their tastes and spending habits, especially since many had experienced bad times for several years.

Cook, with the help of his friend Charlie Shribman, arranged for a "Smiling" Frankie Carle orchestra tour, including a good start to open the season at Bayside Pavilion in Burlington on June 11. And what a reception! Reported the Burlington newspaper (June 12, 1935):

> **Frankie Carle and Orchestra Featured at Bayside Pavilion**
>
> One of the most enjoyable musical attractions of the season at Bayside Pavilion, Malletts Bay, was the presentation last evening of "Smiling" Frankie Carle and famous orchestra in a program of smooth, syncopated melodies.

> When Frankie, who is popularly known as "The Wizard of the Keyboard," bends over the "ivories," his audience is impressed and more than convinced of his outstanding and inspirational talent, as portrayed in the harmonious melodies and even tempo of his playing. The keyboard of the piano is like so much clay in the palm of his hand, so easy is it for him to mould melodies to suit his mood.
>
> Featured with Carle and his orchestra is Bernie Barton, vocalist, whose singing shows rare quality. He is also supported by a group of excellent artists.
>
> Outstanding among the evening's presentations were some of Frankie's own compositions, including "We Still Have Love," and his interpretation of the ever-popular current selections were remembered by the dancers long after the orchestra had ceased to play.
>
> Donald Glynn, popular Burlington tenor, was guest artist during the evening, singing as one selection, "I Love You Truly." Glynn is a regular feature on the "Man-About-Town" program over the *Daily News* radio station WCAX.
>
> Coming from Holyoke, Mass., Carle and his musical organization will play at Ware's Grove, Spofford Lake, Brattleboro, this evening. They are scheduled to play in Fitchburg, Mass., on Thursday and at Winsted, Conn., on Friday evening.
>
> Frankie is well-known in musical centers, having been featured as pianist with Mal Hallett and McEnelly's orchestra. He now has a band of his own, having organized it about four months ago. Members of his orchestra include men from Cincinnati, O., Louisville, Ky., Bedford, Pa., and Springfield, Mass. Frankie does all of his own arranging.

As reported in the newspaper article, the Frankie Carle orchestra was to play that evening (June 12) at Ware's Grove, Spofford Lake. The article failed to mention, however, that the Ware's Grove one-nighter was the band's premiere in the practice of the battle of bands, doing this one with Shribman's Doc

Peyton orchestra. That same week was a "good" week. But not all the weeks were that active. After Winsted, the Frankie Carle orchestra played only Nutting's-on-the-Charles; then waited almost two weeks to play again, this time at the Butterfly for the July 4 celebration.

Late in July Frankie came to Bedford Grove, Manchester, and a week later, Lake Nipmuc Park. The response was particularly encouraging at Nipmuc, resulting in a return engagement for one week at the end of August. In mid-August (August 13) the band played the Commodore in Lowell, Mass., and Station WLLH Lowell not only carried Frankie's fifteen-minute evening broadcast from the Commodore but also aired a special one-half hour broadcast that night.

The popularity of the Carle orchestra grew, but the popularity was restricted to local New England. On September 1, the band played a one nighter at Meadow Brook, North Adams, and six days later, O'Brien's Ballroom in Holyoke. Two days later, it was Kimball's Starlight. Then, what seemingly was going to be a good "break," Cook succeeded in landing the Carle crew for the season's opening at the Hamilton Park Pavilion in Waterbury on September 14. Frankie returned three times to Hamilton Park, one-nighting at Lake Compounce and Meadowview in between.

The ten-man Carle orchestra persevered even though it was not achieving financial success. The group hung on; trumpeter William Mazur was the only sideman who left.

The orchestra continued to receive favorable reviews in local papers. Frankie himself was usually singled out for his work on the keyboard. Customers would generally find their way to Frankie, as they did in the old days in Springfield. He was still the main attraction. He was always personable and obliging to customers' requests, sometimes even to challenges. One challenge, writes "Slim" Overman, "happened at a dance close to Berlin, N. H. A lady, who was probably a piano teacher, challenged Frankie to play "Rhapsody in Blue" at sight and put $20 on the piano which was his if he played it to her liking—needless to say he did."

But Frankie did not thrive on challenges. He was thoroughly dedicated to shaping up a "dance" orchestra. It looked as though the band was going to make "big time" as some bands did from 1935 on. But such was not the case. By the fall of 1935, the Frankie Carle orchestra simply was not making it.

From the debut at the Butterfly, May 24, to the farewell dance there on October 23, the Frankie Carle orchestra played sixty-two dates, including the first week and four additional dates at the Butterfly. The remaining fifty-three dates were scattered over thirty different spots, not quite averaging two playing dates per ballroom. The only extended engagement—one week—occurred at Lake Nipmuc. Broadcasts occurred only at Manchester, N. H., and Lowell, Mass. Sidemen were earning $6 per date, about the same for the leader. (Frankie had to play approximately six dates to pay for music stands, and that would mean "zero" take-home pay for those six dates.) Cook was sufficiently attuned to the business world to realize that the Frankie Carle band was not making it financially.

During his renewed association with the Cook-McEnelly organization, Frankie had received a steady salary. Most of that went into his orchestra. On his own now, he no longer enjoyed that steady income. The orchestra needed more extended engagements, and it needed a New York City exposure. It landed neither. It needed some recordings, at least one, to boost its popularity above the local level. But the recording companies that waxed Frankie's style of music did not seek the Frankie Carle orchestra. At this time Brunswick was pressing the sounds of Ozzie Nelson, Glen Gray, Cab Calloway, Louis Prima, Freddy Martin, and Red Norvo. Victor waxed Henry Busse, Ray Noble, Tommy Dorsey (who earlier recorded on Columbia), Rudy Vallee, and Benny Goodman (also earlier on Columbia). Columbia engaged Will Osborne, Eddie Duchin, and Glenn Miller; and newly formed Decca was pressing Bob Crosby, the Dorsey Brothers, and Dick Jurgens.

Frankie became depressed as he realized that the band was not working out. He thought about the months prior to his organizing the band and the many opportunities that he had turned down or the opportunities that might have been in the offing had he been interested in playing for someone else. He thought about the moral support given to him by Rudy Vallee when Vallee had introduced Frankie to the audience at the Hollywood Club in New York and had praised the pianist who was about to embark upon a new career as a bandleader. Ozzie Nelson did the same thing when Frankie was in Nelson's audience one night. Frankie recalled the $125 per week offer from Enric Madrequera to play in New York. (Frankie even went to rehearse with Madrequera one day.) Frankie thought about the plaudits given him by the Dorsey Brothers band when it came to the Butterfly; Frankie remembered meeting Bob Crosby that night. "I could have just about picked any band at the time, "recollected Frankie, "but I just wanted my own. I'd have been better off—lost everything."

At the last engagement at Hamilton Park, the Waterbury newspaper appraised the Carlemen as the "latest orchestra sensation to take the East by storm" and referred to Frankie as the "debonair wizard of the ivories" who now "goes to New York." Frankie went to New York, but not New York City. When Frankie and the crew came into Waterbury, a Connecticut booker, Norman Flewelling, had made Frankie a proposition to play an Albany spot. In Albany the advantage would be a regular broadcast. Frankie, of course, consulted with Cook, with whom he was in constant communication, particularly since the band was in dire straits. The venture of Cook and Carle, which had begun six months earlier, was approaching almost a $20,000 loss. Prospects of the band about the time Flewelling came along were meager, with only two one-nighters on the docket. There was no hesitation on Cook's part as to what Frankie had to do, and at Cook's insistence, Frankie would take Flewelling's offer. If it were not for Cook, Frankie would have "thrown in the towel." Thus, when the newspaper article mentioned that the Carle band now goes to New York, the connotation and the actuality were miles apart.

Flewelling had booked the band into the Edgewood Club, a dine-dance spot in East Greenbush, N. Y., just outside of Al-

Ware's Grove, Spofford Lake, N.H.

TOMORROW NIGHT, WEDNESDAY, JUNE 12
THE SEASON'S GREATEST DANCE EVENT

Battle of Music

DOC PEYTON

and

SMILING

Frankie Carle

25 Musicians 25

CONTINUOUS DANCING — 9 P.M. TO 2 A.M.
One Small Price of Admission for This Great Dance Event—75c, (incl. tax)

LAKE NIPMUC PARK
MENDON

ANOTHER DANCE HIT!
SMILING FRANKIE CARLE and Orchestra
TONIGHT—CHECK DANCING—5c A DANCE
WEDNESDAY—SPOT DANCING

At RUSTIC THEATRE :
On the Stage—5 ACTS OF VAUDEVILLE
On the Screen—"HELL'S ANGELS"
With Jean Harlow, Ben Lyon, James Hall.

All Next Week—Old Home Week!
At Ballroom—McENELLY'S ORCHESTRA
At Theatre—Big Musical Comedy Show
Featuring Mae Ross and David Reid in "TAKE THE AIR."
Nipmuc Is the Center of All New England Amusements.

KIMBALL'S STAR LIGHT
On Route 128, at South Lynnfield, between Newburyport Turnpike and Wakefield
TONIGHT—CHECK DANCING
FRANKIE CARLE
TOMORROW NIGHT
AL ROSEN and his
Hotel Biltmore Orchestra

ROSELAND
ON THE MERRIMACK—LAWRENCE
TONIGHT—SMILING
FRANKIE CARLE
AND HIS ORCH.—ADM. 40c
SAT.—CHECK DANCING

Lake Compounce
Bristol
SUN., SEPT. 15
FRANKIE CARLE
AND HIS
ORCHESTRA
ADM. 40c

COMING
SUN., SEPT. 22
Joe Rines
AND HIS
Celebrated Band
Direct From
The Famous Mayfair Club of Boston

GALA FALL RE-OPENING

HAMILTON PARK PAVILION

"The Ballroom Supreme With Music to Match"

Tomorrow Night

THE NEW DANCE BAND SENSATION!

"SMILING FRANKIE"

CARLE

AND HIS OWN ORCHESTRA
RADIO AND RECORDING ARTISTS
Featuring the inimitable "pianoistics" of Frankie himself
and grand vocals of Bernie Barton.

Coming Thursday
DON FELIX AND HIS BAND

ADMISSION 40c

BEDFORD GROVE
Dancing Outdoors — Manchester, N.H. — Dancing Indoors
TONIGHT --- FRANKIE CARLE
THIS AD AND 20c ADMITS ONE TONIGHT

COMING FRIDAY
RUDY VALLEE IN PERSON
and His Company of 30 Stars

ADM. BEFORE 8 P.M., 90c   REG. ADMISSION, $1.10
Bus leaves Stark St. Every 15 Minutes

On the State Highway

MEADOW BROOK BALL ROOM
North Adams

America's Greatest Pianist
Composer and Arranger

"SMILING"
FRANKIE CARLE
AND HIS
SENSATIONAL ALL STAR
ORCHESTRA
PLAYING
DAWN DANCE
SUNDAY, SEPT. 1
Doors Open at 10
11 till 4 a.m.

WLLH—Lowell (219m) 1370k; 25 miles
7:00 P.M.—Lowell ERA Orchestra.
7:30—Same as WAAB.
8:45—Frankie Carle's Orchestra.
9:00—Concert from Frant Park, Chicago.
9:45—Margaret Roy, classical pianist.
10:00—Tuning Around.
10:30-11:00—Frankie Carle's Orchestra.

WCSH—Portland (319m) 940k; 40 miles
6:00 P.M.—Flying Time—adventure in aviation.
6:15—Dawn Melody Lane.
7:00—Amos 'n' Andy.
7:15—Hall and Gruen, piano duo.
7:30—Gale Page, popular singer.
7:45—Same as WEEI.

Carle billings, circ. 1935

bany. Some adjustments were needed in the band. Andy Methot left; Jimmy James took the trombone chair and doubled on guitar. Hack O'Brien replaced Herbert Renth on drums. Paul Robillard left and Frankie decided to go on with one brass less. Joe Duren and Ralph Overman also left, and Frankie landed his old friend from the McEnelly days, tenor saxman Percy Booth, who had recently left Carmen Cavallaro. Booth recruited another tenor and arranger, Bob Noble, who would be available for a short time. Flewelling found a good alto sax in the person of Ben Puglia of Bridgeport.

The Edgewood was some ninety miles from Springfield, a popular club with tea dances on Sunday afternoons. The owner was a meticulous fellow, an arthritic, who would personally supervise the breaks in between sets. "He was a regular time clock," quipped Frankie.

Although the boss's habit of checking the band was an annoyance, Frankie and the crew did not let it thwart their desire and drive to perform. They grinned and bore it as a matter of survival, especially since big bands had come into their own at this time. Names like Count Basie, Artie Shaw, Gene Krupa, Glen Gray, Larry Clinton, Bunny Berigan, Horace Heidt were few among a score of big bands that had gained national acclaim. There were hundreds of bands striving for recognition and the Frankie Carle orchestra was one of them. No petty annoyance was going to stand in the way. The orchestra concentrated more on prospect and performance, and the Frankie Carle crew had come to expect better things since the Edgewood was beginning to "pack 'em in."

Frankie had paid salaries between $30 and $35 per week, he himself realizing about the same. His income was far from proportionate to his investment, and, to be sure, an income far from what he would have commanded as a sideman, let alone leader. "Piano players in other bands were making more," offered Frankie, squinting his eyes, trying to remember names to back up his statement. "[Joe] Bushkin, [Milt] Raskin, [Tom] Fulford, [Bob] Zurke, [Jess] Stacy," he added. (Piano players with Bunny Berigan, Krupa, Chick Webb, Bob Crosby, Benny

Goodman, respectively.) "I'm sure I could have made more money playing for someone else," he continued, shaking his head as if to say 'I was foolish.' But the inclination to lead was inexorable. "At least the Edgewood gig was steady," he interjected, as we ended the conversation.

As Flewelling promised, Frankie broadcast locally over WGY from 4:30 to 5 P.M. on Sundays and from 6:45 to 7 P.M. on Thursdays. The *Knickerbocker Press* of Albany (December 29, 1935) announced the orchestra's network airing, and at the same time, suggested "that young man should be in the big time." About a month later, *Variety* publicized the Frankie Carle orchestra in connection with the WGY broadcast and also with one of the biggest events in that area, the A & P Managers' Benefit, a gala affair which catered to 800 people.

As a consequence of his successful run at Edgewood and his broadcasts, Frankie landed additional jobs, like the Knights of Columbus ball in North Adams and the Middlebury College prom. The additional exposure was good, seemingly only a question of time before the Frankie Carle orchestra would be singled out for national prominence. By spring, Frankie Carle and his orchestra reached the status of a celebrated band, whose leader exercised some influence. Through Frankie, the Lang Sisters performed over WGY, a breakthrough for them, even though their potential eventually fizzled out. *The Schnectady Sun* (May 31, 1936) appraised the Frankie Carle crew: "Prospective commercial sponsors now looking him over. Likely timber."

Frankie never exerted so much energy in pushing for the band as he did during this period of time. He devoted countless hours to polishing the band for those "big time" bookers and "prospective commercial sponsors." Neither had materialzed.

It was disconcerting to Frankie and the boys that after some eight months at Edgewood, at best the Frankie Carle orchestra could only come up with a two-week billing at Sherman's in West Caroga Lake. Frankie and the boys knew well that they had reached their peak. They just couldn't make it over the "hump."

Late that summer, Frankie called Shribman. As Shribman had always said, "If anything goes wrong, Frankie, you always got a job with me."

Frankie Carle became a sideman once more.

CHAPTER 8

Hallett was playing Philadelphia when Frankie rejoined him on September 24, 1936. Frankie was to resume his previous status, the only difference being a raise in salary, to $125 per week. Remembering the extensive travelling Hallett had done the first time with him, Frankie anticipated a like itinerary. For the first week, Frankie was not disappointed. The orchestra played Philadelphia, Lawrence, Mass., then Portland, Me., Bridgeport, Conn., and then Springfield, Lowell, and North Adams, Mass. It seemed as though the one-nighters would go on and on, but such was not the case. Shribman booked Hallett into the Commodore Hotel in New York where Hallett remained for an unprecedented engagement, four and one-half months, from October 2, 1936, to February 18, 1937!

Teagarden, Krupa, Mondello, Jenney, and Murphy were gone. Buddy Welcome was now on saxophone; Clark Yocum, on guitar; and Dick Taylor, on trombone. Yocum and Welcome both sang, Yocum later becoming one of the Pied Pipers. Frank Ryerson (who wrote Hallett's theme) was on trumpet, as was Bob Alexy who later (August, 1937) went to Jimmy Dorsey and then on to Glenn Miller. Art Lombardo replaced Bob Alexy. Then Al Buntman left, being replaced by Doc Spears. It remained for Joe Carbonero to be the only sideman with Mal Hallett from beginning to end.

The Commodore gig (the term "gig" became popularly used by this time) proved to be Frankie's most propitious opportunity in establishing, once and for all, his rightful place as a nation-wide pianist *par excellence*. And in no small way did the Commodore bill help Frankie obtain not only a recording contract but also the cognizance of William Lackenbauer, a publisher who was to play an important part in Frankie's career. For Hallett, the Commodore proved that his band did, in fact, become one of the regulars in the big band era.

The Commodore Hotel was the right place. It meant that places like the Savoy Ballroom, the Meadowbrook, or the Glen

Island Casino in all likelihood would follow. It meant broadcasts over WOR and WNEW, regularly reaching coast-to-coast listeners. With its clientele and excitement, the Commodore was the logical place to lure artists and repertoire men (a&r) of recording companies and music publishers; these entities were the *sine qua non* of fame in the big band era.

I

One recording company in particular, Decca, which had come into existence (out of Brunswick personnel)* in mid-1934, was now competing in the rapidly growing industry. At its inception Decca had pressed Dick Jurgens and Bing Crosby. It followed with Bob Crosby and the Dorsey Brothers in 1935. Decca was making it, despite doubts by the thriving bigger companies. "They said we'd fold in short order," reminisced "Decca" Joe Perry.

The earlier Hallett aggregation, unfortunately, had travelled too extensively; such an arrangement did not lend itself to attracting recording executives. "As a matter of fact," recalled Frankie, "the only time we stayed put was at the Commodore Ballroom in Lowell (Mass.) and at the Kentucky Hotel in Louisville." Now, a reputed one-nighter band notwithstanding, Hallett enjoyed more prolonged engagements. This made the difference. Thus, by the third week into the Commodore Hotel stand, Hallett landed a Decca contract.

Hallett recorded for the first time on October 23, 1936. Bob Stevens was recording manager. Hallett cut "Where the Lazy River Goes By" and "There's Something in the Air" (993A and B); "Sweetheart, Let's Grow Old Together" and "Moonlight on

---

*Brunswick was selling to Warner Brothers and in the interim, Jack Kapp conceived the idea of a new label. Hence, Kapp, with four or five Brunswick personnel, including Joe Perry who got Bing Crosby and Dick Jurgens to record on the new label, and Bob Stevens from Columbia, launched the new enterprise. Sterling Lewis of London Decca was the backer; thus the label assumed the Decca name.

the Chesapeake" (984A and B); and "Good-Night My Love" (1047A). The B-side to "Good-Night My Love" was done at the second recording date, November 4, when Hallett pressed "One Never Knows, Does One?" On that November date, Hallett also did "In the Chapel in the Moonlight" and "Let Me Sing in Echo Valley" (1033A and B).

Then, in January, 1937, Decca gave Hallett one of the most popular tunes of the time, "Big Boy Blue" (1163A), even if the Andrew Sisters, Count Basie, and Les Brown were now in the Decca fold. Needing a B-side for "Big Boy Blue," Stevens suggested a number that Hallett played often at the Commodore and one which WOR and WNEW had aired numerous times—"Ridin' High," a number in which the Hallett pianist excelled in solo.* A month later, Hallett recorded "Rockin' Chair Swing" (1190A) and for a B-filler used "Humoresque," with solo in Frankie's own rendition, the one he had copyrighted in 1929, and one which had also been performed often at the Commodore and in broadcasts.

"Ridin' High" and "Humoresque" eventually found their way into one platter (25147), but the record was not released until September 8, 1947! And then re-released in the album, Piano Magic, (DL 5087) in February, 1950, and again in March, 1970, on platter (VL 3622), along with other numbers Frankie played with a rhythm section under separate contract with Decca.

*The artistry of Frankie Carle on this number has been unsurpassed. Chuck Cecil, dj whose chronological compilation (from *Cashbox & Billboard* information) of million-sellers used previously in this book, relates the following incident, some 34 years after that 1937 recording. "It was 1970 or '71," began Cecil. "I had just played Hallett's 'Ridin' High.' That was at KFI. George Shearing called. I took the call myself. Shearing just had to know who played that great piano on the record. I told him, 'Frankie Carle.' "

II

Primarily because of his solo work with Hallett and the broadcasts over WOR and WNEW, the artistry of pianist Frankie Carle became recognized by an important segment of music-America, the New York scene. "The first broadcast from New York was on October 5, 1936," Frankie asserted positively, checking a very small diary he kept of those years. "The next day we played for the Yankees, a party for their winning the '36 series," he added.

Of the forty-six broadcasts from the Commodore Hotel, Frankie was featured forty-two times, playing fourteen numbers in forty-four solos. He played "Doll House," "Vipers' Drag," and "Spring Fever" once; the others, and times played, were "Ink Spots" (5); Frankie's "Estelle" (4); "Would Do Anything for You" (2); "After You've Gone" (2); "I Got Rhythm" (4); "Ridin' High" (8); "Alligator Crawl" (3); "Tea for Two" (5); "Nola" (2); "Canadian Capers" (3); and "Humoresque" (3). Most of these numbers were requested by listeners, some requests coming from Nova Scotia. "Tea for Two" was the most popular, and often requested was "Canadian Capers," a tune which listeners had been requesting since the days of WBZ! Decca, which had already recruited the Hallett swing, now singled out Hallett's featured artist.

Thus, the Tuesday following the Hallett closing in Atlantic City—September 7, 1937—the Carle-Barbour-Weiss-Stephens quartet recorded its first session. That session included thirteen tunes, including three of the most popular tunes of the time, "Afraid to Dream," "You Can't Have Everything," and "The Moon Got in My Eyes." (See Discography) It was a capable quartet, with Dave Barbour on the guitar, Sammy Weiss on the drums, Dave Stephens on bass, and Frankie.

At a second recording session on October 26, 1937, the quartet pressed "Rosalie," "Why Should I Care," "Who Knows," on one side and "In the Still of the Night," "I've a Strange New Rhythm," and "In My Heart" on the flip side of one platter (29214). On a second platter (29215) Decca packed "Nice Work

If You Can Get It," "A Foggy Day," "Things are Looking Up," and "I Can't Be Bothered Now" on one side and on the filler, "Have You Met Miss Jones," "I'd Rather Be Right," "Sweet Sixty Five," and "Take and Take and Take."

By the third and last recording session on January 3, 1938, Frankie had already left Hallett. At this time the quartet cut three records, but the platters were not jammed with numerous tunes. "Kitten on the Keys," the Confrey number Frankie had mastered in the 1920's, appeared on side A (25144) and "Holiday" on side B. "Flapperette," and "Dancing Tambourine" appeared on platter (25145) and "Doll Dance" and "Wedding of the Painted Doll," on another (25146). (See Discography for release and re-release dates.)

III

Charlie Shribman continued to push the Hallett image, and through Charlie, whose many friends included Frank Dailey, better engagements were in the offing. Six days after closing at the Commodore, the Hallett orchestra landed a Roseland Ballroom date. The Roseland was a one-day affair; yet, it was the Roseland! And less than a month later—twenty-seven days to be exact—the orchestra set up at the famous Meadowbrook on March 18 for a ten-day stand. The Meadowbrook meant broadcasts over the ABC and CBS networks; it also meant that, yes, indeed, the Mal Hallett orchestra and Frankie Carle were a part of the big band era.

While CBS and ABC were bringing Mal Hallett to the nation, Martin Block was plugging "Ridin' High" and "Humoresque" over WNEW.

The last date at Meadowbrook was March 28—three days after Frankie's 33d birthday. "The day before we closed," offered Frankie, "I became a New York man (Local, American Federation of Musicians)." He was quite pleased with himself, having precise knowledge at hand rather than going through the alphabet as he had so often done in trying to remember detail.

"After Meadowbrook," continued Frankie, "the one-nighters started again. In Waltham, Mass.," he interjected rather suddenly, "we had a battle of music against Fats Waller." The two piano players had not crossed paths since that time in Springfield. Frankie squinted his eyes, probing deeply for details of that history, but he could not recall whether or not the subject of Zez Confrey came the first or second time that he and Fats met. To be sure, however, Zez Confrey's name did come up. Frankie's version of Confrey's "Kitten on the Keys" had received much favorable comment, including that of Fats Waller. The number also found its way in Decca album (DL 5087) in 1950 and in another album (VL 3622) in 1970.

As the one-nighters proceeded, the Hallett orchestra appeared in ballrooms in which it had not appeared before. The exposure in New York and Charlie Shribman's connections paved the way to different ballrooms, more colleges, theaters, a movie short, and more broadcasts. Eventually the Hallett orchestra spearheaded westward to Indianapolis.

The Hallett aggregation made a Vitaphone movie short in May, 1937. After the two-day shooting, the band one-nighted its way to Detroit. Coming east again, it ended up in Baltimore for a week's run at the Hippodrome Theater, June 17-24. Frankie nursed an injured foot while he vacationed for a week in early July, and after one-nighters in Springfield and Old Orchard, Me., Frankie and the Hallett crew enjoyed a string of theaters unprecedented in the Hallett itinerary. After a Paramount Theater stay from July 21 through August 3, Hallett appeared at the Earle in Washington, D. C., the Nixon in Philadelphia, the Stanley in Pittsburgh, the Capital in Steubenville, and the Michigan in Detroit.

In Detroit Frankie received word that Dora was seriously ill. He wasted no time; immediately he left for Providence. The organist at the Michigan Theater filled in for Frankie for the remainder of the engagement.

Coming home to Providence under these circumstances contrasted sharply with Frankie's usual homecomings. The two youngest Carlone children, Lou and Lucky, were young men. Lucky was the only one yet in school (a basketball star at Hope

Frankie with Hallett the Second Time Around. Frankie was "Ridin' High" in popularity at the time (May, 1937) of this Vitaphone picture.

High). Edith met Frankie in Providence, and together, with the whole Carlone family, waited anxiously until Dora passed through a critical period. On September 3 Dora was admitted to the state's Walum Lake Sanitarium, the condition being pulmonary tuberculosis. Eventually this condition was to cause her blindness.

Shortly after Dora entered the sanitarium, Frankie rejoined Hallett in Atlantic City for a week's run. Hallett returned to Boston for a stay at the Metropolitan Theater, then on to the Earle in Philadelphia, the Stanley in Camden, landing at the Savoy Ballroom in New York on October 3. It was a one-day engagement, but it was the Savoy!

October was a whirlwind. After more one-nighters, including a ball at VMI, the Hallett orchestra opened at the Lyric Theater, Indianapolis, the farthest west the crew had penetrated. Then all over again. Back east for more recording dates, theaters, and ballrooms. "It was about this time I played solo for Martin Block on WNEW Swing Session," related Frankie. "First time for me. There appeared myself, Count Basie, the Andrew Sisters, and James Grundy the arranger." (Date, October 31, 1937, to be exact.)

The Hallett orchestra and Frankie Carle, featured soloist, were making their mark in the 1937 music-America revolution, both presumably reaching status of celebrated personalities. At the pace Hallett was growing and at the momentum Frankie Carle was accelerating, it seemed almost certain that both, leader and sideman, were to achieve the prominence of others who "made it"—names like Larry Clinton, Artie Shaw, Sammy Kaye, Les Brown, Lionel Hampton, Harry James, and a host of others who were proselytizing throngs to "big bands."

But.

Prior to the Vitaphone movie short, Hallett increased Frankie's salary to $200 per week. On that account Frankie was satisfied, a steady income with bonuses on occasion. Satisfaction of remuneration was offset, however, by the change in attitude Hallett had shown his star pianist. Starting sometime after the Vitaphone job and becoming more noticeable after Frankie's appearance on the Martin Block show, the rapport between leader Hallett and assistant Carle skidded. "He was drinking quite heavily by that time," offered Frankie, suggesting that perhaps Hallett's drinking may have contributed to the cooling of the relationship. Hallett began giving Frankie fewer and fewer solos. Hallett further shied away from giving Frankie the responsibilities once afforded him. "Toward the later part of November," remembered Frankie, "we were playing Pottsville (Penn.). I finally approached Mal. Asked him what was the trouble. Why he was avoiding me." Frankie felt he had executed his responsibilities to the satisfaction of Hallett and himself and failed to see any reason for Hallett's disaffection.

Hallett, lacking tact in any encounter with a sideman, merely brushed the inquiry off lightly but boldly. "This is my band," he growled somewhat incoherently. "I'll do what I want."

A stunned piano player, almost always even-tempered but provoked at this treatment, tersely said, "You're drunk. I quit. You got my notice."

The parting was unusually abrupt for such an illustrious association. "I would have walked off then and there," explained Frankie, "but I had to give two weeks. Union requirement."

Frankie's last two weeks with Hallett were uneventful. "Just played my parts," sighed the Hallett star attraction.

IV

A thirty-four-year old Frankie Carle, songwriter, had hardly matched the achievement of Frankie Carle, pianist, in 1937. Another auspicious occurrence resulting from the Commodore Hotel engagement was Frankie's meeting William "Bill" Lackenbauer, owner of Jewel Music. Lackenbauer, a friend of Hallett, would come to the Commodore frequently. He enjoyed listening to Frankie's "licks" between sets (Frankie always played solo between sets), but what struck Lackenbauer's fancy was Frankie's improvisation—or what Lackenbauer thought was improvisation—of established tunes. Having learned that Lackenbauer was a publisher, Frankie approached him regarding a song Frankie had written two years earlier. The song, "Blue Fantasy," Frankie felt, fit perfectly the style of Duke Ellington and wanted Lackenbauer to try getting Ellington to do it. Prior to this solicitation, Lackenbauer had begun to nurture a "hunch" about the capabilities of the Hallett pianist. "Blue Fantasy" was a departure from the music in vogue; nevertheless, Lackenbauer did take it. Though he could not get Ellington to do the number, Lackenbauer did place it with Gene Kardos. Kardos pressed it on a Vocalion label. The song did not become a hit, even though Clyde McCoy pressed it a bit later. But more important—as Lackenbauer himself will, later, relate the details of "Blue Fantasy" and other Carle songs—the die was cast: Lackenbauer's foresight and "guts" and Frankie Carle's music.

Frankie's first compositions were "My Best Gal" and "How I Miss That Sweet Gal O'Mine." "My Best Gal" was a mix-up from the beginning. The song came out "Best Black" by Brunswick-Balke-Collender in 1925 without the composer's knowledge. At twenty-two, an enthusiastic songwriter with the McEnelly band was excited to meet a recognized group, The Mound City Blue Blowers and one William "Red" McKenzie, when that group played the Butterfly. Frankie had performed "My Best Gal" with McEnelly and on occasions between sets and other occasions when added attractions came to the Butterfly. Frankie had forgotten about the songs. He was unaware that "My Best Gal" had been recorded, even though the *Springfield Union* (December, 1925) reported, "the number by Frankie Carle 'My Best Big Black' was recorded by the Mound City Blue Blowers for the Brunswick company." The incident had come to pass. "I forgot about those songs completely," reflected Frankie, "until Shapiro, Bernstein called me in the fall of '37—twelve years later." Shapiro, Bernstein wanted to publish "Georgiana," an instrumental to which they were adding lyrics. The original tune carried the names of "Red" McKenzie and

Frankie Carle and was entitled "Best Black." Frankie never copyrighted the song; McKenzie did. "It was just plain stolen," surmised the pianist. Frankie did go to Shapiro, Bernstein, and, by this time, 1937, the pianist, having nurtured an inclination toward songwriting and anxious to get his name on songs, was satisfied that his name would appear on "Georgiana," which it did, along with the names of "Red" McKenzie and Austen-Croon Johnson. Thus "Georgiana" was published. Shapiro, Bernstein then published an arrangement of the number by Larry Clinton a short time later.

Frankie had not returned to songwriting until 1930 when economic conditions caused a slowdown in the ballroom business. Having ample time on his hand, Frankie began arranging and creating tunes. He was particularly pleased with an arrangement of "Humoresque" on which he had worked at length. It was upon the rejection of that arrangement by Mills Music that another Frankie Carle work became noticed.

Frankie took "Humoresque" to Mills where he performed his arrangement for "a man named Stark," recalled Frankie. "Stark told me Jack Mills was in Europe, and he, Stark, was handling affairs." Frankie played "Humoresque" but Stark was not impressed, asking Frankie if he had anything else. Frankie did have a tune which he had recently completed. He played the number, but Stark showed no enthusiasm for it. As Frankie picked up his material getting ready to leave, Jack Mills darted into the room, "Hey, I like that. I'll take it." A startled Frankie Carle glanced at Stark, but Mills continued talking and asked Frankie what he called the song. Frankie had no name for the tune. "Well, we'll call it 'Estelle,'" said Mills. And "Estelle" it became. Estelle was the name of Jack Mills' wife.

"Estelle" did get some play, but the song never attained "hit" status. Frankie's songs became secondary to Mills, who had come to recognize that the young songwriter was an exceptional pianist. Hence, Mills put together a book, "Piano Stylings," with one Frankie Carle at the keys.

From 1930 on, Mills had always enjoyed first choice at a Frankie Carle tune. In 1931, the lean years for the ballroom

GEORG GEORGIANNA

Featured by Russ Morgan

The Norsemen

DEEP IN YOUR EYES
WORDS BY MITCHELL PARISH AND RUSSELL SNOW
MUSIC BY "SMILING" FRANKIE CARLE

FIRST EDITION

GEORGIANNA

By RED McKENZIE,
FRANKIE CARLE and
AUSTEN CROOM-JOHNSON

SHAPIRO, BERNSTEIN & Co. Inc.
MUSIC PUBLISHERS   NEW YORK

MILLS MUSIC
Music Publishers

business, Frankie worked with Russell Snow on numerous tunes. Of the eleven songs written that year, "most stayed on the shelf at Mills," offered Frankie. However, Mills did publish "Deep in Your Eyes," and this number, too, fell short of "hit" status.

It was not until 1933 that Mills published another number, "Alone with My Tears," the third Frankie Carle composition, and it was not until 1937 that Mills again published anything of Frankie Carle, and then that was not an original composition but a set of arrangements "Modern Hot Piano Solos." Mills had access to twenty-eight original numbers, including "I've Been Dispossessed by You" which Mills did not publish, even though Mal Hallett recorded it.*

Thus, when Frankie befriended Bill Lackenbauer at the Commodore Hotel, a second professional opinion of Frankie Carle music came into existence. Frankie went to Lackenbauer with "Blue Fantasy." Lackenbauer recognized a uniqueness not only in the style of Frankie's playing but in the style of his writing. Lackenbauer felt strongly that the Hallett pianist would, indeed, write great songs.

*Recorded by Mal Hallett, with Teddy Grace on vocals. Decca #1419B. Decca had no record of recording this number. The Frankie Carle catalogue showed no listing of this number. (See Discography)

CHAPTER 9

Transiency had become a way of life for musicians during the rise of big bands in the 1930's. Stories about musicians quitting leaders or leaders firing sidemen echoed widely and rapidly. The credibility of these stories depended upon the personalities involved. When the story of Frankie's leaving Hallett came out, people in the business accepted the story as matter of fact because of Hallett's reputation in dealing with the likes of Krupa, Teagarden, Mondello, and Jenney. Those who knew Frankie intimately thought that it was about time he left; others with a vested interest in the business wondered how Hallett could let his "star" get away.

One such individual who wondered how Hallett could let his "star" get away was Norman Flewelling, who reacted quickly with a trip to Springfield. Flewelling proposed that Frankie once again organize his own band. The Connecticut booker was confident that he could get plenty of work for Frankie and felt that Frankie's reputation in New England would attract first class musicians. Flewelling also felt that the big band market was ripe for a good band. Having experienced the frustration of failure in previous attempts, Frankie was not immediately receptive to the idea. But the lingering, inherent urge to lead, an urge which had matured over the years, effected the response, "I'll think about it." For the time being, Frankie explained to Flewelling, he wanted to spend some time with the family and see what happens. Flewelling had to be satisfied with that decision but would be in communication with Frankie again after the holidays.

Thus, during the Christmas season of 1937, an unemployed Frankie Carle, his wife Edith, and their twelve-year-old Marjorie were on their way to visit with the Carlones in Providence. The thought of unemployment had not dampened Frankie's optimism. He would return to music; in exactly what capacity, was uncertain.

Frankie's thoughts at this particular time were his mother,

father, and brothers and sisters. At home in Providence he would play cards with father Angelo and would surprise him again with a new artificial leg. He would thrill at the details of basketball games in which Lucky starred at Hope High School. He would talk long with brother Louie, who now was a truck driver. He would give piano lessons to the girls—Jenny, Louise, Esther, and Ann. Etta and Evelyn, the only married sisters, would come in from Hoboken to spend the holidays. Frankie would live, in a word, *family*. Then he might visit with old friends, like Addeo, his childhood chum whose band had become a figurehead at a dinner-house in Providence.

Dora was still at Walum Lake Sanitarium, where the family would visit her at every opportunity. Dora, always mindful of her son's involvement in music, was inquisitive; she knew he was out of work. She appeared to be in good spirits when Frankie related his good fortune of a recording session with Decca at the beginning of the new year. He told Dora about Flewelling's proposal for another orchestra. Dora was elated at this news. "Yes," she agreed, "that's for you." But Frankie purposely avoided discussion, and he was happy when Dr. U. E. Zamborano interrupted their conversation with a request for Frankie to play. In the meantime, implored Frankie, as he escorted his mother to the recreation room, Dora was not to worry the slightest about him or the family, but to get well and come home.

At his visits to Walum Lake, Frankie would always anticipate and readily accept Dr. Zamborano's invitation to play a "duet" with the piano-playing doctor for the entertainment of the patients. These performances with the doctor became routine at every visit. Frankie enjoyed playing there; the patients loved it; Dora was particularly delighted.

During the Christmas season Frankie and Edith discussed the Flewelling proposal. Edith, too, agreed that Frankie ought to go ahead with the plan. She had saved some money. They did some accounting, and though they would sink everything into the venture, they decided to call Flewelling. "If it didn't work out," they jested, "well, what the heck, we've been broke before."

I

Hurriedly, Frankie rounded up some of the crew he had in 1935-1936. Available were Frank Granato, Ben Puglia, Gus Benvenuti, and Percy Booth. Frankie then recruited Ben Funk and Irving Berger on trumpets, Sam Salomone on tenor sax, and Bob McDonald on guitar. Drummer Hack O'Brien could only help out temporarily because of previous commitments but he was happy that Frankie was getting back at the helm. Evie Vale would soon replace him. Frankie had little time to shape up the band, but by the time the Frankie Carle orchestra opened at the Seven Gables in Milford, Conn., Frankie was quite pleased with the sound. And the orchestra proved successful. Joe Casillo, owner of the Seven Gables, had come to appreciate the group, especially since the Gables was showing a steady increase in patronage. In the beginning, Casillo, hesitant to go with an unknown bandleader, agreed only to a six-week run. Flewelling, in the meantime, continued pushing for long-term jobs, and he was successful in landing a stand at the Edgewood Club, where Frankie last played before the Hallett sojourn. When the engagement at the Gables finished, Casillo was sorry that he had not acted sooner, for he really had grown fond of the Frankie Carle orchestra and now could only wait until other commitments had been satisfied.

Frankie returned to Edgewood early that spring. Evie Vale of Hartford was now on drums. The sidemen who played with Frankie in 1936 joked about their last job at Edgewood, with the owner himself escorting the band back from a break. This time the owner surprised the band with a new contrivance. He rigged up an electrical device that would signal the band when the break time was over. "Even if his toy finally bothered us," explained Frankie, "I felt very sorry for him. He was really plagued with arthritis. He was quite irritable and began picking on us. We were glad to finish there."

Frankie left Edgewood and returned to the Seven Gables. Casillo greeted the return of the Frankie Carle orchestra with enthusiasm. His admiration for the piano player and his satisfaction with the band were attested to by his offering Frankie

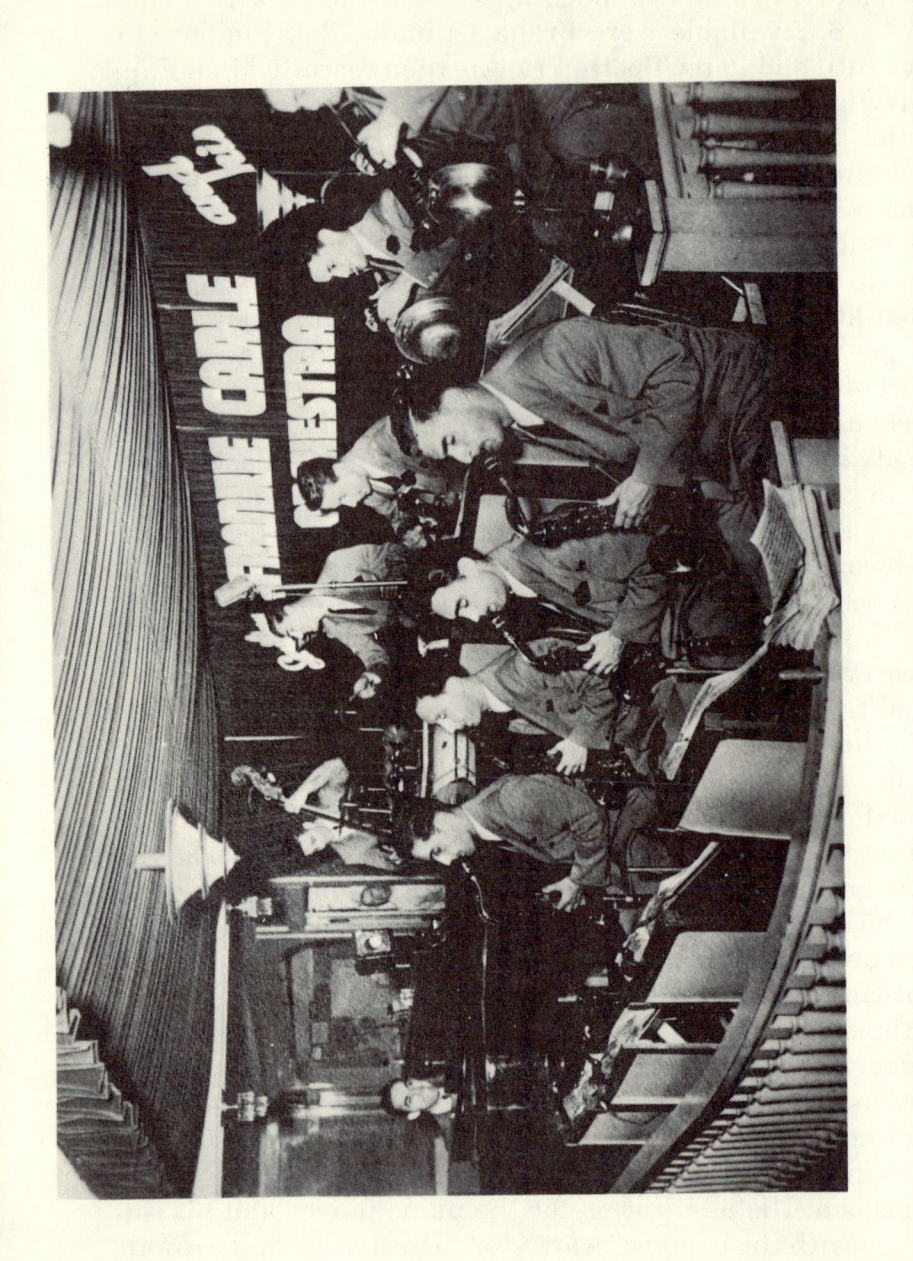

Frankie's 1938 Seven Gables Orchestra. Frank Granato, bass; Evie Vale, drums; Bob McDonald, guitar; Ben Funk, trumpet; Irving Berger, trumpet; Sam Salomone, tenor sax; Ben Puglia, alto sax; Gus Benvenuti, alto sax; Percy Booth, tenor sax.

the job at the Seven Gables for as long as Frankie wanted it. Casillo's pronouncement relieved some of the pressure on Frankie who had been constantly seeking a way not only to enhance the prominence of the orchestra but also to save it from bankruptcy. But Frankie needed an exposure greater than that of the Seven Gables; he needed broadcasts and recordings, especially in 1938 when the "band craze" was evident across the country. Even a "hit" song would have helped. None of these stepping stones, however, were immediately forthcoming. Frankie believed that his musicians were the best, with a sound comparable to a score of sounds of bigger name bands. "What, then, was wrong?" he thought.

The Seven Gables thrived; it catered to a mixed clientele, including important people in the music business either patronizing the Gables by chance or choice or coming there purposely on Frankie's behalf or request.

Frankie had made numerous trips to New York City, trying either to push the band or sell a song. All these trips were frustrating. Tom Rockwell and Corky O'Keefe, management of the Casa Loma band, did come to the Gables and Frankie asked them to appraise the orchestra. "They thought the band was fair," related Frankie, "but were really not sold on it. They wanted me and the band to go to Frisco for a week. I said no."

"Jimmy Dorsey and Helen O'Connell came in one night," continued Frankie, "but that was a social call."

What Frankie meant was that O'Connell and Frankie met some years earlier, as he had met Jimmy Dorsey when the Dorsey Brothers band existed. O'Connell had approached Frankie when the Hallett orchestra was playing Steubenville, Ohio. She wanted desperately to sing with a band, Frankie's band. But the band Frankie was leading at that moment was not his own. He told her that if ever he had his own band, he would hire her. Frankie sent her to Larry Funk, who he thought was looking for a singer. Funk was not, but he referred her to Jimmy Dorsey. O'Connell was not at the Seven Gables at this time looking to be hired by Frankie Carle, for she was already among the top chirpers singing with one of the most popular leaders in the band era.

Although Frankie harbored a secret disappointment that the orchestra had remained at a plateau, his dealings with everyone, socially or professionally, were congenial. After several months at the Gables, he had suspected that the Seven Gables was the top of the world for the Frankie Carle orchestra. But the job was steady, he rationalized, and it was his for life, at least, that is what Casillo had reiterated. But then Joe Casillo died suddenly.

The affable Casillo suffered a heart attack at his wedding anniversary celebration at the Gables. Having grown fond of the Casillo family—Joe, his wife, and the two children—Frankie felt the loss deeply. He understood well the attachments in a closely knit family.

"After Joe died," imparted the Gables' house-bandleader, "it wasn't the same."

When Joe died, his son Lenny assumed control of the Gables. "Lenny was a good kid," continued Frankie, "and knew the business well enough. I'm sure Joe's passing hurt the business a little."

About a month later, Lenny had forewarned that the orchestra might have to take a cut in salary. Frankie's savings were gone, his portion of the band-take was inadequate to keep meeting expenses, the band's general fund was bankrupt, nothing promising for the orchestra was in store, Frankie's songwriting was not paying off, and the prospect of lesser pay left little doubt that the end of the Frankie Carle orchestra was in sight. Emotionally, Frankie apprised the band of the situation. He suspected that the crew had already come to that conclusion. The Frankie Carle orchestra lasted at the Seven Gables until July of that year. Frankie and the boys had always been on the friendliest terms; that made the parting sad. After one year and five months as a bandleader, Frankie would become, one more time, a sideman.

During the last several weeks at the Gables, Frankie had begun feeling despondent. The more conscious he became of the condition, the more pronounced it appeared. Apparently the strain and stress accompanying disappointment had affected him. Having gone through periods of nervous exhaustion in the past, Frankie was not convinced that his new condition was the same. Whatever it was, it caused him to hold back, eventually convicing him that maybe he was "through."

Thus, when the band was on the verge of folding, Frankie was in a quandary. He was thirty-six years old; frustrations were a little harder to take now. Although Frankie lost some drive, he was still congenial most of the time. Edith detected some cynicism. But one bandleader was not going to take "no" for an answer—Horace Heidt.

The Horace Heidt orchestra, before it was known as Horace Heidt and His Musical Knights, was playing the Arena in New Haven when Heidt visited Frankie at the Gables. Heidt was doing the Allemite program at that time. After a dinner and long discussion at the Gables, Heidt persuaded Frankie to sit in with the band that coming Sunday at least for one performance. Frankie consented to do it. He soloed on the Heidt program in New Haven. The tune was "Sunrise Serenade," a number which Bill Lackenbauer had succeeded in placing with Glen Gray and, a little later, with Glenn Miller.

The following Monday, Heidt called Frankie from New York City, the Biltmore, and wanted Frankie to come to audition for Heidt and Frank DeVol, who was handling music arrangements and personnel for Heidt. Frankie, hesitant, admitted that he simply had no money; he was quite embarrassed about that. But Heidt insisted. "He sent me $1,000 to get there and anything I needed," disclosed Frankie, "more than enough. And he never would take that money back, either," he added.

Toward the end of June, 1939, when a tune, "Sunrise Serenade" was beginning to get much play, Frankie made that trip to New York. Some of the spunk that he had exhibited earlier was gone. He had ventured that great city many times, trying to sell a band, a song. He was on his way to—of all things—audition! A twenty-year experienced pianist, a superstar since he was thirteen—on his way to an audition. Frankie Carle no more needed to audition than Rachmaninoff! And it took less than eight bars to satisfy procedure. Frankie joined Heidt, July 15, 1939.

II

The experiences of the Frankie Carle band at the Edgewood before and after Hallett, and the extended engagement at the Seven Gables were far from losses. Quite the contrary. Frankie may have suffered the loss of a band and perhaps his pride, but he gained the respect of the music world as a consequence of his being there. At Edgewood Frankie came to write "Sunrise Serenade" and at the Gables he came into the Heidt organization.

Although Frankie failed to sustain a dance orchestra as leader ever since his first try with the Syncopators, he continued to persevere as a star performer. He had awed audiences with Colangelo, with Yohe, with McEnelly, and with Hallett. Even when he led his own groups, he would capture the attention of audiences and enrapture his following of admirers. When his orchestra played the Edgewood Club in 1936, one such admirer was Johnny Quinn of Troy, N. Y. Quinn and his wife Grace frequented the Edgewood, as they did other ballrooms wherever Frankie appeared. The Quinns had been admirers of Frankie from the McEnelly through the Hallett years. Along the way, Edith and Frankie Carle had established a friendship with the Quinns long before the engagement at the Edgewood Club. Johnny Quinn, a man of means, but by what means Frankie could only conjecture, was a man of some influence in Troy. He knew and had dealt with some of the more prominent citizens.

Thus, the Frankie Carle orchestra in Edgewood afforded the Carles and the Quinns many occasions to socialize, even if the socializing occurred after the job and generally centered around highballs and a Chinese game—Mahjong—which the Quinns taught the Carles to play.

It was a warm night in early summer when the Quinns asked Frankie and Edith to join them for a nightcap and maybe a little Mahjong. Edith encouraged accepting the offer. She knew that Frankie had been experiencing some depression because the band had not realized its potential after many months at

Edgewood. This would be diversion. They accompanied the Quinns to Troy.

After better than an hour at the game of Mahjong, the group conceded to enough cards, the ladies comforting themselves on the couch. Quinn asked Frankie to play a little piano while Quinn fixed another round of drinks. Quinn intimated his preference in Frankie's style; he particularly enjoyed Frankie's licks between sets when Frankie would improvise a tune or randomly finger the keys while he seemingly fell into a sort of reverie.

"Why not compose a tune in that style," suggested Quinn, as he mixed the drinks.

Frankie understood immediately what Quinn meant and went to the piano. He rolled his fingers over the keys randomly.

"You mean like this," as he touched tercets in varying combinations with no definite arrangement.

"Yeah, like that," agreed Quinn, shaking his head in approval.

Frankie continued, and about several minutes into the manipulations, a "thump, thump" resounded from the ceiling, flooring the occupants in the apartment upstairs.

Frankie ceased, but Quinn was quick to say, "Hell with 'em. Keep playing Frankie."

There was a second warning and a third from the occupants upstairs, but Quinn each time insisted that Frankie continue, for, thought Quinn, that's the kind of playing that typifies Frankie.

Before the quarter hour had elapsed since the last interruption, Frankie had come up with a melody that struck his and his host's fancy. But at the same moment, which by the clock was long past four in the morning, a visitor knocked at the front door. It was no visitor but a police officer. Almost apologetically, as the officer recognized Quinn, he delivered the complaint of disturbance. Quinn, who had had occasion in the past to become acquainted with the police and had even remembered the name of this particular one, very congenially escorted the officer into the apartment. He introduced him to Frankie and explained what Frankie was doing. Quinn proposed that the officer himself listen to Frankie's tune and then weigh the complaint of disturbance. Somewhat reluctantly the officer agreed, although he did refuse the drink Quinn offered him. Frankie played the tune, and Quinn immediately wanted the officer's reaction.

"It's very nice," he said. "What do ya call it?"

Frankie just shrugged his shoulders and continued very softly with repeated chords to give the tune a finality. Quinn, almost immediately realizing the horizon breaking with dawn, interjected, "Sunrise—that's it."

"Nay," uttered Frankie inaudibly as he rose from the piano stool. He observed that the officer was more relieved that perhaps the "noise" would now cease, than he was anxious to pursue the insignificance of a song title. The word "Sunrise" stuck in Frankie's mind however, for as he rose, he unconsciously added, "Serenade—yeah, Sunrise Serenade."

The officer prepared to leave, satisfied by inference that the party, and, therefore, disturbance, was terminated. His leaving prompted the Carles' leaving. And that was the sum and substance of the birth of one of the world's great standards.

Frankie had never written down the notes; he did not have to. They were implanted in his soul. By the end of that summer, Frankie had given up with the band and returned to Hallett. Only occasionally in the next couple of years, in the quiet of his solitude and his piano, would he finger that tune.

III

During Frankie's second tenure with Hallett, "Sunrise Serenade" remained in the back of Frankie's mind. It was not until early 1938 when the tune became a topic of recollection. Frankie had garnered another band and at one of his dates, Quinn came in. Reminiscing, he asked Frankie, "Frankie, remember that tune you made up the night the cop broke up our party?"

Frankie had not thought of it for a long time, but once he began playing it, every note fell into its proper place.

"Yeah, that's the one," said Quinn, "gee, that's pretty."

"Doesn't mean a damn thing," stammered Frankie, "nobody wants it."

What Frankie meant was simple enough; nobody wanted "Sunrise." With his 1938 band, Frankie sought ways to enhance the Frankie Carle orchestra. Besides trying to land bigger places for the band, he was pushing his songs, about six or seven, including "Sunrise," which he had not written down yet. Perhaps by landing a hit, the band would become recognized. Before he left Hallett, "Georgianna" was out; even "I've Been Dispossessed by You" came out on Decca with Hallett. Mills had published "Modern Hot Piano Solos" with Frankie on the keyboard and did publish "In Spite of the Way Things Are," but Mills wouldn't touch "Sunrise." Frankie had tried with "Blue Fantasy," the one he gave to Lackenbauer, and another "If You Please," but to no avail. "Leo Geist, and even the Berlin group didn't want "Sunrise," said Frankie, "they said it was too hard to sing. I didn't write it to be sung."

Shortly after being reminded of "Sunrise," Frankie made one copy—only one—and sent it off to Washington.

It was not until the fall of 1938 when Bill Lackenbauer came to the Gables on Frankie's request to hear some new material. Frankie had played a couple of other tunes but Lackenbauer insisted on something that was uniquely Frankie, the kind of stuff that Frankie would play when all familiar music was eradicated from his mind. When Frankie had nothing more to offer, he returned to the piano to play some licks before the next set. He began playing "Sunrise Serenade" and before he finished the piece, Lackenbauer was back at the piano.

"Now, that's what I want," he said, smiling as if he were sure Frankie would surprise him with something.

"Nay, Bill," protested Frankie, "You're too good a friend of mine to get stuck with this."

With words to the effect that he wouldn't mind getting stuck with it, Bill insisted that Frankie give him the music. Having no music, Frankie scribbled the song on the back of an envelope. Lackenbauer took it. And the account of "Sunrise Serenade," plus other Carle tunes, is best told by Lackenbauer himself.

Our first association in the music business was with the song called "Blue Fantasy." This song was recorded by Gene Kardos on the Vocalion label about 1936 or 1937. Shortly after, Clyde McCoy recorded it on Decca. It was the "B" side to his theme song "Sugar Blues." Though "Blue Fantasy" did not enjoy the hit status of his later songs, it did convince me that this was a man of exceptional talent and if we worked together, we would eventually come up with a song that would be played as long as good music was performed. When Frankie was playing with Mal Hallett at the Commodore Hotel in N. Y., I used to enjoy listening to Frankie play between dance sets. I often thought, if he would put some of those distinctly Frankie Carle's licks into a song, we would both make music history. When Frankie came to my table, I would suggest he put into a song that great talent he was wasting on other composers' songs. This he did with "Sunrise Serenade."

I am reminded of an incident three years later when Frankie was visiting me, and Frank Ryerson, co-composer of "Blue Champagne"—a song I was working on at the time—came into the office. Frank Ryerson was playing trumpet in Mal Hallett's band when Frankie Carle was in it. Frank Ryerson said to Frankie Carle, "Do you remember when Bill left the Commodore, you said to me, 'I think Bill's crazy with his suggestion.' " Frankie Carle's reply was "Yea, how do you like that." I only bring this out because artists with the abundance of talent of a Frankie Carle need a third person to show him that great talent he is letting go to waste. After Hallett, Frankie Carle formed his own band. One day when he was playing at the Seven Gables Inn, Milford, Conn., Frankie called me, asked if I would drive up to hear a song he wrote. Larry Wagner, who afterward became the arranger for Glen Gray and the Casa Loma Band, drove up to Milford with me. Frankie played the song he wanted me to hear. To me it sounded like something Billy Hill would write. I said to Larry, 'Why doesn't Frankie use the great God-given

*talent he has instead of writing like a million other writers.'
When Frankie came to our table and found I was not impressed,
he left and went up on the stand and started what I thought
was improvising. I said to Larry Wagner, 'Now that's Frankie
Carle.' I went up to Frankie and said, 'Now that's a pretty tune.
Whose is it?' Frankie said, "Mine, doesn't mean a thing." I asked
if anyone had it. He said "no." I said, 'I'll take it.' Frankie said,
"You're too good a friend of mine. I don't want to stick you with
it. I had it all over the street. Even Jack Mills wouldn't take it."
I said, 'Frankie, that's the kind of song I would like to be stuck
with.' He had no lead sheet so he wrote it on a manila envelope
I had. Frankie had made an arrangement for his band using
clarinets and rhythm section and he played it for me. The sound
to me was very good. I gave the manila envelope to Larry Wagner
and asked him to make an orchestration arrangement as soon
as possible, and incorporate Frankie Carle's clarinet sound in
the arrangement.*

*I distributed the orchestrations to all the major radio stations,
also all the major bands on the air. Followed up these contacts
every week for weeks, with no results. I sent a copy to Down Beat
magazine for a review on the song. The review was almost disastrous. When the review was published, they said, quote, "This
is the first time a music publisher was foolish enough to try to
make a popular song hit out of piano licks." My partners, when
they read that, tried to persuade me to drop the song and work
on a song that two of them wrote. When I refused, the three of
them went to my wife to try to get her to talk to me. They said
I was making the firm the laughing stock on the street. My wife
refused and said she never interfered in my business. She told
me of this meeting months later. One of my weekly contacts on
"Sunrise Serenade" was Jerry Sears, one of the conductors of
the house band on NBC. When I asked him if he had looked at
the tune yet, he said yes, but had tossed it aside when he saw
all those black notes in each bar. He said, "Bill, you are in
charge of the music on one of our shows and know we have only
15 minutes rehearsal for an hour show." After about an hour
of persuasion, he agreed to put it up at every rehearsal until the*

band got it down pat. After about two weeks, it was ready to be programmed. I took an off-the-air recording of the rendition and took this recording to Cork O'Keefe, Glen Gray's manager. He or Glen Gray never listened to it. After about 10 days, I tried a new approach. I got Glen Gray's secretary to play it every time I went to their office. She got to like it and played it very often. One day Glen and Cork were having a meeting and she started to play it in the outside office. Glen asked her what was that thing she was playing. She said, "That's Bill's tune 'Sunrise Serenade.'" Glen called me and asked me to bring two orchestrations over to the Waldorf where he was playing, as he wanted to put it in rehearsal that night. The next week I went to the Waldorf and as soon as I went in, Glen put it up on the stand and played it. After the set, he and Pee Wee Hunt came over to my table and told me everytime they played "Sunrise Serenade," dancers would stop and ask what was the name of that pretty song they were playing. Glen told me as soon as they got the song down the way they wanted it, they would put it on the air. After it was on the air a few times, they started to get fan mail on it. The mail became so big that they put it in their next recording session. But Jack Kapp, president of Decca records, red-penciled it out. After several such incidents, Glen suggested I see Jack Kapp. Jack said to me it was only a piano solo and maybe someday he may let Frankie Carle make a piano record of it. When I told Glen Gray what Jack said, Glen blew his top and said," I record it on my next session or I don't record." Rather than lose Glen, they recorded it on the "B" side of "Heaven Can Wait."

 When the record came out, Walter Winchell raved about "Sunrise" and Frankie Carle as composer, as did Dorothy Kilgallen, Earl Wilson, Walker, Jimmy Fidler, and scores of other writers. Calls came in from all over the country. Connie Boswell called and said she must have a lyric, as she wanted to do a vocal record on it. Glenn Miller called me the day after I had Leonard Joy, then recording manager for Victor, listen to Glenn when he was playing at the Paradise Restaurant. Glenn said he was going to record "Sunrise" on the Bluebird label. He also asked *if he could put his theme song on the back of "Sunrise." As he had no title for it, he would call it "Moonlight Serenade" with "Sunrise" on one side and "Moonlight" on the other. He would cover the whole day. I spoke to Leonard and that's the way the record came out. Miller used to open his stage show in theatres with a backdrop of a rising sun and then announce that "Sunrise Serenade" played the most important part in his early rise to success. Miller's record became the number one record in the nation when it took the play away from Glen Gray. Give a big plus to Frankie Carle and "Sunrise Serenade" for its outstanding contribution to the success of the nation's all time number one band, Glenn Miller's Orch.*

Horace Heidt's manager called and said Horace Heidt was going to record "Sunrise." Horace also heard Frankie played a pretty good piano. Horace could use him. Frankie joined Horace Heidt's Orch, and this was the beginning of Frankie Carle becoming one of the top band leaders in the country.

Frankie and I were fortunate in that neither he nor I belonged to any performance rights society at that time, so therefore we received no performing rights payments. If any commercial program wanted to use "Sunrise Serenade" they had to get my permission as the copyright owner. To receive that permission they had to announce on their program Frankie Carle's name as the composer every time they performed "Sunrise Serenade." As "Sunrise Serenade" was performed on every commercial program that used music many times, Frankie Carle and "Sunrise Serenade" became a household word.

SUNRISE SERENADE
Featured and Recorded by
GLEN GRAY
and the
CASA LOMA ORCHESTRA
Glen Gray
Casa Loma
CARLE
LYRIC BY
JACK LAWRENCE
JEWEL MUSIC PUBLISHING CO. INC.,
1674 BROADWAY, NEW YORK, N. Y.
Barbelle
MADE IN USA

CHAPTER 10

What if Frankie Carle had never gone with Heidt? Would "Sunrise Serenade" have given him the thrust needed to catapult his Seven Gables orchestra into the "big" time?

Frankie is not one to brood over "what if's." He is the first to give credit where credit is due, and Horace Heidt, to this day, enjoys the respect and gratitude of one Francisco Nunzio Carlone.

Horace Heidt, two years Frankie's senior, had a similar musical beginning to Frankie's. Heidt's mother, too, resorted to spankings for Horace's neglect at the piano. She, too, was the principal influence in Horace's initiation into show business.

After a not too impressive piano debut at age fourteen, Heidt entered Culver Military Academy, with ambitions of becoming an athlete. He did try out for the Culver Jazz Band, a band which nurtured the likes of Red Nichols, but Heidt was unsuccessful. Thus, he pursued his athletics, eventually winning "best all around athlete" award for his prowess in football, baseball, boxing, swimming, and track.

Heidt's athletic aspirations ended, however, when Heidt suffered a fractured spine when playing for the University of California. During his convalescence, he decided to return to music, as a singer or a piano player. He failed at both. Determined not to be embarrassed further in either category, Heidt organized his own band in the mid 1920's. He was "in" and "out" of the band business several times before he met with a sustained tour in Europe in 1931. (The first American band to play the Riviera.) Success was short lived. Returning to the United States, he settled in San Francisco where he created a band-training concept. He would train local musicians specifically for placing them on the stage to support the acts. Heidt worked out this scheme with the management of the Golden Gate Theater, and from that time on, Heidt began a series of firsts in entertainment.

By accident, Heidt conceived an idea from which evolved a

program called "Answers by the Dancers." While he was playing the Drake in Chicago, a microphone fell to the floor. To cover up the embarrassment, Heidt jumped down from the bandstand, picked up the microphone, and started asking the audience questions. The questions and responses were ad libbed, hence uncensored, and a whole new idea began in show business. In 1934 Heidt contrived Treasure Chest, a gift-giving bonanza which gave away vacations, plane trips to exotic places, etc., to couples celebrating wedding anniversaries. That program was successful. He followed with Pot O' Gold in 1938, another gift-giving program which utilized a wheel of fortune to determine the identity of the lucky one who would get a crack at the Pot O' Gold. This program led to a full-length movie. After the tremendous success of Pot O' Gold there was no end to the continued successes of the Heidt organization in the full spectrum of the entertainment business. At one time or another, many great performers were part of the Heidt family, and many of them eventually went out on their own to establish names for themselves. Art Carney, Al Hirt, Bobby Hackett, Frank DeVol, Gordon MacRae, Fred Lowery, and Dick Contino were some.

Yes, indeed, Horace Heidt was really "big" time.

Frankie joined Heidt in the summer of 1939 and remained with him until the fall of 1943, a tenure about the same length of time as that with Hallett. Heidt and Hallett had one thing in common—showmanship, the scope of Heidt's far greater. The Hallett orchestra was far more "hep" than Heidt's, but there was no comparison in all other respects. "Heidt didn't drink, either," quipped Frankie.

The Heidt organization, really an institution in the early 1940's, provided a talent such as Frankie Carle with every outlet to capitalize on that talent. Heidt played the best hotels, the theaters and ballrooms; he flooded the air waves coast-to-coast with his two successful give-away programs and broadcasts from the ballrooms; he recorded for Columbia, and even if his band was "corny," he managed to produce top-ten ratings in some recordings. And Horace Heidt played the whole country perhaps more than any other big name in the late 1930's and 1940's.

What Frankie had to do now was to live up to the reputation he had so very solidly gained in New England, a reputation leaping, perhaps, beyond local boundaries before he had joined Heidt. Ken Smith, former N.Y. Mirror sportswriter and, at this writing, director of Baseball's Hall of Fame and a Frankie Carle fan, recalls the popularity of the pianist:

> During the 1930's when I was on the N.Y. Mirror traveling with the N.Y. Giants, in Chicago, I'd drive with broadcaster Hal Totten sixty miles, after the Cubs-Giants game at Wrigley Field, to his home in Crystal Lake. Off with our coats, Hal would put on a stack of Carle records, and relax. That was the type of his following, there were many great ones but Frankie came through with the most melody.

Both the popularity of the pianist before Heidt and the success of "Sunrise Serenade" notwithstanding, Horace Heidt was the best thing that happened to Frankie Carle.

Heidt treated Frankie generously. The contract gave Frankie feature billing and at least one solo at all broadcasts. Frankie would receive additional monies for other appearances, commercials, movies, and recordings. Heidt eventually negotiated a Columbia recording deal for Frankie with a rhythm section made up of Heidt's sidemen. It was now up to Frankie.

And how did Frankie respond? Could he sustain the rigid discipline under which Heidt functioned and the glamorous but very hectic itinerary which Heidt pursued? Would Frankie live up to his expectation as a songwriter and a performer? And where would Heidt's bandwagon lead to?

I

The discipline maintained by Heidt, similar to the kind in the Edwin J. McEnelly orchestra, presented no obstacle to

The Heidt Troupe 1939-40.
(Left to Right) Front Row: Fred Lowery, Peggy Adams, Larry Cotton, Horace Heidt, LeAnn Sisters, Bobby Hackett, Henry Russell. Second Row: Frankie Carle, Bob Knight, Mary Drane, Beatrice Perrin, Virginia Drane. Third Row: Bernie Matthewson, George Dessinger, Jimmy DeMio, Bob Riedel, Jerry Kasper. Fourth Row: Eddie McKimey, Jerry Borshard, Wayne Webb, Warren Lewis, Frank Strasek. Back Row: Art Carney, Red Ferrington, Bob McCoy.

Top: Frankie received top billing with Heidt. Below: Frankie with the Wood sisters, Gloria, left, and Donna.

Frankie. Heidt and Frankie worked together, friendly and efficaciously. In his long association with Heidt, Frankie had experienced only two confrontations, both arising out of Frankie's vulnerability in matters of his music and family.

Frankie had been with Heidt not quite two weeks when the first occurred. Heidt was playing the Biltmore in New York. He programmed "Sunrise Serenade" for Frankie to solo over the air. As Frankie played, Heidt quickened the tempo—the usual Heidt tempo—but Frankie boldly ignored the leader. Several times Heidt made facial gestures to bounce in unison with his hands, but Frankie proceeded and finished "Sunrise Serenade" in the tempo he wrote it. Heidt was angry; he protested vehemently Frankie's disregard of his direction. "Did you not understand me," Heidt began, rhetorically, and in the same breath, "We play in one tempo."

"I didn't write it that way," interrupted Frankie, "and that's the only way I'll play it."

"I'll set the pace for the music," replied Heidt, but before he could finish, Frankie interrupted again, his face flushed, one of the few times in his life displaying that kind of emotional reaction.

"Your music, not mine. Do you want my two weeks' notice?" Frankie blurted out.

Heidt did not answer to that. Both adults, somewhat embarrassed, walked away from each other. The sidemen were astonished.

Larry Cotton, Heidt's singer, came to Frankie. Cotton had sung "Sunrise" several times and admitted that he had had much difficulty in singing the tune in the Heidt tempo. "All of Heidt is too fast," said the newcomer who dared defy Heidt.

"You're right, Frank. The song should be as you played it," agreed Cotton.

Less than one-half hour later, with tempers cooled, Heidt and Frankie faced each other. Both agreed to respect each other's principles; both apologized and decided to drop the matter. However, Heidt had not programmed "Sunrise Serenade" for a few weeks after the incident, but the tune, getting nationwide play, could not remain in solitary confinement much longer. Heidt scheduled it again, and after Larry Cotton's rendition, Cotton leaned over to Frankie and said only, "Thanks, Frank."

The orchestra played "Sunrise" in Frankie's tempo, and Cotton was able to sing a "difficult" song reasonably well.*

The only other Heidt-Carle confrontation occurred in Houston some four months after Frankie had joined Heidt.

Heidt was doing the Pot O' Gold and Treasure Chest programs each week. His engagements at the big hotels ran, generally, six weeks. He would do radio broadcasts and theater engagements and ballrooms, sometimes concurrently. Then there would be rehearsal *every morning.* The band had made its westward and southwestward sweep, and from Houston, it would come up to the Cocoanut Grove in Los Angeles for an extended engagement. Usually, then, Heidt would go up to the Golden Gate Theater in San Francisco, returning to the Los Angeles area. From there the band would go to Salt Lake, its turn eastward. It would be April by the time Heidt landed on the east coast. In Frankie's mind, about spring before he got home.

Edith and Marjorie remained in Springfield when the Heidt troupe came west. Once Frankie had acclimated himself to the Heidt policy and itinerary, he became very lonesome. He was not in the habit of being away from the family, both his families, for very long periods of time. In September, his mother Dora, after a three-year confinement at Walum Lake Sanitarium, was released. She had recovered well enough but she was going blind. Edith's letters would keep Frankie abreast of developments. "I guess it was a combination of things that made me homesick," reflected Frankie, not being even slightly embarrassed that a thirty-seven-year old man got homesick.

Thus, Frankie had asked Heidt for some time off. Heidt thought that a couple of weeks might be arranged. About a

---

*Connie Boswell, according to Frankie, was the only singer who sang "Sunrise Serenade" reasonably close to the tempo in which it was written.

week later, however, after a usual morning rehearsal, Heidt informed the band that all vacations were cancelled. Frankie spoke up immediately.

"Look, Horace, you promised me a vacation. I'm . . ."

Heidt cut him off. "Don't talk to me unless I ask you questions," he said, meaning that at the conclusion of a rehearsal, a regular meeting was in progress, and Frankie was out of order. Heidt continued, ignoring Frankie further, "we have additional dates to meet."

Before Heidt finished, Frankie again interrupted, "I'm going home, regardless," then sat down, fuming.

Heidt did not add much more to the announcement and dismissed the meeting. He took Frankie aside.

"You should never talk to me like that," Heidt said in a rather irate tone.

"Well, you promised me a vacation," Frankie reminded him.

"I know," interrupted a still irate Heidt, "but it can't be worked out just yet," and he quickly walked away.

Frankie, too, walked away, grumbling under his breath. He was not satisfied with the outcome; he did not get his vacation. Instead, for several weeks he got the "cold shoulder" from his boss. After three weeks of virtual silence and *no* solos, Frankie contacted his lawyer Zissu. Zissu contacted Heidt, reminding him of the contractual agreement stipulating solos. Heidt and Frankie then met privately, each apologizing to the other. Frankie admitted his candor and Heidt admitted his rancor, and both agreed to iron out differences before differences became issues. "I was going to give you a vacation anyhow," confessed Heidt. "Well, I didn't know that," said Frankie, and the two shook hands and smiled.

Thus, on two accounts, both within the first six months of the Heidt-Carle association, had the relationship suffered any hard feelings. From then on, the relationship was friendly in every respect. Heidt even had grown to rely more on Frankie, as McEnelly and Hallett had done earlier. Heidt had automatically included Frankie in all appearances, whether promotional or social, and he had come to realize the extent of dedication and loyalty of his star attraction. Heidt remembers the following incident, early March, 1941:

> Once on the stage in N.Y., he [Frankie] complained of pains in his lower right side. He refused to have a doctor, so when he got on the stage, I explained to the audience [typical of Horace Heidt] his problem, and should he or should he not go to the hospital. The audience was 100 to 1 to go, so we called an ambulance and packed him out. He probably would have passed on if he had not gone. He had acute appendicitis, but it goes to show his loyalty to his audiences.

As the Heidt-Carle association developed, Frankie's popularity accelerated. Frankie began receiving coverage in the trade magazines, *Billboard, Down Beat, Orchestra World*, and others. Newspaper accounts of performances were plentiful and complimentary. Frankie had not only met well known personalities but also appeared in person with them on numerous and sundry programs. While at the Grove in Los Angeles in early 1940, he met Bob Burns, and that meeting resulted in a continued friendship until that performer's death. At the Tin Pan Alley Ball in Chicago in March, 1940, Frankie enjoyed the company of Eddie Howard, Ted Weems, Larry Clinton, and Chicago's dean of music, Lou Breese. His long-standing friend was there too, Ozzie Nelson. In Detroit in June, he headlined and socialized with Martha Raye, Al Jolson, Milton Berle, and Cab Calloway, with whom Frankie would meet and socialize whenever their paths crossed. Frankie's personal appearance on the Al Jarvis program (Make Believe Ballroom) in Los Angeles would be one of many such appearances. (Al Jarvis KFWB, Los Angeles, was the counterpart of the Martin Block show WNEW, New York.) That October in Glendale, Frankie appeared with Phil Harris, Gertrude Niesen, Freddy Bartholemew, and Sunny Dunham on KFWB, having enjoyed guest Tommy Dorsey on the Pot O' Gold program a couple of days before. Frankie's personal appearances at the big department stores to autograph records became routine. Frankie accompanied Heidt, Cotton, Ronnie Kemper, and Phil Harris at the Coin Machines Operators Convention in Los Angeles shortly before the Heidt troupe would begin making the Pot O' Gold movie in December, 1940. And in the same year, Frankie relocated his family to the San Fernando Valley, becoming Heidt's neighbor. The arrangement was more convenient.

With Heidt there would be many more personal appearances, new acquaintances, new friendships, and heavy dosages of the glamour indigenous to the "big" time.

These new experiences and plaudits Frankie was receiving had almost come to a sudden stop in 1941, when he suffered the worst setback of his career. Heidt was playing the Rialto Theater in Louisville. During the first show on June 11, Frankie began "struggling" with the keys. His right hand felt numbness. As the band played, Frankie signaled to the drummer and left the piano. He collapsed in the wings. Stagehands administered some first aid, and when Heidt heard what had happened, he immediately called for an ambulance. A general examination at St. Anthony's Hospital in Louisville ruled out a stroke and further examination was inconclusive, although "nervous breakdown" was suspect. Doctors observed and treated Frankie, but after eight days in the hospital, they could do no more for him. Frankie did not respond well to treatment; he had very little coordination in his right hand. The doctors released him and prescribed rest. Frankie, not wanting to alarm Edith and the Carlones back home who were unaware of what was happening, instructed Heidt to say nothing of the illness. Heidt used to write Edith when the band was away for long periods. After another week and no sign of recovery, Frankie began to worry. "I really thought I was through," reflected the pianist, "and to think I was doing so well then."

Heidt insisted that Frankie no longer keep this illness from Edith and that Frankie should send for her. This Frankie did, and since Chicago was the next stop on Heidt's schedule, he asked Edith to meet him there.

Edith came to Chicago. Since Marjorie was out of school for the summer, Edith brought her along. Edith was not so much

4

THE HORACE HEIDT HERALD

Our thanks to Johnny Miles, the Publicity Staff, and Ned Scott, Photographer.

ACTION ON THE "POT O' GOLD" FRONT!

1. "Dr." Heidt looks for a Patient!
2. A Knife, a Fork, and a Spoon!
3. "You see Paulette . . ."
4. A tintype . . . and how . . . it's Mr. and Mrs. Horace Heidt!
5. Your "Pot O' Gold" Stars.
6. "Pete the Piper!"

LISTEN TO THE POT O' GOLD PROGRAM THURSDAY NIGHTS ON NBC BLUE NETWORK
HEAR THE TREASURE PROGRAM TUESDAY NIGHTS ON THE NBC RED NETWORK

TUESDAYS   THURSDAYS
8:30 - 9:00 E.S.T.   8:00 - 8:30 E.S.T.
Watch your local newspaper
for station and time.

Yes, Horace Heidt had his own newspaper. This issue covered the completion of the Pot O' Gold movie with Paulette Goddard and Jimmy Stewart.

concerned with Frankie's physical illness as she was with his mental attitude. Rest was what the doctors ordered and Edith arranged, to be sure, that Frankie got just that. She rented a cottage in the woods near Hatfield,* Wisconsin, a very quiet hideaway where Frankie would not be bothered. She made sure there was no telephone in or near the cottage. Frankie was to do nothing but rest. "I had tried to get him three or four times," remembered Heidt, "but he said he had a defect in the fingers of one hand, and was afraid he was through."

"I don't know how he found me," pondered Frankie.

Heidt was not one to accept setbacks lightly. He managed to get Frankie to come to Chicago and actually talked him into doing a recording. Frankie did play, but his performance provoked him more than it pleased him. His appraisal of his playing was disastrous and Frankie was convinced that he couldn't play anymore.

Heidt, however, was unwilling to accept Frankie's attitude of hopelessness. He was certain that Frankie would get well and suggested that he go to Mayo Clinic.

> I made an agreement with Frankie and Zissu his attorney that if I sent him to Mayo Clinic in Rochester at my expense, then upon his return, he would join me. If it did not work out, I would, of course, lose him.

Frankie went to Mayo where doctors concurred with the diagnosis of "complete exhaustion." In the two months following Frankie's earlier illness, which well might have been some kind of warning, he had overworked himself. As one trade magazine put it, Frankie "suffered a relapse in Louisville." Even days off were spent at the piano practicing or composing. An eighteen-hour day at one's work is apt to overtax the nervous system, particularly in Frankie who did not know how to relax. There was always something on his mind—his job, his music, his family. Simply, he was too conscientious. Whenever the band came into a new place, Frankie would even tune the

*Black Falls, Wisconsin.

148

piano himself to make sure the tone was to his satisfaction. Each and every detail had to be supervised by Frankie himself.

At Mayo Frankie regained confidence in himself. "He lived at a Dr. Louis Buie's house," remembered Heidt.

"When the doctor came home at night," related Frankie, "he would fix me a drink. We'd sit and talk. Then he'd ask me to play a bit."

After one week at Mayo, the doctors assured Frankie that it was only a question of time before he would be himself again. In the meantime, Frankie should take it easy, relax. And how was Frankie to do that? Just as he and Dr. Buie had done every night for the whole week!

Thus, to last in the Heidt organization, Frankie first had to get along with Heidt. This he did well. Then he had to sustain a nerve-wracking pace. Although Frankie suffered illnesses, half of all 1941, he came back, in no way impairing his activity in performing with Heidt, in making records with and without Heidt, or in writing his songs.

II

The encouraging happenings with "Sunrise Serenade" in the early months of 1939 shortly before Frankie joined Heidt had convinced Bill Lackenbauer that he was right in his hunch about Frankie's music. Although Frankie remained pessimistic with that tune, he had continued composing. His mood was often reflected in the moments alone at the piano after the job, playing bars of "Sunrise" mingled with bits and pieces of other unfinished tunes. These moments appeased Frankie's moods. On one of these occasions early that spring, Frankie finished a piece. He printed "Nightfall" across the top of the music sheet and put it with other papers he was taking home that night.

Some weeks later, Lackenbauer came to see Frankie, to apprise him of the latest development on "Sunrise." Lackenbauer had become so very confident in "Sunrise" that he wanted Frankie to do a sequel to it. Frankie agreed to think about a sequel, but, in the meantime, he gave Lackenbauer "Nightfall" to see what could be done with it. At this particular time, Frankie was not so much concerned with his own music as he was with the prospect of losing his Seven Gables orchestra, especially since young Casillo had informed Frankie of an impending cut in salary.

The dining and dancing continued at the Seven Gables, as usual, into the spring, even though the days there were numbered for the Frankie Carle orchestra. And it was on one such usual night of dining and dancing that a young couple caught Frankie's attention. This couple had danced most of the evening, often dancing close to the bandstand. "You could tell these kids were in love just by the way they embraced and the way they'd look at each other," analyzed the thirty-six-year old leader.

Toward the end of the evening, the couple had reached a spot close to the piano at the conclusion of the number and the set. They smiled at each other and at Frankie when they became aware that Frankie was looking directly at them. "I'm gonna write a song about you two," Frankie said, winking his eye and pointing at the couple as he rose from the piano stool. The couple just giggled and smiled as Frankie walked away. The incident passed, but the vision of that tender, loving moment of a boy and a girl on the dance floor remained with Frankie. Within two days of that seemingly insignificant incident and within two nights of Frankie's reverie at the piano, that recurring vision of the two lovers effected "Lover's Lullaby." Frankie tucked the music away, and not too long afterwards, just about the time the Frankie Carle orchestra was to play its last bars at the Seven Gables, he gave "Lover's Lullaby" to Lackenbauer as the sequel to "Sunrise Serenade."

By the end of the year, "Sunrise" had become the hottest tune in the business, and Frankie, who had joined Heidt in the meantime, had enjoyed numerous occasions to solo with it over the Heidt broadcasts. "Sunrise Serenade" received the Song Hits Award (1940). "Nightfall," which had been changed to "Shadows," appeared in sheet music; Artie Shaw eventually recorded it. It was not until early 1940 that Lackenbauer decided to go ahead with "Lover's Lullaby," and because of Larry Wagner's great arrangement in helping sell "Sunrise Serenade," Frankie gladly consented to include Wagner's name on "Lover's" in the Jewel release. Frankie first performed "Lover's Lullaby" on the Pot O' Gold program on March 12, 1940. If "Sunrise Serenade" and "Lover's Lullaby" were not enough to cement Frankie's reputation as a composer (which they were, and ASCAP accepted Frankie into the Society), then another tune would certainly have forced recognition—"Falling Leaves."

The following is Bill Lackenbauer's account of "Falling Leaves."

Now this again is an example of the Frankie Carle genius. I was driving home from Frank Dailey's Meadowbrook in Cedar Grove, N.J. one night and listening to Horace Heidt broadcasting from the Biltmore Hotel in N.Y. Larry Cotton was singing a ballad—title I don't remember—but the Frankie Carle personality playing behind Larry made the most beautiful theme for a song. When Horace Heidt went off the air, I called Frankie at the Biltmore and said 'Don't leave until I get there.' Frankie waited and about 2:30 a.m. we drove out to my home and finished (on what Frankie used to call 'his lucky piano') in my estimation, one of the outstanding standards "Falling Leaves."

Just about three months after Frankie had performed "Lover's Lullaby" for the first time, Heidt introduced "Falling Leaves" at the Eastwood Gardens in Detroit on July 2, 1940. Before Frankie had celebrated his first anniversary with Horace Heidt, he himself had become celebrated as the composer of "Sunrise Serenade," "Lover's Lullaby," and "Falling Leaves." Frankie Carle, who had lived up to his image as a virtuoso at the keyboard, had now become a recognized songwriter. These successes alleviated some of the pangs he secretly harbored, those secret disappointments known only to bandleaders who experience failure.

"Lover's Lullaby," like "Sunrise," flooded Lackenbauer not only with requests but also with headaches. The recording of "Lover's" angered a few, including Glenn Miller to whom Lack-

"Sunrise Serenade" received the Song Hits Award (1940). William "Bill" Lackenbauer of Jewel Music shares the honor with Frankie.

enbauer had given priority. (For years this writer—an addict of the big bands since the mid-thirties—erroneously thought that Miller had recorded the song. I must have heard Miller's sound in "Lover's" only in my subconscious!) Lackenbauer himself relates the story of "Lover's."

Miller was doing a dress rehearsal for Chesterfield in the CBS Broadway Theatre across the street from my office. I went over and asked him if, after rehearsal, would he stop at the office and listen to a new Frankie Carle tune—he did and liked it. As a matter of fact, he suggested a few minor changes. Glenn asked if he could introduce it on the Chesterfield Show; I agreed. The date was set . . . before he put the song on the air I had to leave for California. This is where our problem began. Two days before Glenn Miller's introduction of the song, my professional manager, Joe Whalen, went to the Commodore Hotel where Sammy Kaye was playing. Sammy asked Joe if we had a new tune, as Miller was doing "Lover's Lullaby" in two days. Joe figured it was safe enough to give a copy to Sammy—Joe was wrong. Sammy immediately made an arrangement and introduced "Lover's Lullaby" on his Wings Cigarette Show one day before Miller was to introduce it on his Chesterfield Cigarette Show. Miller tore up the arrangement and swore he would never do a Jewel Music tune again. After I arrived in California, I went up to Frisco to see Frankie Carle who was playing the Golden Gate Theatre with Horace Heidt—Frankie said, "Bill, don't go near Horace, he heard Kay Kaiser doing "Lover's" and is he mad!" I said to Frankie, 'that was impossible as Kay Kayser has never even seen the tune'—it was Sammy Kaye he heard. After I straightened Heidt out on that, he called Joe Higgens, the recording manager for Columbia Records, that he wanted to record "Lover's" when he arrived in L.A. Joe Higgens told him he was too late as Gene Krupa had already recorded it. Gene was managed by the same manager as Sammy Kaye—that's how Gene got the tune. However, Horace insisted and recorded it on Columbia. On my return to N.Y., my secretary told me about Miller not doing another tune for us. Though I was tired from the trip, I went to the "Cafe Rouge" in the Pennsylvania

Hotel where Glenn was playing. After staying there till closing time, I finally succeeded in convincing Miller that it was one of those thousand to one shots that such a thing could happen. Glenn said he would never play "Lover's Lullaby," but he would take my word and record my next tune which he did—the title: "Falling Leaves."

"Falling Leaves," as Lackenbauer would concur, is, too, the "perfect marriage."

It was Lackenbauer's belief that "Frankie introduced a new vogue in popular music with 'Sunrise.' " After Miller established his sound and before Glen Gray recorded the number, Lackenbauer had conceived the notion of a Miller-Carle union. "Miller's sound and style in arranging that made me think—what a perfect wedding that would make—"Sunrise Serenade" with a Glenn Miller arrangement." For this reason, Lackenbauer's principal choice for "Lover's Lullaby" was Miller, but the unfortunate—yes, really unfortunate—circumstances intervened. Happily, though, Miller did take "Falling Leaves," and his rendition, in this writer's opinion, compares with the greatest in the Miller sweet book. Unfortunately, "Falling Leaves" was denied the play and popularity of "Sunrise Serenade," simply because of the ASCAP hassle in 1941.

The friendly association between Heidt and Frankie nurtured a conducive atmosphere in which Frankie could write. Frankie even penned a tune as a theme for his boss' "Pot O' Gold" program. Appropriately, the tune was entitled, "Pot O' Gold in the Air." The gesture was well taken by Heidt who introduced it on that popular program on January 23, 1940. The tune, however, did not nearly approach the prominence of Frankie's earlier songs.

Heidt had come to expect new tunes from the hand of Frankie, and Frankie was always obliging. When Frankie was recuperating in the Wisconsin woods, Heidt once telegrammed Frankie:

JUST TO LET YOU KNOW THAT EVERYTHING IS GOING FINE AND WILL HAVE "WHISPERS" AND

FALLING LEAVES
Piano Solo

COMPOSED AND ARRANGED BY
FRANKIE CARLE

JEWEL MUSIC PUBLISHING CO. INC.,
1674 Broadway, New York, N.Y.

JEWEL MUSIC PUBLISHING CO., INC.

"JUST LAZY" ALL SET TO GO ON THE AIR IMMEDIATELY WITH SIGNING OF ASCAP SO DONT WORRY ABOUT ANYTHING AND LET ME KNOW IF THERE IS ANYTHING I CAN DO. GET WELL QUICK WE LOVE YOU. YOUR PAL HORACE

The trade papers and magazines would generally mention a new release. Sometimes the newspaper columnist would lend some editorial comment to a new tune. Nick Kenny in his column (August 11, 1943) mentioned: "And speaking of songs, Old Sailor, keeps your seagoing eyes on "I Still Care," written by Frankie Carle and Hank Russell, of Horace Heidt's band. I heard the Heidt band play it Saturday afternoon on WOR. It is Hit Parade material."

In his years with Heidt, Frankie had composed forty-one songs. Some, like "When Your Lips Met Mine,"* "Whispers," "With My Heart in My Hand," "I Still Care," and "Next Saturday Night" met with some success, but none had made the impact on music as the more popular songs already noted.

Thus, Lackenbauer's expectation that Frankie Carle would write beautiful music became a reality in the Heidt years.

III

The style of Frankie Carle was recognized when Mills published "Piano Stylings by Frankie Carle" (1930), the same time "Estelle" came out. Basically, the Carle piano had persisted in that same style, a style characterized by simplicity of melody. When Frankie played a tune, there was always a distinctive quality in the touch, the "Golden Touch" as it was later referred to. Of the thousands upon thousands of times that Frankie played, that distinctive touch, coupled with a distinctive mel-

---

*This song was Gordon Macrae's first Columbia recording. Frankie went "to bat" for the NBC page boy to help get his audition with Heidt. The audition took place in the men's room on the sixth floor of NBC ten minutes before show time. Heidt used Macrae in solo on the program that night.

ody, captured listeners' attention, a fact well realized by showman Heidt and apparent in all Frankie's performances, including recording with or without Heidt.

Of the hundreds of broadcasts aired by Horace Heidt, Frankie performed repeatedly tunes that have come to be identified with Frankie. "Barcarolle," Frankie's favorite piano piece, "Humoresque," an arrangement Frankie worked out in 1929, Confrey's "Stumbling" and especially "Kitten on the Keys," the one Fats Waller particularly liked by Frankie, "Hindustan," which Ken Smith observed when Frankie played the number in the 1973 Cavalcade of Bands program . . . "they drooled when he played "Hindustan" . . . and "Prelude in C Sharp," a frequently requested number, were among the tunes which Frankie performed time and time again. "Tea For Two," "Nola," "Chinatown," "Sweet Lorraine," "Ma, Making Eyes," "12th Street Rag," "Dark Eyes," and "Melody in F" were others which pleased audiences and, hence, repeated often.

Frankie's own compositions, too, enjoyed repeated performances. His tunes that were accepted more than others naturally received more play. Frankie played "Blue Fantasy" regularly until "Sunrise Serenade" became popular; then hardly a week passed when "Sunrise" was not played two or three times. After Heidt introduced "Lover's Lullaby" in early 1940, then "Lover's" appeared regularly. A like pattern followed after "Falling Leaves." As a matter of fact, Heidt programmed a streak of Frankie Carle tunes over the air for an extended period of time. On all broadcasts from June 2, 1940, when Heidt introduced "Falling Leaves" at the Eastwood Gardens, through the entire engagement at the Edgewater Beach Hotel in Chicago (ending August 15, 1940), Frankie performed repeatedly "Falling Leaves," "Lover's Lullaby," "Sunrise Serenade," "Blue Fantasy," and "Estelle." The only other tunes played—and then only *once*—were "Sweet Lorraine," "Stumbling," "Sophisticated Lady," "Tea for Two," and "12th Street Rag." Yes, indeed, Heidt provided Frankie Carle with an outlet not only for Frankie's virtuosity at the keyboard but also for his talented songwriting. And in no small way did such exposure enhance the Carle personality and reputation.

Had the three-month illness in 1941 debilitated Frankie's performance? On the contrary. Frankie came back stronger than ever. At the end of the year (1941), the traditional all star poll in *Down Beat* showed Frankie Carle ranking sixth in piano players, right up there with such greats as Jess Stacy, Mel Powell, Joe Bushkin, John Guarnieri, and Art Tatum. He would, from then on, receive recognition and numerous coveted awards in the music business for years to come. The *Orchestra World*'s "year's outstanding musician award" naming Frankie Carle in 1942 and 1943 sufficiently attested to Frankie Carle's prominence as a performer in the "Big" time.

The notices of the Heidt pianist steadily progressed into raves. An early *Billboard* review (February 17, 1941) mentioned ". . . Frankie Carle is the right kind of pianist to place in the spotlight. He plays smoothly and with a smart mixture of tricky technique." The mixture of tricky technique no doubt referred to Frankie's playing backwards, a novelty also exploited by Hallett, and boogie, which Frankie did not care to play. However, Heidt the showman could not let Frankie's boogie go unnoticed. Writes Heidt: (of an engagement at the Capitol Theater in N.Y.)

> Frankie had never liked to play Boogie and wouldn't, but the audience could not get enough of him on the show, so I stepped to the mike and announced that Frankie was now going to play Boogie and there was nothing he could do but play Boogie. The house started to clap, in time with his music, and almost shook the house down.

Yes, there was boogie and playing backwards; Heidt promoted more of this technique than Frankie cared to exhibit. But with or without the "gimmicks," within a couple of years, reviewers almost always singled out and raved about Frankie Carle. In Minneapolis, the *Tribune* (May 16, 1943) stated that "the high spot is the Frankie Carle piano appearance. His liquid, effortless playing of his own and other tunes, all of high caliber, is something to keep even a tough audience entranced." Most reviewers would comment on other attractions in the show. Donna Wood, the Don Juans, Henry Russell, and Fred Lowery the whistler would receive favorable appraisal. The antics of Ollie O'Toole and Art Carney would evoke praise. Solo performances by Bill Mustard on trombone, Irving Fazola on clarinet, Hugh Hutchins on tenor, and Buddy Yeager on trumpet were usually lauded, but it was Frankie Carle who enjoyed the greatest praise. Typically, the *Indianapolis News* (May 29, 1943) contended:

> Any discussion of the music in a Heidt show naturally gravitates to Frankie Carle and stays there. How to describe what this man does with ten fingers? Magic seems to flow from his hands to the keyboard, so that while he is playing one wishes that he would keep playing for a long, long time.

Regardless of where the Heidt band went, the reviewers continued their praises. W. Ward Marsh in the *Cleveland Plain Dealer* (June 19, 1943) said "in a class by himself is pianist-composer Frankie Carle . . ." Harold C. Eckert in Columbus (June 16, 1943) referred to a "revue-stopping pianolog" and maintained that "kids and oldsters whistle and stomp for Frankie, their boy." In the McEnelly days, reviewers freely praised Frankie's performance alone being worth the price of admission. Not much has changed some twenty years later. *The Boston Herald* (July 30, 1943) speaks of Carle, "whose renditions of "Moonlight Cocktails," "Lover's Lullaby," the Barcarolle from "Tales of Hoffman"—in jazz rhythm—and other selections are worth the price of admission . . ." In Detroit, one reviewer (July 3, 1943) tersely surmised, "You can listen to him all day . . ." Perhaps best to summarize Frankie's performances is Mitch Woodbury's account (Toledo, June 12, 1943): "Highlight of the hour's entertainment, of course, is Frankie Carle's specialty. This smiling young man is indubitably the band world's foremost piano stylist."

No doubt about it, Frankie was a performer, and his talent was not restricted to the Heidt shows or evidenced in Heidt's recordings. There were Frankie's own recordings, also.

One facet perhaps more than any other of Frankie's prodigious talent was that of a recording artist. "Sunrise Serenade" undoubtedly introduced Frankie into the "big" time. When Lackenbauer granted permission for the use of "Sunrise" in broadcasts, he stipulated Frankie's name be mentioned as the tune's composer. That Frankie Carle, piano player, had never been west of Indianapolis before Heidt, left little doubt that the mention of Frankie's name would evoke the query, if any query at all, "Frankie who?" But Frankie's records, and even his part in recordings of others, would change that.

Frankie had recorded earlier on Decca with the Carle-Barbour-Weiss-Stephens group, but the recording avenue was closed to him with the Edgewood and Seven Gables orchestra. With Heidt, Frankie returned to recording with rhythm section, Heidt being instrumental in getting a Columbia contract. He did other recordings, too, either with Heidt or with a complement of Heidt's men, such as the records he did in late 1939 with Bobby Hackett.*

In 1940 he did his first album (C-23) with rhythm section. Later, he also handled the piano in the Irving Fazola Hot Eight recordings. Although not intended to be featured in Heidt records, Frankie, nevertheless, was singled out by reviewers. For example, "On the Records" column in *Billboard* (February 15, 1941) appraised Heidt's "Out of the Gray" and "Dark Eyes" disc (Columbia 35918) thus: "Reverse ['Dark Eyes'] has a Frankie Carle piano bit in particular to recommend it, the sort of passage that gives a disk a permanent place in a record library, if only to play the particular 16 bars over and over again." Another *Billboard* appraisal (March 29, 1941) of Heidt's "Friendly Tavern Polka" and "Broadway Caballero" (Columbia 36006) maintained "it contains another superior Frankie Carle hit."

But it was Frankie's Columbia presses with Bob Knight,

---

*"Chico's Love Song" and "It's A Whole New Thing" (catalog #5155) and "Night Glow" and "Blue Fantasy" (#5241) recorded October 5, 1939, released in 1939.

guitar, Edward McKimey, bass, and Bernie Matthewson, drums, that made Frankie Carle Columbia's leading recording artist in the early 1940's. People who never saw Frankie Carle with Heidt at the hotels, theaters, ballrooms, or at radio shows or who had never heard him over the air, knew him via recordings.

Most of the solos Frankie performed in the Heidt broadcasts eventually found their way into recordings. When Frankie left Heidt in 1943, a *Variety* story estimated that Frankie "last year [1943] . . . had 4,000,000 individual pressings." There were yet to come many more Columbia recordings (not even to mention additional recordings for ten years at Victor!).

Thus, Frankie Carle with Horace Heidt had lived up to his expectation as a performer, to say the least.

IV

As Frankie pursued his career, another Carle career was beginning, that of his daughter Marjorie. Marjorie, studying voice under Stepson "Doc" Humphrey, noted teacher of Mary Martin and Carol Landis, appeared with a local group, Art Whiting, in the Los Angeles area. Art Whiting appeared at a war bond rally in Glendale, with Bob Crosby on the bill. *Down Beat* carried a brief story of the rally and told of the sixteen-year old thrush's appearance there. This development was virtually unknown to Frankie. This was more of Edith's doing, kept secret to surprise Frankie later. He was aware, however, that his little Marjorie was studying with Humphrey.

V

On Thursday of the first week in December, 1941, Frankie and Heidt spent the off-day autographing records in Hollywood. Heidt was enjoying two smash hits. His "B-I-By" recording ranked third, behind Miller's "Chattanooga Choo-Choo" and

"Elmer's Tune" as the most popular record in coin machines. Heidt's "Shepherd Serenade" was second to Bing Crosby's rendition. The Heidt orchestra was coming into the Casa Manana in Culver City in a couple of weeks, and the Heidt crew was doing some Columbia recordings and the Tums and Fitch broadcasts in the interim. The coming Sunday was Pearl Harbor.

Although the Fitch broadcast went on the air as usual that Sunday, the thoughts of the Heidt crew, as those of a stunned nation, were perplexed. The broadcast that day was perfunctory.

America was about to enter into war, and the war would bring about numerous changes in all aspects of life. Changes in the band business, in its activity and in its musicians and leaders, were quick to come about. Within a few months, many musicians and leaders either enlisted or were drafted.

Heidt was already forty-years old when the war broke out; Frankie was going on thirty-nine. Their conscription was unlikely, at least not immediate. But the Heidt organization was well aware of all the ramifications of America's involvement. In a word, Heidt and his organization would be ready for whatever exigency confronted the war effort in the area of entertainment.

Heidt came into the Orpheum in Omaha in the summer of 1942. It was at the Orpheum that Frankie received a telegram from Eddie Duchin, who was joining the Navy.* Duchin wanted to know if Frankie was interested in taking over the Duchin orchestra. Although Frankie still harbored a desire to lead his own band, he did not jump at this opportunity. He knew Heidt was encountering enough problems with a beefed-up itinerary in the war effort and a rapid loss of sidemen to the service. Heidt had treated Frankie kindly and generously, and Frankie felt he owed it to Heidt to stick it out in the present crisis. Frankie and Heidt, nevertheless, did discuss the Duchin pro-

---

*An officer on the USS Bates, a destroyer escort which participated in Omaha Beach. Enroute to the South Pacific, Duchin was transferred. Shortly afterwards, the USS Bates was sunk by Kamikaze.

At Boston Gardens, entertaining 35,000 soldiers and war workers to raise "smokes for the boys."

For the Navy boys at Grosse Ile, Detroit

From the stage of the Palace Theatre in Cleveland, we entertain the Air Cadets of Fenn College

We entertain 10,000 boys at the Fargo Naval Detachment Center, Boston Massachusetts.

posal, and the result was Frankie's getting five percent of the Heidt band. In addition, Heidt gave him a basic salary of $500 a week. Frankie would handle all the chores of the band,* including the hiring and firing of personnel, but Heidt would continue to emcee programs and shows. With this arrangement, Heidt would be able to spend more time on business matters. All the trade papers and magazines carried the story of the Heidt-Carle pact. And with the addition of engagements at the army camps, hospitals, war bond campaigns, and servicemen clubs to the already busy Heidt itinerary, the move might have been the only way for the Heidt organization to survive without more "nervous breakdowns."

It was not much of a surprise that Duchin thought of Frankie in this regard. The reputation of Frankie Carle as being a very reliable and conscientious person, as well as a virtuoso, had become common knowledge in the business. Ken Smith recalls the following pre-war incident: ". . . once I was introduced to Eddie Duchin, by Eddie Brannick, Giants' secretary, at Shor's. I was described as a friend of Frankie Carle's. Duchin said, 'Tell him to stop being so damned good.'"

Frankie was quite capable of recognizing talented musicians. As a matter of fact, when Frankie first joined Heidt, it was Frankie who suggested Bobby Hackett. Heidt hired him, and although pleased with Hackett's ability, Heidt was displeased with Hackett's drinking. The Hackett tenure with Heidt was short lived, unfortunately, and Frankie could do little to change Heidt's mind when Heidt fired him. "The situation got bad on New Year's Eve," remembered Frankie. "Hackett was drunk. I knew Heidt would fire him this time, and I couldn't do anything about it."

After Omaha, the first engagement of the Heidt band with Frankie as musical director occurred at the Edgewater Beach Hotel in Chicago. Frankie was determined to change the image of the Horace Heidt band, especially the image suggested in the annual *Down Beat* polls showing Horace Heidt usually in

---

*Called the Heidt-Carle orchestra.

the category of "corn." Once, to the chagrin of Heidt, Frankie fired five musicians in rapid succession. When the band played a Milwaukee engagement, several musicians met one another for the first time the night of the job. "And we played pretty good," remarked the new musical director, although the reviewer in the *Milwaukee Journal* (May 8, 1943) discerned "bugs" in the stage show and attributed these bugs in part to "no rehearsal, four new men in the band, timing difficulties, etc." (No rehearsal because of a late train from Chicago.)

In reshaping the band, Frankie released two trombones, one trumpet, a sax, and a drummer. He brought in two of his former sidemen, Percy Booth on sax and Hack O'Brien on drums. Personnel being scarce in the war years, Frankie luckily landed very capable musicians, including noteworthy trombones in Harry Ziele and Warren Covington. Heidt, who hired Irving Fazola before Frankie became director, was also responsible for getting Bill Finnegan, the arranger, when Glenn Miller went to the service. With these new capable sidemen and an excellent arranger, Frankie was able to eradicate the reference "corn" when Heidt's band was the topic of shoptalk. *Metronome*'s George Simon observed:

> But it's Carle also, who in many, many ways is responsible for the vast improvement in the band's music. Not only to the musicians, but to the observer out front, it's obvious that he is the chief musical director of the band, for it's Frankie who does most of the actual directing; it's Frankie who sets the tempos, and it's Frankie whom the men watch carefully for all musical cues, etc.

At the time of the Heidt-Carle partnership, Heidt fully realized that Frankie not only would be a capable bandleader for him but should have an organization of his own. And he encouraged Frankie in that regard. Some three or four months after Frankie became musical director, Heidt arranged for Tom Rockwell of General Amusement Corp. (GAC) and James McCabe, president of Pennsylvania Hotel, to come to the Capitol Theater for the express purpose of observing Frankie, which Rockwell and McCabe did on two consecutive nights. When Heidt suggested that Frankie was ready for his own band, Heidt thought of a small group, like a rhythm section with which Frankie recorded. Heidt felt that Frankie's piano in that situation would not get lost as might happen in a large band. Besides, there would be fewer headaches with a small group and just as much money for Frankie. However, Rockwell, who concurred with McCabe that, yes, Frankie was a great prospect, was thinking in terms of a "big" band. So was Frankie. Nevertheless, in spite of the differences of opinion, Heidt encouraged Frankie who, obviously, needed some moral support to undertake such an enterprise. Rockwell had agreed to handle a Frankie Carle orchestra and, confidently, predicted that Frankie would gross a quarter of a million dollars in his first year. Frankie left Heidt with Heidt's blessing in September to organize, one more time, a band of his own.

Thus, Frankie's reward for his efforts in the Heidt-Carle relationship was not so much the money Frankie realized but, rather, one more chance—the last chance perhaps—to satisfy his life-long desire to lead and be accepted as a bandleader.

Heidt and Frankie made a great combination. As a consequence of his achievement, Frankie got a percentage of the Heidt Orchestra and equal billing as the music director.

Heidt introducing Gordon Macrae

Hack O'Brien

Henry Russell

Percy Booth

Breaking all records at the Palace Theater in Cleveland

Frankie and Bobby Hackett

Records were broken on our last week of our 1942 tour in Boston

Heidt-Carle Finale. Frankie leaves Heidt to front his own orchestra.

CHAPTER 11

The debut of the Frankie Carle orchestra at the Pennsylvania Hotel in New York was no less than starting at the top. Unusual? Yes. But GAC's Tom Rockwell and Pennsylvania's James McCabe were not completely unaware of Frankie's twenty-eight years in the business. They were not totally ignorant of his part with Hallett and with McEnelly before Hallett. They were not derelict in recognizing Frankie's leadership in the Heidt-Carle orchestra. (Rockwell, remember, also observed Frankie in 1939 at the Seven Gables. "Ironic," commented Frankie, "he could have gotten the band for $500 a week in '39—now it cost seven times that!") And Rockwell and McCabe were not blind to Frankie's other assets, his work as a recording artist and composer. Hence, when all parties agreed to go with the big band, Frankie enjoyed financial backing from GAC, a generous affiliation with the Pennsylvania Hotel on a return basis for ten years, and a start in the big time at a place, about which hundreds of other bandleaders dreamed. The anxiety Frankie felt was not so much the loss of money if he failed, as it was frustration of his firm conviction that he could "lead a big band in my own style and be successful." Even if the year 1944 was not the most propitious time, as explained earlier, it was "now or never" for the forty-one-year old music man. Thus, in the fall of 1943, Frankie set out to form his band; he was apprehensive, to say the least, of the challenges awaiting him.

I

Getting a band together in wartime was itself a challenge. Some bands were folding because of the lack of personnel. However, Frankie managed. He mustered Artie Mendelsohn, his lead sax, a sparkling alto from Bradford, Pa., who had played with Bob Crosby; Percy Booth, 2d tenor-man, a long-standing friend of Frankie's who had played in the Seven Gables band and had later been recruited by Frankie for Heidt; Danny Small, baritone sax out of Pittsburgh, formerly with Jan Garber; Julian Pete Johns, 3d alto and flute, from the Woody Herman Herd; and first tenor, Irving Trestman, a Minneapolis product who had played with Gus Arnheim. On trumpets, Frankie carried Heidt's former sideman, Bernie Mitchell, on 1st trumpet; Dudley Santin (Santoniello), 2d trumpet, a Providence boy and solid swinger with Hallett's crew; and 3d man, Roger Bacon, the boy from Iowa who doubled on vocals for Frankie, formerly with Charlie Spivak. The trombones included Eddie Lucas, slick performer from Louis Prima; Harry Zeile, 2d, from Ohio, who had played with Dick Rogers; and 3d trombone, Brooklynite Bert Prager, a newcomer to the big bands. On drums, of course it was Hack O'Brien, who left Heidt to be with Frankie and then went into teaching drums a year later when Frankie came west. A Bostonian radio-station staff musician, Lee Columbo, came aboard to perform the dual role of guitarist and vocalist, and on bass, Frankie secured Maurice Roy, a Connecticut musician who had played with Tommy Tucker. Al Avola, a Californian who had done most of Artie Shaw's arranging at one time, became Frankie's principal arranger. Percy Booth did some arranging also.

Harry Zeile, 37, was the oldest member of the crew; Pete Johns, Arthur Mendelsohn, Percy Booth, and Maurice Roy were in their 30's. All the others were in their 20's. Mendelsohn and Trestman had already received their discharges from the service.

No band would be complete without a song thrush. For this chore Frankie recruited pretty Betty Bonney, who, however, would last only through the initial hotel engagement. Phyllis Lynne, an attractive twenty-one-year old who had sung with Vaughn Monroe and Russ Morgan, joined Frankie shortly before Frankie went on the first theater tour. Warren Pearl, Frankie's personal manager, recommended Paul Allen for male vocals, and Allen joined shortly after the Pennsylvania opening.

The staff that would handle the new Frankie Carle orchestra consisted of GAC's Warren Pearl, personal manager, who also handled Sunny Dunham; Al Rylander, publicity agent, who also served in that capacity for Xavier Cugat; Leonard Zissu, and his associates Abe Marcus and Alan Stein, attorneys; Harry Geist, accountant; and Andy Travers, road manager.

Warren Pearl had booked the new orchestra into Boston for one week, the week prior to the Cafe Rouge opening at the Pennsylvania Hotel.* That move was tantamount to doing a Broadway play elsewhere before bringing it to Broadway.

Thus, on February 17, 1944, Frankie Carle gave the downbeat at the Cafe Rouge, a downbeat which was twenty-seven years in the making. Not only Frankie but also the crew anxiously awaited the reviews. In general, they were favorable reviews. The one thing on which reviewers seem to agree was the commercialism of the new Frankie Carle aggregation. Critic Gary Stevens, a lone dissenter in Frankie's favor, thought the leader fabulous, but the band, at best, "mediocre." Metronome's George Simon, however, rated the band B musically, 1 commercially, and prediction—success. Characteristic of the band was its "simplicity," which, contended Simon, "will undoubtedly make the Frankie Carle band successful." Not overlooking Frankie as the focal point, Simon surmised "sections are whipping themselves into shape nicely." And of the vocals—Bonney, Columbo, and Bacon—"all three add to the Carle commercialism, which from the looks and sounds of things, should make his a highly successful dance band. It's already doing very good business at the Pennsylvania in New York."

---

*Despite the time and concentration Frankie needed to ready the band for his debut, he took the time to oblige the parents of an aspiring young singer, Betty George. Frankie listened to George's audition and advised and encouraged a voice teacher for her. Almost two years later, Betty George returned to Frankie, but being set in that department, he recommended her to Glen Gray, who hired her. After a time with the Casa Loma, she went on to make a name for herself on Broadway.

Frankie Carle Debut, Hotel Pennsylvania, 1944: Betty Bonney, vocals; left to right, reeds, Danny Small, baritone sax, Percy Booth, tenor, Artie Mendlesohn, lead alto, Pete Johns, alto and flute, Irv Trestman, first tenor. Trombones, Bert Praeger, Eddie Lucas, lead, Harry Zeile. Trumpets, Roger Bacon, Bernie Mitchell, first trumpet, Dudley Santoinelli. Lee Columbo, guitar; Maurice Roy, bass; Hack O'Brien, drums.

Indeed, the Frankie Carle orchestra did do good business at the Pennsylvania, and, undoubtedly, the showing there had much to do with Frankie's landing the Old Gold radio program which Sammy Kaye had vacated. After the Pennsylvania, also, the Frankie Carle orchestra was to play the prestigious Terrace Room in Newark for a two-week engagement in May, the New York Theater Authority's opening at Central Park Mall in June, and Atlantic City's Steel Pier in July. Not bad for starters.

A band two months old hardly lands a "biggie" in radio. Apparently the Old Gold people had not considered the age of the Frankie Carle orchestra. Whatever Old Gold's reasons for going with Frankie will be left to conjecture. More importantly, the Old Gold program meant coast-to-coast radio with a tremendous following; it meant exposure to the whole country of Frankie's brand of music; and it meant recognition of the Frankie Carle orchestra. Getting the radio show was as much a surprise to Frankie as it was to other bandleaders who had been around longer.

Booked with Allan Jones, who at the time had recently finished the Broadway musical "Jackpot," and Red Barber, famed sportscaster and announcer, Frankie entered another avenue from which to "sell" his kind of music. All the trade slicks and daily newspapers carried the story, and almost invariably the copy identified Frankie Carle with the phrase "golden touch." Whether or not the phrase was inadvertently ambiguous would be hard to say. Some writers perhaps construed "golden touch" to connote "Midas touch," but, mostly, the phrase referred to Frankie's keyboard finesse. Nevertheless, the *New York Mirror* attested and quipped, "His first broadcasts with Allan Jones for their new ciggie sponsor are the rave of the industry and to top it off, Chicago hoodlums stole a truckload of his [Frankie's] records bound for coin machine operators . . . this proves he is good." The first Carle-Jones show was broadcast on April 5.

First the Pennsylvania, and then the Old Gold program! Frankie was pinching himself. But that wasn't all!

The same month Frankie took over the Old Gold program, he landed another "mecca" of the big bands—New York's Capitol Theatre. The theater circuit would be Frankie's trial as a showman. On the bill with Ginny Simms, who also starred in the movie "Broadway Rhythm" playing concurrently, dancer Mitzie Mayfair, and mimic Arthur Blake, Frankie had sufficiently great talent with which to work. His debut in this area was characteristically with aplomb. However, *Variety* (April 19, 1944) observed, "Carle's new orchestra, playing its first theatre date, does a fine musical job, but its leader's lack of experience in handling himself and a show is lessening its impact. However, when Carle sits at his keyboard things hum and the band justifies itself." Frankie's prime concern was shaping up a dance band, and on that score, he accomplished, what *Billboard* (April 22, 1944) proclaimed, "listenable quality few orks achieve in so short a time." Even if his showmanship was wanting (Frankie never admitted to being a showman), he had experienced, in addition to vaudeville, two great showmen, Hallett and Heidt. Certainly some of them rubbed off on him. When Allan Corelli, head of the New York Theatre Authority, introduced Frankie at the Central Park opener, Corelli stated Frankie's feat of playing with his back to the piano—a novelty initiated by Frankie himself out of pure challenge when Krupa, in the early 1930's, asked Frankie to "liven things up." Hallett continued with the gimmick, as did Heidt. Corelli knew of this novelty, but, it is safe to assume that Corelli unconsciously included the phrase "with his hands tied behind his back," and a startled Frankie, having always accepted challenges to his talent, intuitively handed Corelli a handkerchief with which to bind Frankie's hands. Frankie did play in that manner, surprising himself in the process. What Frankie did here suggests some inherent quality of the showmanship, but the real proof came a few months later in Columbus at the Palace.

The Carle orchestra readied for its show at the Palace. However, because of transportation difficulties, common in wartime, the instruments had not arrived in time for the first

Frankie Carle's debut in the theater. The novelty act that's hard to beat. With Allan Jones and Red Barber on the "Old Gold" program.

show. They had not arrived in time for the second show, but Frankie was not going to disappoint the customers. He stepped out onto the stage and conducted a one-man show. For thirty-five minutes he played requests, did a dance, led the audience in song, accompanied volunteer singers, and brought some jitterbugs on stage. When the instruments did arrive, it bothered no one in the audience that the setup took place while there was yet action on stage. The one-man show concluded with some contribution from the band, which by now was ready. The audience responded enthusiastically. Paul Hornung of the Columbus paper, in the audience that matinee, lauded the way Frankie handled the situation. Quickly the wire services had the story all over the country. William W. Howard of RKO in New York wrote Frankie: "Had a note from Jerry Shinbach of the Palace Theatre in Columbus, telling how well you handled the emergency that arose when your baggage failed to show up . . . I cannot resist telling you what a big kick I got out of what you did. It is nice to know there are still troupers left in the business."

Indeed, Frankie handled himself as well in the role of a showman as he did in his own individual performances. And he is the first to admit that with good talent on the theater bill, breaking box office records was not due to his singular participation. Ginny Simms was a "hot" item when she appeared with Frankie at the Capitol. Mitzie Mayfair had already made her mark as a dancer. At the State in Hartford, the newest comedian to crack-up audiences was Jan Murray, and Murray, along with Ollie O'Toole of Heidt fame, complemented Frankie's part on the bill. Another talented comedian, Henny Youngman, appeared with Frankie at the Earle in Philly. And when Frankie brought his revue into the RKO Boston, the *Evening Globe* (July 21, 1944) judged "no better place to go this week than RKO Boston theatre . . ." The *Youngstown Vindicator* appraised, "If his reception here is any indication, he [Frankie] is set for a successful future in the new field." After the Columbus incident, Frankie became the talk of the theater-stage business. By the time of his Oriental Theatre show in Chicago in early September, he was nearing record crowds. *Billboard* (September 9, 1944) reported "looks like a winner . . . record breaking week." In that same issue, *Billboard* broke the story, "Frankie Carle and band will go to RKO for a one-picture deal." The movie development in the midst of the theater momentum was unexpected, particularly since the practice of using bands in movies waned, as *Variety* (September 6, 1944) pointed out, the studios' "use of name bands easing off the past year."

The prospect of a movie had not nurtured a "big head" in Frankie Carle. On the contrary, he worked even harder in shaping up his band and giving ballroom and theater audiences their money's worth. The favorable responses on tour continued through Minneapolis, the last stop before the band headed east to arrive in time for a second Pennsylvania Hotel stand and a return to the Old Gold program in October. One of the biggest successes on the eastward trek in mid-September occurred in Detroit at the Michigan Theater, where Frankie, billed with lovable Gil Lamb, amassed a near-record gross.

Even if the Frankie Carle orchestra was unable to traverse the country, it received, by the end of September, recognition of nationwide proportions. *Billboard* reported its 1944 service camp music polls (bands-on-their-way-up) showing Frankie Carle in the third spot, behind Stan Kenton and Les Brown. Another surprise? Not quite. The Frankie Carle orchestra was eight months old, but, really, the age of the band was of little consequence in the area of Frankie's contributing to the service camps and all other war-related or charity-related causes.

The practice of bands playing army camps, hospitals, war bond drives, and sundry other benefits was widespread during and after the war. Heidt had contributed much in this area, and almost immediately after Frankie had organized his own band, he assumed the practice. By the time the orchestra was but a few months old, Frankie had performed at the WAC Fox Hole in Hartford, where, among other things, wives of overseas servicemen would come to learn the what and what nots about shipping packages overseas; played a lunch-hour at the Veede-

Root war plant to help promote the war effort and attainment of the E-flag; appeared with Jeanne Cagney in the Bid For Victory program from an army hospital; and performed at the Waterbury Tool Company in a war-loan drive. When the March of Dimes staged one of the biggest conga lines down Broadway in early 1945, Frankie Carle led the parade. Wherever Frankie and the orchestra appeared, Frankie was ready to contribute to the cause, be it war effort or home front or charity. When he played Indianapolis, he appeared and played for the wounded at Ft. Benjamin Harrison; when he played Madison, Frankie performed at Truax Field. After his mother Dora died, his activity in this area increased, particularly in benefits for kids. Boys Town was always a stop when Frankie was in the Nebraska area. Cedric Adams (*Minneapolis Star-Journal*, January 2, 1945) best summed up Frankie in this regard: "Frankie Carle, current band leader at the Orpheum, is probably one of the most generous musicians this town has ever had when it comes to devoting time and talent to extracurricular activities. There hasn't been a hospital, shut-in or kiddy performance he's turned down in five days, and he'd break his neck to squeeze in special appearances for our wounded veterans. It's that sort of spirit that makes a gem out of a guy."

Thus, when a preference for Frankie Carle appeared in a poll of service camps, it was understandable. If there existed an installation in the area of Frankie's engagement, he played it. The only other way service camps could have become acquainted with Frankie's music would be radio, unless service camps still confused Frankie with the Heidt-Carle orchestra. Certainly not the Carle band on recordings. That would not occur until the end of 1944.

Nevertheless, before its first anniversary, the Frankie Carle orchestra was enjoying raves in its hotel engagements, in the theater, in the ballrooms, and in radio and, indeed, the service camps. The progress and popularity of the new band—perhaps the last band of the big band era—did not escape the syndicated columnists and other perspicacious writers in other media. Walter Winchell (June 26, 1944) divulged "Frankie Carle's

Thousands of GIs will remember Frankie Carle at the camps. Frankie also derived particular pleasure in playing at Boys Town. Pictured above with Boys Town founder, Fr. Flanagan.

five-month old band is getting 3½ Gs against a percentage. A record for any crew playing one nighters." Dorothy Kilgallen (June 27, 1944) posed the question, "Isn't Frankie Carle, the new skyrocket bandleader, being tempted by the Shuberts to appear in their forthcoming revue, 'The Passing Show'?" Even some things of a more personal nature began to crop up, a sure sign of one in the public's eye. Reported Ed Sullivan (September 30, 1944), "Frankie Carle's daughter, Margie, will wed Hugh Backenstoe, the band pianist." When the AFM held its convention of bandleaders at the Roseland in July to discuss problems besetting the bands,* Frankie Carle was among the group of the most celebrated names in the business—Tommy Dorsey, Woody Herman, Duke Ellington, Harry James, Paul Whiteman, Benny Goodman, Vincent Lopez, to mention some. In August, Jim Bishop, associate editor at *Collier's* at the time, had done a feature story on Frankie. And in another *Collier* issue (December, 1944), a fiction story by Nancy Lyon, *Maud*, had Maud, a volunteer in a hospital loaded with G.I.'s, come in with a stack of her records to play for the boys. "Jive," she said, "from way back. Tommy Dorsey, Cab Calloway—a touch of Frankie Carle." In October, cartoonist Ham Fisher used Frankie Carle and His Orchestra in the Joe Palooka strip, and in that same month Frankie made personal appearances on the Kate Smith show, with Mary Astor and the Ink Spots, and on the Ralph Edwards' Truth or Consequences program. As a matter of fact, GAC itself ran an advertisement in *Billboard* (September 30, 1944) setting off in bold caps, GOLDEN TOUCH, followed by a blurb and then a message—PREDICTION FULFILLED. By the time Frankie returned to the Pennsylvania, as one writer put it, "Reservations at the Penn for the evening of Frankie Carle's return are harder to get than fourth-row tickets to 'Oklahoma.' "

---

*Two important issues: "stealing" of men by orchestra leaders by offering more money. (Hedit was accused of this practice.) And, placing musicians in work after the war.

See this handsome young man, a jive artist of note? Being a band leader, you'd know he's not too young—say 27, 28, wouldn't you? See the pretty singer? She's with his band. How old would you say she is? Maybe 19, maybe 20? Well, actually she is his daughter, but she doesn't use daddy's name. That would be a giveaway. She uses the name Marjorie Hughes. Her daddy is Frankie Carle. They'll be here soon.

Frankie's popularity was evident everywhere. Supposedly kept secret, the father-daughter team hit the newspapers nationally. Above, Frankie appears with Ralph Edwards on "Truth or Consequences" and in Ham Fisher's "Joe Palooka" strip.

Fan mail began to multiply. Some fans wanted advice on piano technique; some wanted him to recommend a piano teacher for a child; some wanted his picture; some just wanted to say they enjoyed him here or there or on radio or on records; and some wanted odd things—like money, love affairs, and even marriage.

Oddities almost always accompany popularity. One woman had written Frankie love letters every day, all year long, for fifteen years! Another woman had followed the band from Ithaca to California. Her presence became quite obvious and Frankie assumed that she was following a sideman. But when he was apprised that he was the "object of her affection," Frankie went to Zissu his lawyer who eventually managed to discourage her continuance of the practice. But most of the fans were fans of the regular kind. Even to this day Frankie enjoys the admiration of long-lasting fans. "Perhaps the most lasting fan," related Frankie, "is Paul Dubé." Dubé has followed the Carle career since the early 1940's. He collected every recording, writeup, notice, picture, in general, Carleana, over all these years. Dubé finally visited with Frankie in 1978.

Richard Bellamy of the *Milwaukee Journal* (November 26, 1944) conceived what he called "The Billion Dollar Band," a band made up of high grade musicians who reached their peak of fame and wealth. It was a band not all sweet, not all true hot jazz, one catering to dancers and fans of sweet, swing, and jazz. Bellamy named Paul Whiteman, leader. Duke Ellington would be arranger and writer of originals. Harry James, and Charlie Spivak, and Tommy Dorsey made up the brass. Benny Goodman, Woody Herman, and Charlie Barnet comprised the reed section. Gene Krupa handled the drums. No guitar. (Alvino Rey in the service, says Bellamy.) For singers, he named Bing Crosby, Frank Sinatra, and Dinah Shore. And on piano, Frankie Carle. (Who by no means had reached his peak of fame and fortune.) "Many might protest," claimed Bellamy, "that Count Basie or someone else would make a better keyboard choice than Frankie Carle, but we'll counter by pointing to Frankie's record sales. No doubt about it, as a soloist Carle is a great draw. And don't forget that for several years he played satisfactory "rhythm piano" in the ensemble with Horace Heidt."

With all the attention given the new big-band leader, 1944 ended on a sad personal note for Frankie.

After the orchestra closed at the Pennsylvania in early December, it was scheduled for a one-nighter at the Ritz in Bridgeport before opening a theater engagement in Akron. Enroute to Bridgeport, Frankie went to Providence. He could spend a little time with his folks before the evening performance and then spend the entire next day. Edith and Marjorie, who had joined Frankie that fall, were in Springfield visiting the Georges; Frankie would meet up with them later.

Dora and Angelo were now living in a new house which Frankie had bought for them. Dora was blind, a consequence of her long illness. Angelo had aged but he was remarkably strong. He manipulated his artificial leg as if it were real. Esther, the only one of the Carlone girls who had not married, lived with her parents. Brothers Louis and Lucky were in the service, Lou in Guam and Lucky on Leyte.

Dora and Angelo always got excited when Frankie came home, even if he assumed the role of "boss," emphatically issuing directives aimed at their well being. Frankie had become particularly worried about Dora; to him she did not look good. She assured him, however, that she was just "fine," although she labored to maintain her usual good spirits. She would "perk up" to tell Frankie she was proud and happy that he was doing very well with his band; she really delighted in hearing him over the radio. And the news of the prospect of Frankie in a motion picture thrilled her and Angelo alike. Almost always at the conclusion of salutations, Dora would remind Frankie, "Be thankful to God that things worked out. Don't ever forget poor people—we were poor—especially poor kids. Thank God." Frankie invariably would smile and nod at his mother in agreement.

Frankie remained with his folks most of the day following the Bridgeport one-nighter and was prepared to leave for Akron late that evening. A little snow had fallen during the night. The day was cold, beautiful—the sun gleaming sporadically through the clouds. The house was warm, content. When night came, Dora rose to retire. Frankie kissed her goodnight as she began iterating her exhortation, "Thank God all turned out . . .." Angelo moved to help her to her room. She implored him to stay with his son, who in a little while had to leave to catch a train.

Angelo, too, expressed his contentment, especially that his son was doing "whatever he wants to do" and he was doing it well. Angelo, who had never given up his preference for some good Irish whiskey, thought there was ample time for a snort and, perhaps, a quick game of cards before Frankie left.

The train left Providence that night. Several days later, Harry Neigher, Frankie's friend with the *Bridgeport Herald*, wrote (December 17, 1944):

> Many nights I sat with Frankie Carle at the Seven Gables and consoled and encouraged the curly-haired pianist-composer and tried to snap him out of his lethargy. He used to plead with me to be his manager and to write the words to some of his songs that have since become hits. Frankie didn't want success for himself alone, but he wanted it to give his mother all the nice things in life. Frankie became a success, and in his first 10 months as a bandleader broke all orchestra business records and made more than a half-million dollars. But Frankie wasn't happy and to the casual observers and even to those who knew him well, Frankie appeared glum, possibly high hat. He appeared to snub his friends who came to see him at the Ritz Sunday night. But Frankie wasn't snubbing anybody. He was worried and grieving. For his mother was gravely ill. Monday she died. And all that he had worked so hard and longed for, died with her. Frankie has become a great success—but right now he is one of the unhappiest men in the world.

CHAPTER 12

Although the Frankie Carle orchestra seemed to have established itself well in its first year, the first year was by no means a "peak" year. (Actually, Frankie's net pay the first year was less than that of his last year with Heidt. The expenditures in running a big band shocked Frankie.) Frankie himself had reservations as to the musical merits of his crew. The apparent success, i.e., more than the predicted ¼-million dollars (actually, $281,057.05), and the real success as Frankie envisioned success, were incongruent.

Winning the Adam Hats 1944 Popular Bandleader award and receiving other recognition, attested more to Frankie's popularity than they did the merits of his band. Underlying his impressive rise, he thought, were his own compositions, especially "Sunrise Serenade," and the recordings which he had pressed with rhythm section before the recording ban went into effect. Frankie realized that the war had drained most bands of good talent, and although he drew audiences, he suspected that perhaps the "mediocre" was all that was remaining. He further pondered the fact that his band had not appeared in many areas, particularly the west coast.

Nevertheless, the recognition of the band, in the first year was not too far fetched from the apparent sensationalism of the plaudits. What Frankie had not considered was that in the mid-1940's, the public was already leaning more to the sweeter music with vocals and less on jive, as pointed out earlier. And Frankie's was basically a sweet band; of course he had a swing book, too. Besides, although he had not toured extensively and had not played the west coast, his style of music was reasonably well known around the country. Finally, there were top-notch musicians and bands around, despite the war.

Gary Stevens, the earlier dissenting critic, reported "marked improvement in both arrangements and performance of the aggregation" the second time around, which would have made the band some six months old. Stevens yet asserted "the most important asset is still Frankie Carle"—no one ever denied that.

True professional that he was, Frankie met every situation with objectivity and confidence, but at no time departing from his basic style. Frankie's plan was simple enough: syncopate each of the sections for danceable music and play a tune in which everyone can follow in his mind from the first note to the last. "I figured it'd take a year or so," reflected the maestro, "that is, if enough money came in to pay the bills. And I figured some recordings were needed—the ban had to go sooner or later—and some new material, new songs."

The public's acceptance of his style of music, the acceptance of recordings by his band, when and if they could record, and the acceptance of new material which Frankie had been working on all along, were all contained in the notion of success as he envisioned it.

I

Recordings and new material were definitely necessary for a successful, i.e., "top", band. Frankie's contributions here had already begun before his first trip to the west coast in 1945. His successes in these two areas complimented his performances in 1945 and 1946, the years considered by Frankie his "peak" years.

It was not until November, 1944, that Columbia, along with Victor, settled with AFM on the recording fight. "Columbia's first release, following the Petrillo deal," reported the *Boston Traveler* (November 16, 1944), "will be recordings by Frankie Carle, for which they have advance orders for one and a half million."

Remember, when the two-month old orchestra went into the Capitol Theater in April, 1944, Columbia distributed Frankie's five-millionth record. Al Rylander, Frankie's capable publicity agent, could not resist the promotional advantage of such an eventuality and arranged for Frankie to present that five-millionth record to Ginny Simms. A photograph of that presentation appeared in newspapers and slicks all over the country. In June, Columbia released Frankie's "Girl Friends" album (C-97); the "Encores" album (C-70) and "At The Piano" album (C-23) were already in circulation. But these were not the Frankie Carle orchestra, and, as already mentioned, a band needed recordings. This is an accepted rule in the business.

The first record the Frankie Carle orchestra pressed was "I Had A Little Talk With the Lord" and "A Little on the Lonely Side" (36760), with Paul Allen on vocals. In January, 1945, "A Little on the Lonely Side" appeared (or "hit", as they say) the charts (*Billboard*'s Music Popularity Chart of tunes most played on juke boxes). Three months later, when Les Brown's "Sentimental Journey" hit the chart, "A Little On the Lonely Side" was yet holding steadily in its rating, behind the seeming monopoly of "Rum and Coca-Cola" (Andrew Sisters), "Ac-cent-tchu-ate the Positive" (Johnny Mercer), and "Don't Fence Me In" (Bing Crosby-Andrews Sisters). This was a good start in the area of recordings, making it unanimous that Frankie had a good start in everything he did. The orchestra next did "Evelina" (36764), with vocal by Allen, and this tune received great reviews and much play; but the instant favorite was "Carle Boogie" (36777). This pianistic jazz piece was the tune people wanted to hear most when Frankie went on tour. "Carle Boogie" eventually won second place in *Billboard*'s "favorite hot jazz record."* However, the recording that was to put Frankie on top was not "Carle Boogie" but Frankie's "Oh, What It Seemed To Be"** (36892), with daughter Marjorie on vocals, in 1946.

This tune was the song most nearly approaching the fervor generated by "Sunrise Serenade." Charles Schneider (*Cleveland Press*, January 4, 1946) wrote, "I don't know where the tune came from or where it's headed, but it's good enough to

---

*Some jazz critics protested vehemently because Frankie was not "jazz." He was not, nor did he purport to be, a jazzman. But history and authority tell us that he could play jazz with the best.
**With Ben Benjamin and George Weiss.

Frankie presents Ginny Simms with his 5-millionth record (1945), and still many recording years to go.

be a hit." Within a couple of weeks, the tune hit the charts in the 10th position. Two other recordings of the number were in contention: Frank Sinatra and George Paxton. By February the race was on; Sinatra's rendition assumed 3d position; Frankie's, 4th. In this same month, a host of others—including Dick Haymes teamed with Helen Forrest—were recording the tune. Carle's recording "sold more than 100,000 in two weeks," reported Dorothy Kilgallen (February 7, 1946), and by March, Frankie Carle's "Oh, What It Seemed To Be" hit the top position, with Sinatra holding 6th. *Variety* listed the tune 4th among best sheet music. By the end of March, "Oh, What It Seemed To Be" not only maintained the top spot in record machines but also hit #1 in sheet music, the top ten on radio, and *Billboard*'s Honor Role of Hits. For the first six months of 1946, this Carle tune was tops, before it bowed to "The Gypsy."

However, by the time "Oh, What It Seemed To Be" had begun its downward slope—and all hits follow a like pattern—another Frankie Carle orchestra recording, with vocals by Marjorie, was sweeping the country—"Rumors Are Flying" (37069). Back to back big hits!

"Oh, What It Seemed To Be" and "Rumors Are Flying" not only solidified the image of the Frankie Carle orchestra but also made Marjorie Hughes a star in her own right. Family man Frankie could not have been more pleased.

With the success of Carle recordings in 1945 and 1946, plus the Carle recordings pre-band, the Frankie Carle orchestra was amassing a strong following, along with selling an unbelievable number of records. "By mid-1945, Columbia Records will shortly announce that Frankie Carle has sold 12 million piano recordings to date," reported Irving Hoffman (*The Hollywood Reporter*, July 2, 1945), "more than any other pianist, including Paderewski, who heretofore held the record." If the reporting is accurate, that means from January, 1945, when Columbia distributed the 5-millionth disc, to July, Columbia distributed seven million platters! And yet there were six months to go before Frankie kicked off 1946 with "Oh, What It Seemed To Be" and followed with "Rumors Are Flying."

When Lee Morris of the *Philadelphia Record* (February 15, 1946) said "Frankie Carle, who has made so many records for Columbia that it would take a year to count them all," he wasn't fooling!

As far as new tunes were concerned, Frankie's contributions continued. One wonders how Frankie Carle found time to write songs, but he did.

Most of the first year with the band kept Frankie concentrating on refining the danceable qualities of the music and presenting a decent stage show; yet, he wrote four tunes. "Carle Fantasy" and "A Dream So Heavenly," two unexploited tunes, remained unpublished. "Moonlight Whispers," a tune he introduced at the first Capitol engagement, played rather well, and eventually Paul Weston recorded it. "My Topic of Conversation," penned late 1944, appeared in sheet music and did get some play on the air.

Early in 1945 Frankie wrote "Travelin' Mood," a tune picked up and published eleven years later by Shapiro & Bernstein, and he followed "Travelin' Mood" with "Carle Boogie." This one became a classic in boogie piano. Frankie, who did not really like to play boogie, conceded to the expectation of audiences and often closed a show with that number. Toward the end of 1945, he wrote "Ten Little Indians" and "Don't You Remember Me," both with lyrics by Sunny Skylar, the latter tune published by Edwin Morris & Co. By the end of the year, Frankie collaborated with Ben Benjamin and George Weiss and produced "Oh, What It Seemed To Be." (Incidentally, "Rumors Are Flying" was a Benjamin-Weiss tune.)

Riding chiefly on "Oh, What It Seemed To Be" in 1946, other Carle tunes received meager exposure. "A Passing Fancy," "I'm No Good Without Love," and "Chick With the Band," a novelty, were all 1946 vintage. "Chick With the Band" received most play, mainly because it gave the show a dash of family spice. What better tune could follow Marjorie's rendition of "Oh, What It Seemed To Be" in performances, since hubby Hugh Backenstoe and daddy were in the lyrics?

There was no doubt about it: in 1945 and 1946 Frankie's pen, piano, and baton were very much in evidence everywhere here and abroad. These years essentially were "peak" years in Frankie's estimation, even with what Frankie refers to as his "biggest goof" in 1946. What he meant was that he turned down an audition of one of the later great thrushes in the business. The audition was a Mercury recording of "I Can't Help Loving That Man," sung by Patti Page! The next time Frankie and Patti Page met, at the chocolate Christmas party at Hershey Park, Pattie Page was enjoying a fabulous success, "Tennessee Waltz."

As the tunes and recordings became popular, so did the Frankie Carle orchestra, and the drawing power in the ballrooms and theaters was proof. And as the country went "sweet," Frankie's band berthed comfortably in music consciousness.

II

The west coast debut of the Frankie Carle orchestra occurred at the end of March, 1945, at the Palladium Ballroom in Hollywood. The Palladium contract was a most satisfying development, Frankie getting an eight-week engagement with annual return-engagements for five years. The Palladium was to Frankie on the west coast what the Pennsylvania Hotel was on the east coast—a sort of starting-ending focal point around which Warren Pearl could arrange itinerary.

Coming into Los Angeles was "homecoming" for Frankie, who had been gone for over a year. Edith and Marjorie usually remained in California when Frankie toured, except after Marjorie's graduation from high school. Edith and Marjorie had been with Frankie in the east in the fall of 1944, and after Dora's funeral, they returned home. The Carle family now could resume some semblance of home life, and Marjorie started it off in grand style, marrying dad's pianist, Hugh Backenstoe, that same month of the opening.

Horace Heidt introduced Frankie to a huge crowd at the Palladium opening night, which, according to Jerome O'Shea

(*Palladium Life*, April, 1945) "was the glamour event of the current season. All Hollywood turned out . . ." More importantly, Frankie's music was well received. "Even the reporters from the trade papers were dancing," said O'Shea, "so you know the music must be catching."

The music was "catching." It had been "catching" all along for the past year. Frankie had made few adjustments, notably getting Evie Vale on drums when Hack O'Brien decided to stay in the east, and adding to the payroll a young arranger, Nelson Riddle,* to complement Al Avola's work.

From the Palladium it was a tremendously successful four-week stand at Mission Beach in San Diego, where Frankie was performing when the war ended in Europe. A few months later, the war with Japan would end, and for the remainder of 1945 and 1946, Frankie's band catered to a post-war changing society, as explained earlier.

After Mission Beach, Pearl had booked one-nighters in northern California before touring Frankie east. In the interim, though, there did materialize a movie with the Frankie Carle orchestra.

RKO, which was delayed with a "go" sign because of a National Labor Relations Board inquiry regarding Frankie's salary, used the band in its "River Boat Rhythm" film, with Paulette Goddard and Leon Ames. That movie would be the first of several that Frankie would make a little later in his career. But this the first, along with shorts and Columbia's "Mary Lou," with Joan Barton, attest to the image of the Frankie Carle orchestra at the conclusion of the big band era.

When Frankie's part in the movie was finished, the orchestra continued with one-nighters in the Oakland-San Francisco area, in Santa Cruz, Stockton, and San Jose. In northern California he would cross over to Salt Lake City, the jump off spot for his eastward trek.

*This was a "big break" for the young arranger. Frankie's popular recording of "Let A Smile Be Your Umbrella" is a Nelson Riddle arrangement.

Shortly before Frankie's Salt Lake City engagement and, hence, eastward tour, Edith had connived a date to take Frankie to a night club in Southgate in South Los Angeles. Phil Martin, a local band who played Southgate on weekends, was featuring a thrush by the name of Marjorie Carle, and, unbeknownst to Frankie, this was Marjorie's audition for her daddy's band.

Daddy Carle was so very satisfied with Marjorie's performance that he agreed she should sing with the Carle band. The only misgiving, however, was the daughter-dad relationship. But the name was camouflaged, Marjorie taking the first name of her husband and becoming Marjorie Hughes. The disguise hardly fooled the syndicated columnists! Nevertheless, Marjorie would tour with her daddy on his eastward tour.

By the time Frankie reappeared in New York in late 1945, the band had blossomed into a *bona fide* "big time" orchestra, with a great "commercial" sweet book and a "peppered up" swing book. Marjorie proved to be a valuable asset, as did Urby Green, a young, brilliant trombonist whom Frankie used in numerous solos. And as the popularity of the band grew, so did the number of bookings. And, then, when he left New York on his way to the west coast in 1946, the orchestra was five times as active as the preceding year. Warren Pearl had extended the itinerary through St. Louis, Kansas City, and Norman, Oklahoma, and into Texas, Fort Worth, Dallas, Houston. In Houston, Frankie followed Russ Morgan, whose orchestra had opened the brand new Shamrock Hotel.

When Frankie Carle returned to California in 1946, the popularity of his band and the enthusiasm shown in his forthcoming appearances were not confined to Hollywood and a few northern spots, but extended along the entire coast from the Baja peninsula to Canada. He added additional engagements, including, eventually, the Cocoanut Grove in Hollywood. (One of Frankie's favorite places, because "I loved doing the specials, like the Harry Warren Night or Johnny McHugh Night where the songs of these great writers would be featured.") The orchestra crossed the northern California border, Frankie doing a smash week at the famed Jantzen Beach in Portland and appearing in Seattle.

Thus, knowing well his limited itinerary in 1944, including no appearances in the southwest and west coast, Frankie saw a substantial increase in hotel and ballroom bookings in 1945. That told him he was on the right track, i.e., success as he envisioned it. In 1946, there were perhaps very few ballrooms and hotels which would not have welcomed an appearance by the Frankie Carle orchestra. Ballrooms, in particular, feeling the pinch of a waning business, as explained earlier, would gamble with Frankie Carle to bring in the big crowds.

What was occurring for the orchestra on the hotel and ballroom scenes was occurring also on the theater circuit. The up-and-up (box office gross) trend of the Frankie Carle orchestra, which had begun in 1945, reached its peak the following year.

III

In early 1945 when the Frankie Carle orchestra returned to the Capitol in New York—with Marilyn Maxwell sharing the bill—it had surpassed the box office figures of its first appearance there. When Frankie reappeared in December, 1946, Danton Walker of the *News* (December 8, 1946) reported, "Frankie Carle broke opening day records." At the Orpheum in Omaha in 1945, Frankie came within $500 of Tommy Dorsey's box office record; when he returned there in 1946, he "broke Tommy Dorsey's record by 1 G," reported the trade papers. When Frankie returned to Minneapolis in April, 1946, he did not play the Orpheum, a house he would ordinarily play, simply because the theater had discontinued stage shows—a trend quite evident in 1946. Instead, Radio City Theater made a last ditch effort to save the stage show, and who was selected for the test to draw the customers? Indeed, Frankie.

With a polished aggregation, with some outstanding solo work by Urby Green, plus a great hit in the making for Marjorie with "Oh, What It Seemed To Be," plus Frankie at the keys with both "Sunrise Serenade" type numbers and "Carle Boogie" type numbers, the Frankie Carle orchestra elicited such great response that the theater decided to continue with the stage shows as long as possible.

Frankie recruited Gregg Lawrence in May, 1946, and the addition of this big, good-looking, ex-P-51 pilot, complemented Marjorie on the vocals. Lawrence, too, evoked "swoons" from the females. He, too, helped the box office.

And, again, Frankie is the first to admit that the talent appearing with the band on the same bill had much to do with his box-office ratings. "Especially the Mills Brothers," disclosed Frankie. "We played a lot of bills together. The father was part of the group at that time. They also had a guitar player who was not one of the brothers. They were—still are—" mused Frankie, "the greatest."

Frankie had always fared well in Chicago. His three-week Sherman Hotel engagement in April was a first for a sweet band at the traditionally swing-band hotel. But when he returned to the Oriental Theater later in 1946, he drew "57G—$9,000 over house average," reported *Billboard* (November 15, 1946). Simply, Frankie Carle was a drawing power, and that charisma developed, in part, because of the total image of the Frankie Carle orchestra, which, observed Omar Ranney (*Cleveland Press*, November 15, 1946), "comes up with a better band show everytime he appears here." Hence, when Frankie returned to New York at the end of the year, he not only broke opening day records at the Capitol but hit the "top." Danton Walker observed, (*News*, December 25, 1946), "Frankie Carle's sensational success in an era of flopping bands."

Everybody in the business knew of Frankie Carle, but it took Nick Kenny (*Mirror*, December 5, 1946) to refer to, for the first time, what Frankie Carle really was to the business—a triple threat. "You horn and fiddle boys have always known that Frankie Carle was a triple threat fellow, equally facile at the piano, the baton and as a songwriter, but even you would be surprised at the way he stops every show at the Capitol. Sensational."

About the same time Frankie was performing in Minneapolis, Frankie Carle Fan Clubs were cropping up around the country. Olga Dunbar, who had handled the Horace Heidt Fan Club since the very early 1940's, initiated the club in April, 1946.*

What was happening in this part of Frankie's life is the way Frankie Carle envisioned success.

IV

When *Cash Box* counted its 250,000 ballots for the top band in 1946, the standings came out Eddie Howard, Frankie Carle, and Vaughn Monroe. (Singer-piano-singer: more evidence of the trend, as described earlier.) Not bad. And there was more.

When Frankie was visiting his father Angelo, a less vigorous Angelo, during the Christmas season in 1946, Frankie handed his father a telegram from *Billboard*, revealing the music record industry's annual poll. "See, Pa . . ." That was all Frankie said. Angelo stared at the telegram; he looked up and glanced momentarily at Dora's picture on the mantlepiece. Dora's spirit was reflected in the quiet smile on Angelo's face.

WESTERN UNION

Z62CC 65/63 3 EXTRA EJ   NEWYORK NY DEC 28 1115A #2

FRANKIE CARLE, CARE WARREN PEARL GENERAL AMUSEMENT CORP

THE RESULTS OF THE MUSIC-RECORD INDUSTRYS MOST EXHAUSTIVE MOST THOROUGHLY DOCUMENTED ANNUAL POLL BASED ON MORE THAN 106000 REPORTS WILL APPEAR IN THE JANUARY 4 ISSUE OF THE BILLBOARD WE ARE HAPPY TO INFORM YOU THAT YOU WERE FIRST IN THE YEARS TOP BANDS ON DISK JOCKEY SHOWS AND FIRST IN THE YEARS TOP SELLING BAND OVER RECORD COUNTERS CONGRATULATIONS

THE BILLBOARD JOSEPH CSIDA   EDITOR IN CHIEF.

*By mid-1947, more than 750 clubs with over 25,000 members sending more than 650 letters and telegrams.

And there was more yet. Recognition in Europe and South America was evident. *The Musical Express* in London followed Frankie's career, the recording industry in South America advertised Frankie's records, and in France, *Le Monde Musical* named Frankie Carle "most popular maestro" in 1946, an honor he would repeat in 1947 and 1948.

Had Frankie Carle finally made it as a bandleader? By what gauge had he not? Yes, let the record read: Frankie Carle—top pianist, top songwriter, top bandleader.

V

Francisco Nunzio Carlone, son of immigrant parents, organized a group of musicians to play for dancing in and around Providence, R. I. That was toward the end of World War I. He was a very young man and a small man, with a small group in a small place, and he contributed in a small way to popular music in America. He lived music. He played it, wrote it, and led it. Almost thirty years later, after the end of World War II, Francisco Nunzio Carlone was not so young but a big man, with a big group in a big place, and he contributed in a big way to popular music. As one of America's beloved personalities, James Cagney, put it: "People should know more about Frankie Carle whose sensitive playing has made life more worthwhile for me and so many others."

Indeed, so very many others.

As history of popular music describes various eras in music, the big band era being one, let it record that Frankie Carle not only was a part of that era but he preceded it by thirty years. And he followed it by twenty-two years—but that's another story.

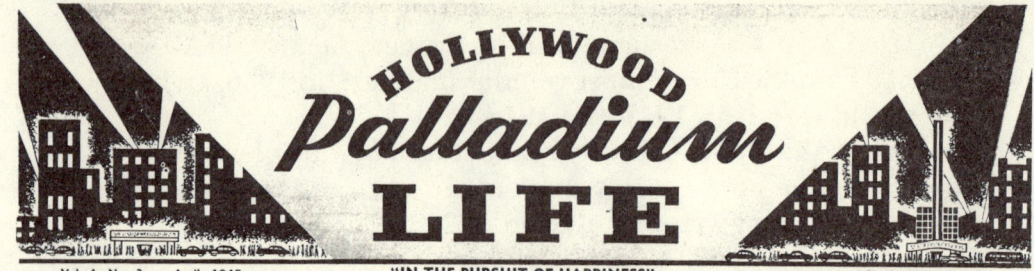

HOLLYWOOD Palladium LIFE

Vol. 4, No. 3 — April, 1945   "IN THE PURSUIT OF HAPPINESS"   Single copy price, 5c

HOLLYWOOD WORLD SHOWTOWN

the bandstand
By BUD MAJOR

It was just little over a year ago when your columnist sat with Frankie Carle and his charming wife on the famed Palladium Terrace and listened
(Continued on Page 8)

This picture montage provides a quick tour of Hollywood. Above left is a crowd shot at the Palladium, with Maestro Frankie Carle seated at the piano below. Lower left show a premier night at Grauman's Chinese. In the center is an exterior view of the Florentine Gardens, while alongside is the "Wall of Fame" at Earl Carroll's, with the Palladium neon sign above. Below is the NBC studio and a panoramic view of the famous Hollywood Bowl.

Film City Now Famed Hub of Entertainment

Not so many years ago, Hollywood was a land of orange groves, bean and barley fields and wide open spaces. Scarcely 30 years have elapsed since the first motion picture studio was built here. Today, it is the film capital of the world.

More than that, Hollywood is the greatest showtown on the face of the earth. Endless opportunities for en-
(Continued on Page 6)

Opening—May 1
TONY PASTOR

Now — FRANKIE CARLE

COMING
TOMMY TUCKER

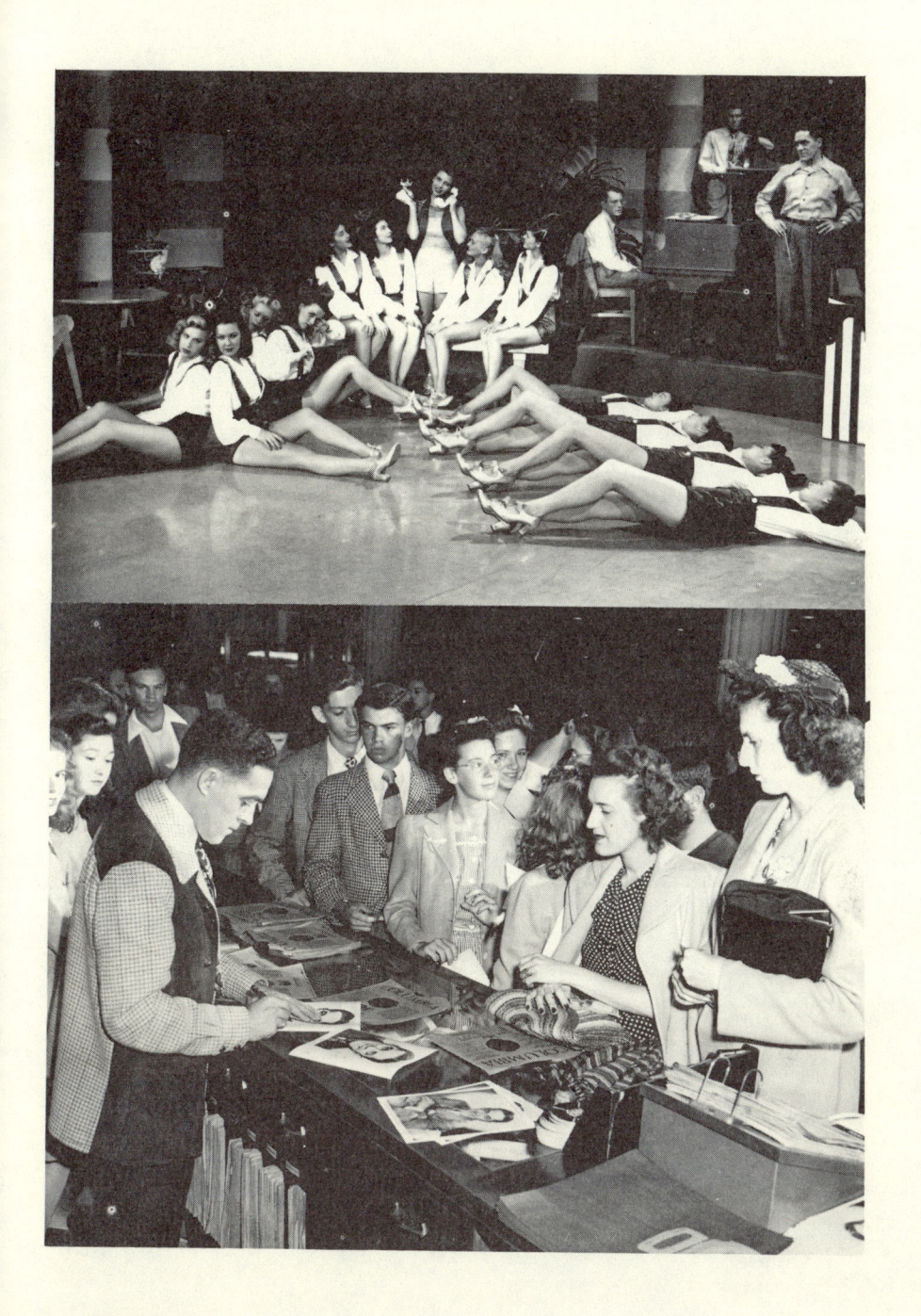

Top: Scene from movie "Mary Lou." Bottom: Everywhere Frankie played or appeared, people jammed for autographs.

The Frankie Carle show at the Orpheum—a record. Upper right, Urby Green and Lee Columbo. Sidemen in San Francisco: left to right, Mitch Zaremba, Evie Vale, Joe Amato, Irv Trestman, Eddie Lucas, Gus Benvenuti, Eddie di Santis, and Ray Hopfner.

FRANKIE CARLE
& HIS ORCHESTRA
EXTRA ADDED
SENOR WENCES
ORIENTAL
STAGE FRANKIE CARLE & HIS ORCHESTRA WITH THE CAITES ★ PAUL ALLEN EXTRA ADDED ATTRACTION SENOR WENCE
STAGE - FRANKIE CARLE HIS PIANO & HIS ORCHESTRA WITH PAUL ALLEN
EXTRA ADDED - SENOR WENCES ★ JOE, LOU AND MARILYN CAITES ★ OTHERS
MERRICK
STARS ON PARADE
LARRY PARKS
GIMBEL'S RESTAURANT

STANLEY
STANLEY THEATRE
FRANKIE CARLE WITH HIS OWN ORCHESTRA
FIBBER McGEE AND MOLLY
STAGE-FRANKIE CARLE AND HIS OWN ORCHESTRA-PHYLLIS LYNNE-LEE COLUMBO-PAUL ALLEN
EXTRA ADDED-ROY DAVIS AND ROBERT SISTERS AND FRANCES WHITE
SCREEN-FIBBER McGEE AND MOLLY IN "HEAVENLY DAYS"

Theater Date
WITH FRANKIE CARLE

1. Proof of the drawing power of Frankie Carle's name was the block-long line which formed outside Chicago's Oriental Theater the night that Frankie opened his engagement there. This stop was one of many on a tour of theaters and one-nighters. Top bands play theaters for a guarantee plus percentage. Frankie's date brought $39,000 into the kitty.

2. What a schedule! And Frankie was overwhelmed by it, too, although he managed to take the six-a-day in his stride. Schedules like this mean less private life, but more money. With him is his pretty vocalist-daughter, Marjorie Hughes.

5. Frankie and his manager, Andy Travers, check light cues at the switchboard with electrician, Dave Oaks. Footlights, house and backstage wing lights are operated from this switchboard, according to the schedule. One of Andy's jobs is to double-check lights on the first show. "They worry like expectant fathers," says Dave of managers in general.

7. The movie in its final reel, the sax section—Dean Sayre, Pete Johns, Tony Johnson, Irv Trostman, Ray Hopfner—warm up. Formal rehearsal was not necessary.

8. Curtain! The show starts off with a deft-fingered solo by the maestro, while the band mates rhythm behind him. They're bouncing on the swingy "Hindustan."

Smash on the theater circuit, especially with the Mills Bros., upper left, Herb, Don, (guitar player unidentified), Frankie, Harry, and father Mills. Upper right, Paul Allen, and with Marjorie, Greg Lawrence.

Theater lines and autograph seekers were commonplace. It was at the RKO Colonial in 1946 where Marjorie introduced "Oh, What It Seemed To Be."

HEADQUARTERS OF THE COMMANDANT THIRD NAVAL DISTRICT
FEDERAL OFFICE BUILDING, 90 CHURCH STREET
NEW YORK 7, N.Y.

A6-2(3)/DHq-18(4)
JRO:mek

23 May 1944

Mr. Frankie Carle
c/o Mr. William Pearl
1270 Sixth Avenue
New York, New York

Dear Mr. Carle:

Again my personal thanks for the effort which you and the boys in your band made to play on our "Bid For Victory" program last Sunday afternoon. Not only did it add immeasurably in the recruitment of WAVES but also, as you know already, entertained the wounded Navy men at the hospital. We appreciate the cooperation which you accorded us and wish to thank you sincerely.

Very truly yours,

William J. Murphy
WILLIAM J. MURPHY
Lieutenant, USNR
Radio Section
Public Relations Office

TREASURY DEPARTMENT
WAR FINANCE COMMITTEE
1808 Industrial Trust Building
Providence 3, Rhode Island
GAspee 0974

OFFICE OF STATE CHAIRMAN

June 16, 1944

Mr. Frankie Carle
c/o Warren Pearl
RKO Building
1270 Sixth Avenue
New York, New York

Dear Mr. Carle:

Nobody needs to tell you what the people of Rhode Island think about you! The deafening applause you received from that packed auditorium on Monday night should satisfy you that you are Number One in your profession as far as the State of Rhode Island is concerned.

I want you to know, however, that the War Finance Committee for this State appreciates not only your remarkable talent, but your generosity and unselfishness in coming back to us

RHODE ISLAND DEPARTMENT OF HEALTH
STATE SANATORIUM, WALLUM LAKE, R.I.
U. E. ZAMBARANO, M.D., SUPERINTENDENT

EDWARD A. McLAUGHLIN, M.D.
DIRECTOR OF HEALTH

June 15, 1944

Mr. Frankie Carle
c/o Mr. Warren Pearl
R.K.O. Building
Radio City, N.Y.

Dear Frankie:

I don't know how to thank you for your ki[nd]ness in entertaining our patients during your recent vis[it to] Providence. Everyone was pleased and they are still [talk]ing about it.

Please accept my sincere thanks and I hop[e that] when you visit Providence again you may find it con[venient]

PUBLIC RELATIONS OFFICE
BILLING GENERAL HOSPITAL
Ft. Benjamin Harrison, Indiana

1 December 1944

Mr. Frankie Carle
Circle Theatre
Indianapolis, Indiana

Dear Mr. Carle:

We appreciate your time and effort in bringing a section of your band to Billings General Hospital. The patients enjoyed the show very much.

VETERANS ADMINISTRATION
Minneapolis, Minnesota

January 17 1945

PLEASE FORWARD

Mr. Frankie Carle,
Orpheum Theater,
Minneapolis, Minnesota.

My dear Mr. Carle:

The patients, particularly the younger ones who so much enjoy music are still talking of your appearance before them and you may be sure they appreciated your effort in getting the appearance in between your very busy acts on the professional stage.

HEADQUARTERS ARMY AIR BASE
OFFICE OF THE COMMANDING OFFICER
STOUT FIELD, INDIANAPOLIS 6, INDIANA

AABSS

30 December 1944

Frankie Carle
c/o Orpheum Theatre
Minneapolis, Minn.

Dear Mr. Carle:

Thanks many times over for your delightful performanc[e] on December 20th. Your kindness and generosity will be long remembered by the enlisted men and women of this base.

They are sincerely grateful for your special effort, after a very hard day's work, to play here at Stout Field.

Morale is one of the more important weapons of war. [It] is, therefore, with pride and a sense of worthwhileness that yo[u] may look upon your efforts to play for members of the armed services whenever and wherever possible.

With kind personal regards and best wishes to all members of your band, Paul Allen, Phyllis Lynn and yourself, I remain

Sincerely yours,

Wright J. Sherrard
WRIGHT J. SHERRARD,
Lieutenant Colonel, Air Corps,
Commanding.

HEADQUARTERS, TRUAX FIELD
MADISON (7) WISCONSIN

18 January 1945.

Mr. Frankie Carle,
1902 R.K.O. Building,
New York, New York.

Dear Mr. Carle:

It is with a great deal of pleasure that I write this letter of appreciation to you for appearing at Truax Field on 10 January 1945. I feel that the morale boosting qualities of such appearances to the personnel of the Field are immeasurable.

Thank you sincerely for coming. To you and similarly patriotic minded members of the entertainment world the Armed Forces are very grateful.

Sincerely,

Vincent J. Meloy
VINCENT J. MELOY,
Brigadier General, U. S. Army,
Commanding.

As Cedric Adams said about Frankie's extracurricular activities, "It's that sort of spirit that makes a gem out of a guy."

The Carle orchestra in action at one of the camps. The rhythm section jams at Ft. Benjamin Harrison; the group entertains at the Stage Door Canteen in Cleveland and at a bond rally over WXYZ.

By 1947 Frankie Carle reached top-band status. Pictured above with Marion Hutton and Perry Como at the Terrace Room. And thousands upon thousands will remember the Steel Pier in Atlantic City. The Carle orchestra there in 1947.

By 1948 Frankie Carle landed what he called his "favorite" spot—The Cocoanut Grove in Los Angeles. There pictured with, top left, Peggy Lee, Bill Goodwin, Dave Barbour, and Johnny Mercer; top right, with Jimmy McHugh; bottom left, with Margaret Whiting; and bottom right, with his favorite songwriter, Harry Warren.

APPENDIX: FRANKIE CARLE MUSIC

Music composed or specially arranged by Frankie Carle is listed first alphabetically by title and then chronologically. Collaborators, lyricists, publishers, and other credits where applicable are given along with dates. Where copyright pertains to transcription or arrangement only, arr. follows. Asterisk indicates more detailed information is included in the text.

A separate list of collaborators—lyricists and co-composers—is included, along with the name of the composition.

Music performed or recorded but not published will bear the abbreviation PRNP. Where an exact date is not known, the probable date, as determined by the composer himself, is given in parenthesis.

Frankie Carle and Sherman Woods are pseudonyms of Francis Nunzio Carlone.

AIR COMMANDOS SONG. Music by W. N. Dekker, words by Reed G. Landis. Arr. by Francis N. Carlone and Jane Burroughs. (Air Emergency Relief) Arr. October 29, 1942.

ALOHA, PARADISE. Music by Frankie Carle and Lisa Farrell, lyrics by Dottie Wayne, PRNP. (Victor) 1962.

ALONE WITH MY TEARS. Music by Smiling Frankie Carle, words by Mitchell Parish, piano score by Lou Leaman, with ukulele arr. (Mills Music, Inc.) September 10, 1943.

ALONG CAME GEORGIA LEE. Music by Francis N. Carlone, words by Mitchell Parish. (Mills Music, Inc.) September 10, 1943. Arr. by Michael Edwards. For voice and piano, with chord symbols. (Mills Music, Inc.) May 22, 1946.

AM I TO BLAME. Music by Frankie Carle, lyrics by W. Lewis. PRNP.

APPLE VALLEY WALTZ. Music by Frankie Carle. June 30, 1960.

BECAUSE YOU ARE. Music by Francis N. Carlone. July 6, 1943 (Jewel) PRNP.

BEST BLACK (MY BEST GAL) (GEORGIANNA) Music by Frank Carle and William McKenzie. (Brunswick-Balke-Collender Co.) April 18, 1925.

BLUE FANTASY. By Smiling Frankie Carle. October 24, 1934. Words by Raymond Leveen (Jewel Music Publishing Co., Inc.) July 19, 1937.

BLUES WITH A LILT. By Francis N. Carlone. May 19, 1946.

BRAND NEW BABY. Music by Frankie Carle, words by R. Snow. August 13, 1931.

THE BUSIEST CORNER IN MY HOMETOWN, IS THE LONELIEST PLACE IN THE WORLD. Music by Francis N. Carlone, words by Stanley Adams and Doris Day. (Bristol Music Corp.) August 10, 1950. (Robert Music Corp.) September 19, 1950.

CARA MIA. Music by Frankie Carle. September 17, 1965.

CARLE BOOGIE. Melody by Francis Carlone. (Shapiro, Berstein & Co.) March 10, 1945. (Transcribed for piano from Columbia record No. 36777 by Ludwig Flato. (Shapiro, Berstein & Co. Inc.) June 6, 1945. (New matter: fox-trot) (Shapiro, Berstein & Co. Inc.) November 21, 1945.

CARLE FANTASY. Music by Frankie Carle. September 23, 1944.

CARLE MEETS ALBENIZ. Music by Frankie Carle and Al Avola. Arr. December 1, 1949.

CARLE MEETS CHOPIN. Music by Frankie Carle and Al Avola. (Dreyer Music Corp.) Arr. May 12, 1948.

CARLE MEETS DONIZETTI. Music by Frankie Carle and Al Avola. Arr. December 1, 1949.

CARLE MEETS GRIEG. Music by Frankie Carle and Al Avola. Arr. December 1, 1949.

CARLE MEETS MOZART. Music by Frankie Carle and Al Avola. (Dreyer Music Corp.) Arr. May 12, 1948.

CARLE MEETS SCHUBERT. Music by Frankie Carle and Al Avola. Arr. December 1, 1949.

CARLEANA. (Piano Solo) Music by Francis N. Carlone. November 25, 1941.

CHICK WITH THE BAND. Music by Frankie Carle, words by Bob Merrill. September 17, 1946.

COCKTAILS FOR TWO. By Arthur Johnston and Sam Coslow. Piano solo by Frankie Carle. (Famous Music Corp.) Arr. May 20, 1952.

DANCE AND THE DEVIL WILL PLAY. Music by Smiling Frankie Carle, words by Burt Milton. October 18, 1934.

THE DANCE OF THE SHMOOS. Music by Chris Bowden and Francis N. Carlone, words by Tade Dolen and Frances Dolen. (D. Dreyer & Co., Inc.) July 29, 1949.

DARLING. (Piano) Music by Frankie Carle. January 18, 1939.

DAY AFTER DAY. Words and music by Ed G. Nelson and Frankie Carle. (Dryer Music Corp.) December 23, 1947.

DAY DREAMS. By Frankie Carle, lyrics by R. Snow. May 24, 1932.

DEEP IN YOUR EYES. Music by Frankie Carle, words by R. Snow. June 1, 1931. (Mills Music Inc.) December 29, 1931.

DID YOU EVER HAVE A DREAM COME TRUE. Music by Frankie Carle, lyrics by H. Russell. (1940)

DON'T LAUGH IF I CRY. Music by Frankie Carle, lyrics by Alice Huntington. 1974.

DON'T YOU REMEMBER ME? Music by Frankie Carle, words by Sunny Skylar. (Edwin H. Morris & Co., Inc.) November 19, 1945.

DOWN BY THE OLD MILL STREAM. New Matter: piano arrangement in Frankie Carle style by Frankie Carle, music by Tell Taylor. (Forster Music Publisher Inc.) May 15, 1944.

DOWN YONDER. Music by L. Wolfe Gilbert, piano arrangement by Frankie Carle. (La Salle Music Publishers, Inc.) Arr. October 16, 1951.

A DREAM SO HEAVENLY. Music by Frankie Carle. December 6, 1944.

DREAMY LULLABY. Words and music by Frankie Carle, Bennie Benjamin, and George Weiss. (Oxford Music Corp.) November 24, 1947.

DUNK A DOUGHNUT. Music by Frankie Carle, words by Raymond Leveen. (Jewel Music Publishing Co., Inc.) September 8, 1939.

DUSKY LULLABIES. Music by Frankie Carle, words by R. Snow. August 20, 1931.

EASY PICKIN'S. By Gray Rains, arrangement by Frankie Carle for piano. (Bregman, Vocco & Conn, Inc.) Arr. April 3, 1947.

*ESTELLE. By Frankie Carle. (Mills Music Inc.) November 15, 1930. (For two pianos. Mills Music Inc.) 1945.

EVERY NOW AND THEN. Music by Frankie Carle, Al Avola, and Sherman Woods. August 8, 1952.

EXACTLY LIKE YOU. By James Francis McHugh, piano solo transcribed by Frankie Carle. (Shapiro Berstein & Co.) Arr. July 10, 1946.

*FALLING LEAVES. Music by Frankie Carle, words by David Mack. (Jewel Music Publishing Co., Inc.) July 29, 1940. (Special piano solo arrangement, Jewel Music Publishing Co., Inc., August 6, 1940.)

FALLING IN LOVE. Music by Francis N. Carlone. June 11, 1941.

FALLING STAR. Music by Frankie Carle. January, 1968.

FOR YOU AND ME. Music by Sherman Woods. September 16, 1963.

FOOLED AGAIN. Composer, Francis N. Carlone. January 30, 1940.

FRANKIE CARLE METHOD OF PIANO STYLING FOR BEGINNERS AND ADVANCED STUDENTS. By Frankie Carle, compiled by Lois Steele. June 8, 1949.

*GEORGIANNA. Words and music by Austen Croom-Johnson, Red McKenzie, and Frankie Carle. (Shapiro Berstein & Co., Inc.) September 25, 1937; October 26, 1937; new matter arr. for orchestra by Larry Clinton, January 18, 1938.

GOLDEN TOUCH. Music by Frankie Carle, lyrics by Lois Steele. (Southern Music) April 15, 1959.

GOLDEN YEARS. Music by Frankie Carle, lyrics by Gordon Clifford. (Freddie Martin, Henry Von Tilzer Music) 1964.

THE GUY WITH THE GUN. Melody by Francis N. Carlone, words by Jerry Bowne. (The Infantry Song) (Lead Sheet) November 10, 1942.

HEADIN' SOUTH. Music by Frankie Carle, words by R. Snow. June 1, 1931.

HERE COMES BABY NOW. Music by Francis N. Carlone and Frank Quinn, words by Bob Russell. (Dreyer Music Corp.) September 29, 1948.

HINDUSTAN. Music by Oliver Wallace and Harold Weeks, new matter by Frankie Carle. (Forster Music Publisher, Inc.) Arr. May 15, 1944.

HOW I MISS THAT SWEET GAL O'MINE. Words and music by Francis Carle. December 7, 1925; December 9, 1952.

HUMPTY-JUMPTY. Music by Frankie Carle and Larry Wagner. (Robert Music Corp.) March 29, 1950; January 17, 1951.

I DIDN'T KNOW. Words and music by Francis N. Carlone and Maurice Murray. (Robert Music Corp.) January 10, 1950; June 27, 1951.

I DON'T WANT TO MEET ANY MORE PEOPLE. Music by Frankie Carle, lyrics by Stanley Adams. (Dreyer Music Corp.) July 21, 1947.

I FOUND MY LOVE IN YOU. Music by Sherman Woods, lyrics by Dottie Wayne. December 15, 1960.

I REMEMBER. Music by Francis N. Carlone. October 6, 1941.

I SAY TO YOU.

I SEE IN YOU. Music by Frankie Carle, lyrics by Dottie Wayne. 1962.

I SOLD MY HEART FOR A SONG. Music by Frankie Carle, lyrics by Bob Merrill and George Brown. (Original title, YOU'RE ONLY MAKING BELIEVE)

I STILL CARE. Music by Francis Carlone, words by Henry Russell and Irving Gordon. With diagrams for guitar. (Allied Music Corp.) September 1, 1943.

I TOLD MYSELF A LIE ABOUT YOU. Music by Frankie Carle. (Mills Music) 1954.

I WISH I COULD LOVE YOU. Words and music by Tade Dolen, Frances Dolen, and Frankie Carle. June 13, 1950.

I WISH I WAS A KID AGAIN. Music by Frankie Carle. March 27, 1951.

I WON'T FORGET. (From Pot O' Gold) Melody by Frankie Carle, words by Henry Russell. (Saintly-Joy Select, Inc.) July 6, 1940.

I WOULDN'T MIND, I WOULDN'T CARE. By Smiling Frankie Carle, lyrics by Fred Quinn. January 21, 1933.

*IF YOU PLEASE. Music by Smiling Frankie Carle, words by Chet Thompson. January 21, 1936.

I'M GOING AWAY. Music by Frankie Carle, lyrics by H. Russell. (1942)

I'M NEVER BLUE WHEN I'M STROLLING WITH YOU. Music by Frankie Carle, words by R. Snow. August 13, 1931.

I'M NO GOOD WITHOUT LOVE. Music by Francis N. Carlone, words by Eugene Cines. October 27, 1946.

I'M SO IN LOVE. See LET'S SPREAD OUR WINGS.

IN A WORLD OF LOVE. Music by Frankie Carle, lyrics by Dottie Wayne. 1962.

IN SPITE OF THE WAY THINGS ARE. Words and music by Frankie Carle and Randy Fones. (Mills Music Inc.) May 29, 1938.

IT'S ONLY ME. Music by Frankie Carle, lyrics by Lois Steele. (1950)

*I'VE BEEN DISPOSSESSED BY YOU. Words and music by Frankie Carle, June 30, 1937. (Mills Music Inc.) August 22, 1944. Lyrics by Lige McKelvey.

I'VE FALLEN IN LOVE. Music by Francis N. Carlone and Al Avola. November 8, 1950.

JUNE, JUNE, JUNE. Music by Frankie Carle, words by Bud Green. February 27, 1951.

JUST A LITTLE GOLD RING. Words and music by Francis N. Carlone and Bob Bilder. (Robert Music Corp.) February 7, 1950.

JUST LAZY. Music by Frankie Carle, words by Guy Wood. (Jewel Music Publishing Co., Inc.) January 8, 1942; February 20, 1942.

THE KIWANIS WALTZ. Words and music by Frankie Carle. March 17, 1938.

KNOCKIN' AT THE OLD FRONT DOOR. Music by Frankie Carle, lyrics by R. Snow (1932).

LET ME BE LOCKED IN YOUR HEART. Music by Frankie Carle, words by R. Snow. May 26, 1931.

LET'S SPREAD OUR WINGS. Music by Frankie Carle, lyrics by Gordon Clifford. 1964.

LOLLYPOP BALL. Words and music by Irving Melcher, Francis N. Carlone, Selig Shaftel, and Larry Wagner. (Robert Music Corp.) January 4, 1950.

LOOKING OUT THE WINDOW IN VAIN. Music by Smiling Frankie Carle, words by Burt Milton. October 18, 1934.

LOVE. Music by Frankie Carle. 1966.

LOVE, FOR YOU AND ME. Music by Francis Carlone, words by Oliver Wallace. April 28, 1945.

LOVE ME. Music by Frankie Carle, words by Frank Stanton. (Dreyer Music Corp.) March 1, 1948.

*A LOVER'S LULLABY. Music by Frankie Carle and Larry Wagner, piano transcription by Frankie Carle. Lyrics by Andy Razaf. (Jewel Music Publishing Co. Inc.) March 6, 1940.

A LOVER'S RHAPSODY. Music by Francis N. Carlone. October 16, 1941.

MAKE WITH A DOWNBEAT. Words and melody by Frankie Carle and Joey Sinay. February 11, 1941.

THE MAN IN THE MOON JUST LAUGHS AND LAUGHS. (From Pot O' Gold) Music and words by Frankie Carle and Henry Russell. (Santly-Joy-Select Inc.) July 6, 1940.

MESSIN' ROUND. By Frankie Carle. (1942).

A MILLION DOLLAR INSPIRATION. Music by Francis N. Carlone. November 8, 1950.

MISSOURI WALTZ. Music by John Valentine Eppel and arrangement by Frederic Knight Logan. New matter: piano arrangement in Frankie Carle style by Frankie Carle. (Forster Music Publisher, Inc.) Arr. March 15, 1944.

MODERN HOT PIANO SOLOS. Arranged by Frankie Carle. (Mills Music Inc.) Arr. September 7, 1937.

*MODERN TRANSCRIPTION OF HUMORESKE. By Frankie Carle. July 22, 1929.

MOONLIGHT COCKTAIL. Music by Lucky Roberts. New matter: piano solo arrangement by Frankie Carle. (Jewel Music Publishing Co. Inc.) Arr. March 10, 1942.

MOONLIGHT WHISPERS. Music by Francis Carlone, words by Al J. Neiburg. (Jewel Music Publishing Co., Inc.) January 30, 1944.

MY DREAM SHIP. Music by Smiling Frankie Carle, words by Chet Thompson. December 12, 1935.

MY EYES TOLD MY HEART. Music by Frankie Carle, lyrics by Lois Steele & Terry Thomas. (AMCO Music Co.) 1959.

MY HONEY. Music by Francis N. Carlone. July 30, 1941.

MR. AND MRS. O'SHAY. Words and music by Sherman Woods. February 13, 1953.

MY LIFE. Music by Frankie Carle, words by Phil Barton. February 17, 1939.

MY MELANCHOLY BABY. Transcribed for piano by Frankie Carle. (Shapiro, Bernstein & Co. Inc.) Arr. July 10, 1946.

MY TOPIC OF CONVERSATION. Words and music by Ray Trotta, Jules Loman, and Francis Carlone. June 15, 1944. (Jewel Music Publishing Co.) November 17, 1944.

NEVER SATISFIED. Music by Francis N. Carlone, words by Russell Snow. December 8, 1941.

NEXT SATURDAY NIGHT. Music by Frankie Carle, lyrics by Henry Russell (1942).

A NIGHT TO REMEMBER. Music by Frankie Carle. (1945)

*NIGHTFALL. Music by Frankie Carle. April 21, 1939. (See SHADOWS).

NOBODY CARES ABOUT ME. Music by Francis N. Carlone. December 23, 1941.

NOT A WORD, JUST A TEAR' IN MY EYE. Words and music by Smiling Frankie Carle. December 15, 1931.

NOT FOR ME. Music by Sherman Woods and Al Avola, lyrics by Eliott Daniels. April 25, 1952.

NOTE AFTER NOTE. Music by Frankie Carle. April, 1958.

OFF STAGE, CLOSER. Words and music by Frankie Carle and Ralph Douglas. April 25, 1952.

*OH! WHAT IT SEEMED TO BE. Words and music by Ben Benjamin, George Weiss, and Frankie Carle. (Santly-Joy, Inc.) December 27, 1945.

ON NEXT SATURDAY NIGHT. Music by F. N. Carlone. April 17, 1935.

ON STAGE. Words and music by Frankie Carle and Ralph Douglas. April 25, 1952.

ON THE ALAMO. Music by Isham Jones. New matter by Frankie Carle. (Forster Music Publisher, Inc.) Arr. May 15, 1944.

ON THE SUNNY SIDE OF THE STREET. By James Francis McHugh. Piano solo transcribed by Frankie Carle. (Shapiro, Berstein & Co., Inc.) Arr. July 10, 1946.

ONCE WE WERE SWEETHEARTS. Music by Frankie Carle, words by Chet Thompson. April 6, 1938.

ONE AND ONE MAKES TWO. Music by Francis N. Carlone. January 3, 1941.

THE ONE I LOVE BELONGS TO SOMEBODY ELSE. Music by Isham Jones. New matter by Frankie Carle. (Forster Music Publisher, Inc.) Arr. May 15, 1944.

ONE LOVE. Music by Frankie Carle. April 23, 1946.

ONE NIGHT IN HEAVEN. Music by Frankie Carle, lyrics by Chris Bowden and Tade Dolen. (1943).

ONLY A ROSE. From the Vagabond King, by Rudolf Friml. Piano solo arrangement by Frankie Carle. (Famous Music Corp.) Arr. March 20, 1952.

OUT OF A DREAM. (From Pot O' Gold) Melody by Frankie Carle, words by Henry Russell. (Santly-Joy-Select Inc.) July 6, 1940.

A PASSING FANCY. Music by F. N. Carlone and Al Avola. August 24, 1946.

PAST, PRESENT, AND FUTURE. Words and music by Frankie Carle and Al Avola. April 25, 1952.

PEPINO AND HIS DONKEY. Music by Frankie Carle.

PIANO POLKA. Music by Frankie Carle and Al Avola, words by David Brown. February 8, 1951.

PIANO STYLINGS. By Frankie Carle. (Mills Music) Arr. 1930.

PLEASE DON'T STOP. Music by Francis N. Carlone. June 11, 1941.

THE RAG PICKER. Music by Frankie Carle. February 2, 1939. Words by Raymond Leveen and George Hayes. (Jewel Music Publishing Co., Inc.) September 8, 1939.

RHYTHM CLASSICS. By Frankie Carle, edited by Morris Feldman for piano. (J. J. Robbins & Sons, Inc.) Arr. July 29, 1949.

RIDIN' ON TWO FLATS. By Dick Hummer, arranged by Frankie Carle for piano solo. (Bel-Air Music Corp.) Arr. September 26, 1947.

RIGHT OR WRONG. Music by Frankie Carle. 1964.

ROSE AND A STAR. Words and music by Frankie Carle, Al Avola, and Mack David. (Dreyer Music Corp.) December 23, 1947.

*ROSES IN THE RAIN. Music by Frankie Carle, lyrics by Al Frisch and Fred Wise. Piano solo arrangement by Frankie Carle. (Barton Music Corp.) January 22, 1947.

RUE DE ROMANCE. Music by Frankie Carle, English words by Sunny Skylar. (Robert Music Corp.) February 14, 1949. April 26, 1949.

SAVE A PIECE OF WEDDING CAKE FOR ME. Music by Frankie Carle, words by Fred Meadows. (Dreyer Music Corp.) January 14, 1949.

SAY HELLO TO JOE. Words and music by Frankie Carle and Al Avola. April 25, 1952.

*SHADOWS. Composer and arranger, Frankie Carle. (Originally NIGHTFALL) (Jewel Music Publishing Co.) July 3, 1939. New matter: lyrics by Jules Loman and Chet Thompson. (Jewel Music Publishing Co.) September 8, 1939. (Dorsey Brothers Music, Inc.) February 18, 1959.

SHE'S DA SWEETEST GAL IN ITALY. Music by Francis Carlone, words by Russell Snow and Frankie Carle. January 5, 1932.

SO GREAT IS LOVE. Music by Frankie Carle, lyrics Stella Unger. (1948)

SO LONG, SO LONG, SO LONG. Music by Frankie Carle, words by Ronnie Kemper. April 30, 1953. (Amco Music Co.) June 15, 1953.

SO MY HEART STOOD STILL. Music by Francis N. Carlone. April 19, 1943.

SOMEBODY ELSE. Words and music by Frankie Carle. March 26, 1931.

SOMEWHERE. Music by Francis N. Carlone. July 6, 1942.

SUNRISE BOOGIE. By Frankie Carle and Al Avola. Frankie Carle's original piano solo. (Dryer Music Corp.) July 8, 1948.

SUNRISE IN NAPOLI. See TRINIDAD.

*SUNRISE SERENADE. Music by Frankie Carle. Registered in the name of Francis N. Carlone. March 17, 1938. (Jewel Music Publishing Co., Inc.) November 19, 1938. Words by Jack Lawrence. (Jewel Music Publishing Co., Inc.) April 20, 1939; November 22, 1965.

TAHITI. Music by Frankie Carle, lyrics by Lou Rich. Copyrighted under DARLING.

TAKE ME BACK IN YOUR HEART. Music by Frankie Carle, lyrics by R. Snow. (1932).

TEN LITTLE INDIANS. Music by Frankie Carle, words by Sunny Skylar. December 5, 1945.

TEND TO YOUR KNITTIN' KITTEN. Music by Frankie Carle, James Cremer, and Ray Sterling. (Rayster Music Publishing Co.) 1965.

THAT EVER LOVIN' RAG. By Walter Byron, arranged by Frankie Carle for piano solo. (Johnstone-Montei, Inc.) Arr. March 28, 1952.

*THAT'S ALL THAT IT WAS BUT OH, WHAT IT SEEMED TO BE. See OH, WHAT IT SEEMED TO BE.

THAT'S THE SAME OLD STORY OVER AND OVER AGAIN. Words and music by Frankie Carle. November 27, 1931.

*THERE'S A POT O' GOLD IN THE AIR. Music by Frankie Carle, words by Henry Russell. January 20, 1940. (Jewel Publishing Co., Inc.) March 26, 1940.

THEY'LL DO IT EVERY TIME. Words and music by Frankie Carle and Ralph Douglas. April 25, 1952.

THINGS WILL BE DIFFERENT THIS FALL. Music by Frankie Carle, lyrics by Bob Merrill. September, 1963.

THIS DAY. Music by Francis N. Carlone, words by Jimmy Eaton and George Dessinger. Copyright title: SOMEWHERE. (Jewel Music Publishing Co. Inc.) January 6, 1943.

TILL I FORGET. Music by Frankie Carle, lyrics by D. Parker. 1959.

TRAVELIN' MOOD. (Lead Sheet) Melody by Frankie Carle. February 15, 1945. (Shapiro and Bernstein) February 16, 1956.

TRINIDAD. Music by Frankie Carle, lyrics by Jimmy Eaton and H. Russell. (Now: SUNRISE IN NAPOLI) (1945).

12TH STREET RAG. Transcribed for piano by Frankie Carle. (Shapiro Bernstein & Co., Inc.) Arr. September 16, 1946.

TWO TREES. Music by Francis N. Carlone. July 5, 1941.

VACATION BLUES. Music by Frankie Carle. (Dreyer Music Corp.) September 29, 1948.

VIOLIN. Words and music by Frankie Carle, Imogen Carpenter, and Frank Stanton. (Southern Music Publishing Co., Inc.) February 12, 1948.

WAIT. Music by Frankie Carle, lyrics by Lois Steele. July 25, 1959.

WAITING FOR THE MOON TO RISE. Music by Frankie Carle, words by R. Snow. September 19, 1931.

WE'RE GOING ACROSS (TO SEE THE MADEMOISELLE FROM ARMENTIERES). Music by Francis Carlone, words by Henry Russell and Irving Gordon. (Allied Music Corp.) October 25, 1943.

WHAT A SURPRISE. Words and music by Frankie Carle and Charmaine G. Dice. December 15, 1947.

WE TWO. Words and music by Sherman Woods. September 19, 1951.

WHAT DO WE CARE, WE'VE STILL GOT LOVE. Words and music by Smiling Frankie Carle. February 20, 1935.

WHEN I DISCOVERED YOU. Music by Frankie Carle. (1937).

*WHEN YOUR LIPS MET MINE. Music by Frankie Carle, words by Jack Owens. December 8, 1941. (T. B. Harms Co.) June 22, 1942.

WHEN THE BOYS COME HOME AGAIN. Music by Frankie Carle, lyrics by Frank DuVol. (1942).

WHISPERS. Music by Francis N. Carlone. January 3, 1941.

WHY MAKE BELIEVE. Music by Smiling Frankie Carle. May 5, 1934. December 16, 1936.

WHY, OH WHY? Words and music by Frankie Carle, Frances and Tade Dolen, and Chris Bowden. (Southern Music Publishing Co., Inc.) August 25, 1949.

WITH LOVE TO GUIDE US. Music by Frankie Carle, lyrics by Gordon Clifford. 1965.

WITH MY HEART IN MY HAND. Music by Frankie Carle, lyrics by H. Russell. (1943).

WITH NO MAN OF MY OWN. Music by Isham Jones. New matter: piano arrangement in Frankie Carle style. (Forster Music Publisher) Arr. May 15, 1944.

YOU AND THE STARS AND ME. Music by Sherman Woods. September 19, 1951.

YOU ARE THERE. By Frankie Carle, Dave Lieber, and Vic White. (Stept, Inc.) May 7, 1947.

YOU CAN'T WIN 'EM ALL. Music by Frankie Carle, lyrics by Gordon Clifford. September 12, 1965.

YOU STILL BELONG TO ME. Music by Frankie Carle and Al Avola. January 9, 1952.

YOU'LL BE MISSING ME. Music by Frankie Carle.

YOUR DREAMS ARE MY DREAMS. Music by Frankie Carle, lyrics by H. Russell. (1943)

YOU'RE ONLY MAKING BELIEVE. Music by Frankie Carle. (See I SOLD MY HEART FOR A SONG).

1925	BEST BLACK (MY BEST GAL) (GEORGIANNA)
	HOW I MISS THAT SWEET GAL O' MINE
1929	MODERN TRANSCRIPTION OF HUMORESKE
1930	ESTELLE
	PIANO STYLINGS
1931	BRAND NEW BABY
	DEEP IN YOUR EYES
	DUSKY LULLABY
	HEADIN' SOUTH
	I'M NEVER BLUE WHEN I'M STROLLING WITH YOU

	LET ME BE LOCKED IN YOUR HEART
	NOT A WORD JUST A TEAR IN MY EYE
	SOMEBODY ELSE
	THAT'S THE SAME OLD STORY OVER AND OVER AGAIN
	WAITING
	WAITING FOR THE MOON TO RISE
1932	DAY DREAMS
	KNOCKIN' AT THE OLD FRONT DOOR
	SHE'S DA SWEETEST GAL IN ITALY
	TAKE ME BACK IN YOUR HEART
1933	ALONE WITH MY TEARS
	I WOULDN'T MIND, I WOULDN'T CARE
1934	BLUE FANTASY
	DANCE AND THE DEVIL WILL PLAY
	LOOKING OUT THE WINDOW IN VAIN
	WHY MAKE BELIEVE
1935	MY DREAM SHIP
	ON NEXT SATURDAY NIGHT
	WHAT DO WE CARE, WE'VE STILL GOT LOVE
1936	IF YOU PLEASE
	WHY MAKE BELIEVE
1937	GEORGIANNA (MY BEST GAL) (BEST BLACK)
	I'VE BEEN DISPOSSESSED BY YOU
	MODERN HOT PIANO SOLOS (ARR)
	WHEN I DISCOVERED YOU
1938	IN SPITE OF THE WAY THINGS ARE
	THE KIWANIS WALTZ
	ONCE WE WERE SWEETHEARTS
	SUNRISE SERENADE
1939	DARLING
	DUNK A DOUGHNUT
	MY LIFE
	RAG PICKER
	THE RAG PICKER
	SHADOWS (ORIGINALLY NIGHTFALL)

1940	DID YOU EVER HAVE A DREAM COME TRUE
	FALLING LEAVES
	FOOLED AGAIN
	I WON'T FORGET
	A LOVER'S LULLABY
	THE MAN IN THE MOON JUST LAUGHS AND LAUGHS
	OUT OF A DREAM
	THERE'S A POT O' GOLD IN THE AIR
1941	CARLEANA
	FALLING IN LOVE
	FRANKIE CARLE'S PIANO SERENADES
	I REMEMBER
	A LOVER'S RHAPSODY
	MAKE WITH A DOWNBEAT
	MY HONEY
	NEVER SATISFIED
	NOBODY CARES ABOUT ME
	ONE AND ONE MAKES TWO
	PLEASE DON'T STOP
	TWO TREES
	WHEN YOUR LIPS MET MINE
	WHISPERS
1942	AIR COMMANDOS SONG
	BECAUSE YOU ARE
	THE GUY WITH THE GUN
	I'M GOING AWAY
	JUST LAZY
	MESSIN' ROUND
	MOONLIGHT COCKTAIL (ARR)
	NEXT SATURDAY NIGHT
	SOMEWHERE (THIS DAY)
	WHEN THE BOYS COME HOME AGAIN
1943	ALONE WITH MY TEARS
	ALONG CAME GEORGIA LEE
	I STILL CARE
	ONE NIGHT IN HEAVEN

SO MY HEART STOOD STILL
WE'RE GOING ACROSS (TO SEE THE MADEMOI-
   SELLE FROM ARMENTIERES)
WITH MY HEART IN MY HAND
YOUR DREAMS ARE MY DREAMS

1944   CARLE FANTASY
DOWN BY THE OLD MILL STREAM (ARR)
A DREAM SO HEAVENLY
HINDUSTAN (ARR)
MISSOURI WALTZ (ARR)
MOONLIGHT WHISPERS
MY TOPIC OF CONVERSATION
ON THE ALAMO (ARR)
THE ONE I LOVE BELONGS TO SOMEBODY ELSE
   (ARR)
WITH NO MAN OF MY OWN (ARR)

1945   CARLE BOOGIE
DON'T YOU REMEMBER ME
LOVE, FOR YOU AND ME
A NIGHT TO REMEMBER
OH WHAT IT SEEMED TO BE
SUNRISE IN NAPOLI
TEN LITTLE INDIANS
TRAVELIN' MOOD

1946   BLUE WITH A LILT
CHICK WITH THE BAND
EXACTLY LIKE YOU (ARR)
I'M NO GOOD WITHOUT LOVE
MY MELANCHOLY BABY (ARR)
ON THE SUNNY SIDE OF THE STREET (ARR)
ONE LOVE
A PASSING FANCY
12TH ST. RAG (ARR)

1947   DAY AFTER DAY
DREAMY LULLABY
EASY PICKIN'
I DON'T WANT TO MEET ANY MORE PEOPLE

    RIDIN' ON TWO FLATS (ARR)
    ROSE AND A STAR
    ROSES IN THE RAIN
    WHAT A SURPRISE
    YOU ARE THERE
1948 CARLE MEETS CHOPIN
    CARLE MEETS MOZART
    HERE COMES BABY NOW
    LOVE ME
    SUNRISE BOOGIE
    VACATION BLUES
    VIOLIN
1949 CARLE MEETS ALBENIZ
    CARLE MEETS DONIZETTI
    CARLE MEETS GRIEG
    CARLE MEETS SCHUBERT
    THE DANCE OF THE SHMOOS
    FRANKIE CARLIE METHOD OF PIANO PLAYING
    RHYTHM CLASSICS FOR PIANO
    RUE DE ROMANCE
    SAVE A PIECE OF WEDDING CAKE FOR ME
    SO GREAT IS LOVE
    WHY, OH WHY?
1950 THE BUSIEST CORNER IN MY HOMETOWN IS THE LONELIEST PLACE IN THE WORLD
    HUMPTY JUMPTY
    I DIDN'T KNOW
    I WISH I COULD LOVE YOU
    IT'S ONLY ME
    I'VE FALLEN IN LOVE
    JUST A LITTLE GOLD RING
    LOLLYPOP BALL
    A MILLION DOLLAR INSPIRATION
1951 DOWN YONDER (ARR)
    I WISH I WAS A KID AGAIN
    JUNE, JUNE, JUNE
    PIANO POLKA

	WE TWO
	YOU AND THE STARS AND ME
1952	COCKTAILS FOR TWO (ARR)
	EVERY NOW AND THEN
	MY SILENT LOVE (ARR)
	NOT FOR ME
	OFF STAGE, CLOSER
	ON STAGE
	ONLY A ROSE (ARR)
	PAST, PRESENT, AND FUTURE
	SAY HELLO TO JOE
	THAT EVER LOVIN' RAG (ARR)
	THEY'LL DO IT EVERY TIME
	YOU STILL BELONG TO ME
1953	MR. AND MRS. O'SHAY
	SO LONG, SO LONG, SO LONG
1954	I TOLD MYSELF A LIE ABOUT YOU
1956	TRAVELIN' MOOD
1958	NOTE AFTER NOTE
1959	THE GOLDEN TOUCH
	MY EYES TOLD MY HEART
	TILL I FORGET
	WAIT
1960	APPLE VALLEY WALTZ
	I FOUND MY LOVE IN YOU
1962	ALOHA PARADISE
	I SEE IN YOU
	IN A WORLD OF LOVE
1963	FOR YOU AND ME
	THINGS WILL BE DIFFERENT THIS FALL
1964	THE GOLDEN YEARS
	LET'S SPREAD OUR WINGS
	RIGHT OR WRONG
1965	CARA MIA
	TEND TO YOUR KNITTIN' KITTEN
	WITH LOVE TO GUIDE US
	YOU CAN'T WIN 'EM ALL

1966   LOVE
1968   FALLING STAR
1974   DON'T LAUGH IF I CRY

Collaborators

Music
AVOLA, AL
  Carle Meets Albeniz; Carle Meets Chopin; Carle Meets Donizetti; Carle Meets Grieg; Carle Meets Mozart; Carle Meets Schubert; Every Now and Then; I've Fallen in Love; Not For Me; A Passing Fancy; Past, Present, and Future; Piano Polka; Rose and a Star; Say Hello to Joe; Sunrise Boogie; You Still Belong to me.

BENJAMIN, BENNIE
  Dreamy Lullaby; Oh! What It Seemed To Be
BILDER, BOB
  Just a Little Gold Ring
BOWDEN, CHRIS
  The Dance of the Shmoos; Why, Oh Why?
CARPENTER, IMOGEN
  Violin
CREMER, JAMES
  Tend To Your Knittin' Kitten
DAVID, MACK
  A Rose and a Star
DICE, CHARMAINE
  What a Surprise
DOLEN, TADE AND FRANCES
  I Wish I Could Love You; Why, Oh Why?
DOUGLAS, RALPH
  Off Stage, Closer; On Stage; They'll Do It Every Time
FARRELL, LISA
  Aloha Paradise
FONES, RANDY
  In Spite Of The Way Things Are
JOHNSON, AUSTEN CROOM-
  Georgianna
LIEBER, DAVE
  You Are There

LOMAN, JULES
    My Topic Of Conversation
MELCHER, IRVING
    Lollypop Ball
MC KENZIE, WILLIAM "RED"
    Georgianna
MURRAY, MAURICE
    I Didn't Know
NELSON, ED G.
    Day After Day
QUINN, FRANK
    Here Comes Baby Now
RUSSELL, HENRY
    The Man In The Moon Just Laughs and Laughs
SHAFTEL, SELIG
    Lollypop Ball
SINAY, JOEY
    Make With the Downbeat
STANTON, FRANK
    Violin
STERLING, RAY
    Tend To Your Knittin' Kitten
TROTTA, RAY
    My Topic Of Conversation
WAGNER, LARRY
    Humpty Dumpty; Lollypop Ball; A Lover's Lullaby
WEISS, GEORGE
    Dreamy Lullaby; Oh! What It Seemed To Be
WHITE, VIC
    You Are There

Lyrics

ADAMS, STANELY
    Busiest Corner In My Hometown Is The Loneliest Place in the World; I Don't Want To Meet Anymore People
BARTON, PHIL
    My Life

BOWDEN, CHRIS
    One Night in Heaven
BOWNE, JERRY
    The Guy With The Gun
BROWN, DAVID
    Piano Polka
BROWN, GEORGE
    I Sold My Heart For A Song
DANIELS, ELIOTT
    Not For Me
DAY, DORIS
    The Busiest Corner in My Hometown is the Loneliest Place in the World
DESSINGER, GEORGE
    This Day (Somewhere)
DE VOL, FRANK
    When the Boys Come Home Again
DOLEN, TADE
    One Night In Heaven
DOUGLAS, RALPH
    Off Stage, Closer; They'll Do It Every Time; On Stage
EATON, JIMMY
    This Day (Somewhere); Trinidad (Sunrise in Napoli)
FRISCH, AL
    Roses in the Rain
GORDON, IRVING
    I Still Care; We're Going Across
GREEN, BUD
    June, June, June
HAYES, GEORGE
    Rag Picker
HUNTINGTON, ALICE
    Don't Laugh If I Cry
KEMPER, RONNIE
    So Long, So Long, So Long
LAWRENCE, JACK
    Sunrise Serenade
LEVEEN, RAYMOND
    Blue Fantasy; Dunk a Doughnut; Rag Picker

LEWIS, W.
> Am I To Blame

LOMAN, JULES
> My Topic of Conversation; Shadows (Nightfall)

MERRILL, BOB
> Chick With The Band; I Sold My Heart For A Song; Things Will Be Different This Fall

MACK, DAVID
> Falling Leaves

MC KELVEY, LIGE
> I've Been Dispossessed by You

MEADOWS, FRED
> Save A Piece of Wedding Cake For Me

MILTON, BURT
> Looking Out the Window In Vain

NEIBURG, AL J.
> Moonlight Whispers

OWENS, JACK
> When Your Lips Met Mine

PARISH, MITCHELL
> Alone With My Tears; Along Came Georgia Lee

PARKER, D.
> Till I Forget

QUINN, FRED
> I Wouldn't Mind, I Wouldn't Care

RAZAF, ANDY
> A Lover's Lullaby

RICH, LOU
> Darling (Tahiti)

RUSSELL, HENRY
> Did You Ever Have a Dream Come True; I Still Care; I Won't Forget; I'm Going Away; The Man In the Moon Just Laughs and Laughs; Next Saturday Night; Out of a Dream; There's A Pot o' Gold in the Air; Trinidad (Sunrise in Napoli); We're Going Across; With My Heart in My Hand; Your Dreams Are My Dreams

RUSSELL, BOB
> Here Comes Baby Now

SKYLAR, SUNNY
>   Don't You Remember Me?; Rue De Romance; Ten Little Indians

SNOW, RUSSELL
>   Brand New Baby; Day Dreams; Deep In Your Eyes; Dusky Lullabies; Headin' South; I'm Never Blue When I'm Strolling With You; Knocking at the Old Front Door; Let Me Be Locked in Your Heart; Never Satisfied; She's Da Sweetest Gal in Italy; Take Me Back In Your Heart; Waiting; Waiting for the Moon To Rise

STANTON, FRANK
>   Love Me

STEELE, LOIS
>   Wait; Golden Touch; It's Only Me; My Eyes Told My Heart

THOMAS, TERRY
>   My Eyes Told My Heart

THOMPSON, CHET
>   If You Please; My Dream Ship; Once We Were Sweethearts; Shadows

TROTTA, RAY
>   My Topic of Conversation

UNGER, STELLA
>   So Great Is Love

WALLACE, OLIVER
>   Love For You and Me

WAYNE, DOTTIE
>   Aloha Paradise; I See In You; I Found My Love In You; In a World of Love

WISE, FRED
>   Roses in the Rain

WOOD, GUY
>   Just Lazy

APPENDIX: DISCOGRAPHY

Where it was possible to include recording dates, they appear. The early Victor recordings of the Edwin J. McEnelly band contain all recordings in which Frankie Carle plays. These are listed by recording dates, record number, and identification. Decca recordings of Frankie Carle with rhythm section are also listed by recording dates, numbers, re-releases, and other information according to Decca files. Later recordings, Columbia and Victor, do not carry recording dates except where indicated. Columbia recordings appear by catalog numbers and represent the complate Columbia catalog, both with Frankie Carle and rhythm section and Frankie Carle and his orchestra. Later Victor recordings (from 1950) are listed according to Frankie Carle's personal record collection from which identification comes. Unable to secure a complete catalog from Victor Records, this section may not be inclusive of all recordings under this label.

Victor recordings (78 RPM) of Edwin J. McEnelly and His Orchestra.

Date	Record Number	Title
March 9, 1925	19617-A	Desert Isle
	19617-B	I Like Pie, I Like Cake, But I Like You Best of All. Vocal by Billy Murray & Franklin Burr
November 2, 1925	19841-A	Normandy. Vocal by Lewis James & Elliot Shaw
	19841-B	What a Blue-Eyed Baby You Are. Vocal by Billy Murray
	19851-B	Spanish Shawl
March 18, 1926	19988-A	Moonlight in Mandalay. Vocal by Lewis James

Date	Record Number	Title
March 15, 1926	20018-B	In the Middle of the Night
October 4, 1926	20259-B	That Night in Araby. Vocal by Henry Burr
	20370-B	Blame It on the Waltz. Vocal by Henry Burr
	20379-B	Tuck in Kentucky and Smile
April 1, 1927	20589-B	My Sunday Girl. Vocal by Frederick Wade
	20597-B	I'll Take Care of Your Cares
March 21, 1927	20601-B	Just Across the River from Queens. Vocal by Frederick Wade
October 10, 1927	21011-B	A Siren Dream
December 5, 1927	21164-A	What Are We Waiting For. Vocal by Johnny Marvin
October 8, 1928	21732-A	Jo-Anne. Vocal by Elliot Shaw
	21732-B	All of the Time. Vocal by Jim Miller & Charles Farrell
	21773-B	Take Your Tomorrow. Vocal by Jim Miller & Charles Farrell
	21786-B	Sleep Baby Sleep. Vocal by Elliot Shaw Yodeling by Edwin J. McEnelly
February 21, 1929	21910-A	Dear, When I Met You. Vocal by Frank Munn
	21910-B	Raquel. Vocal by Frank Munn

(Recorded but not released: Alabamy Bound, Butterfly Waltz, and Lonely and Blue)

Decca recordings of Mal Hallet and His Orchestra. Frankie Carle at the piano.

Date	Record Number	Title	Re-Release	Album
October 23, 1936	984B	Moonlight on the Chesapeake		
	993B	There's Something in the Air		
	984A	Sweetheart, Let's Grow Old Together		

235

	1047A	Good-Night My Love
	993A	Where the Lazy River Goes By
November 4, 1936	1033A	In the Chapel in the Moonlight
	1033B	Let Me Sing in Echo Valley
	1047B	One Never Knows, Does One?
January 13, 1937	1163B	Ridin' High
	25147	Oct 15, 1951
	1110A	Timber
	1111A	I Can't Lose That Longing For You
	1110B	If My Heart Could Only Talk
	1111B	Oh, Say, Can You Swing
	1116B	Who's Afraid of Love?
	1116A	One in a Million
February 25, 1937	1167B	I've Got Rain in my Eyes
	1162A	Boo-Hoo
	1162B	I Adore You
	1190A	Rockin' Chair Swing
	1167A	The Trouble With Me Is You
	1163A	Big Boy Blue
	1190B	Humoresque
	25147	Oct 15, 1951
May 10, 1937	1270A	Turn Off the Moon (Have You Forgotten)
	1281A	The You and Me That Used To Be
	1282A	Alibi Baby
	1282B	Easy on the Eyes
	1281B	'Cause My Baby Says It's So
August 2, 1937	1384B	Turn On That Red Hot Heat
	1384A	Moonlight on the Highway
	1402A	Roses in December
	1403B	The Life of the Party
	1403A	Let's Have Another Cigarette
	1402B	Yankee Doodle Band
October 26, 1937	1522A	When the Organ Played O' Promise Me

	1533B	You're Out of This World To Me
	1522B	Sailing Home
	1533A	True Confession
	1532A	I Love To Play A Love Scene (Opposite You)
	1532B	I Want A New Romance
(Not in Decca files:	62491	I've Been Dispossessed by You. Vocal by Teddy Grace)

Decca recordings with Frankie Carle and rhythm section.

January 13, 1937   25147*   Ridin' High Sept 8, 1947
                                                                          Feb 20, 1950 DL 5087
                                                                              (Piano Magic)
                                                                          Mar 2, 1970 VL 3622

February 25, 1937 25147* Humoresque Sept 8, 1947
                                                                           Feb 20, 1950 DL 5087
                                                                           Mar 2, 1970 VL 3622
                                                                               (Ridin' High)

                              *with Mal Hallett

September 7, 1937	1456	I'm Feelin' Like a Million
		Yours and Mine
		Afraid to Dream
		The Loveliness of You
		You Can't Have Everything
	1468	Have You Got Any Castles, Baby
		Moonlight on the Campus
	1457	Remember Me
		Am I In Love?
		The Moon Got in My Eyes
		It's the Natural Thing To Do
	1468	You've Got Something There
		On With the Dance
October 26, 1937	29214	Rosalie June 1, 1947
		Why Mar 2, 1970 VL 3622
		Should I Care
		Who Knows

	29214	In the Still of the Night Jun 1, 1947
		I've a Strange New Rhythm Mar 2, 1970 VL 3622
		In My Heart
	29215	Nice Work If You Can Get It Jun 1, 1947
		Mar 2, 1970 VL 3622
		A Foggy Day
		Things Are Looking Up
		I Can't Be Bothered Now
		Have You Met Miss Jones Jun 1, 1947
		I'd Rather Be Right Mar 2, 1970 VL 3622
		Sweet Sixty Five
		Take and Take and Take
January 3, 1938	25144	Kitten on the Keys
		Sept 8, 1947
		Feb 20, 1950 DL 5087
		Mar 2, 1970 VL 3622
	25146	Doll Sept 8, 1947
		Dance
		Feb 20, 1950 DL 5087
		Mar 2, 1970 VL 3622
	25146	Wedding of Painted Doll
		Sept 8, 1947
		Feb 20, 1950
	25144	Holiday Sept 8, 1947
		Feb 20, 1950 DL 5087
		Mar 2, 1970 VL 3622
	25145	Flapperette Sept 8, 1947
		Feb 20, 1950 DL 5087
	25145	Dancing Tambourine
		Sept 8, 1947
		Feb 20, 1950 DL 5087
		Mar 2, 1970 VL 3622

Columbia recordings with Frankie Carle with Frankie Carle and rhythm section, with individuals from the Horace Heidt group, and with Frankie Carle & His orchestra. Pertinent information given in parenthesis.

Catalog No.	Title

CL 531	Frankie Carle's Piano Party:
	  Sunrise Serenade
	  A Lover's Lullaby
	  Charmaine
	  I'll Get By
	  Swingin' Down the Lane
	  I Can't Believe That You're In Love With Me
	  Runnin' Wild
	  After You've Gone
	  The One I Love Belongs to Somebody Else
	  Sweet and Lovely
	  Rose Room
	  Hindustan
	  Penthouse Serenade

CL 543	Late Music—Volume III: Moonlight Whispers
CL 599	Columbia "Dance Party Series" Saturday Night Mood: Can't You Hear Me Callin' Caroline

CL 642	Frankie Carle And His Girl Friends:
	  Ida
	  Charmaine
	  Margie
	  Louise

                    Mexicali Rose
                    Sweet Lorraine
                    Liza
                    Diane
                    Rose Marie
                    Josephine
                    Estelle
                    If You Were The Only Girl

CL 686   Music For Bachelors:
                    Penthouse Serenade

CL 913   Roses In Rhythm
                    Begin the Beguine
                    Deep Purple
                    Rose Of Washington Square
                    Stumbling
                    Only A Rose
                    Chopin's Polonaise In Boogie
                    Star Dust
                    Roses Of Picardy
                    I Want A Girl
                    My Wild Irish Rose
                    Twelfth Street Rag
                    One Dozen Roses

HL 7140   The Fabulous Frankie Carle:
                    The Glow-Worm
                    Sweet Sue-Just You
                    Honeysuckle Rose
                    I Know That You Know
                    Carle Boogie
                    Somebody Loves Me
                    The Love Nest
                    Moondust Rhapsody
                    That Naughty Waltz
                    Missouri Waltz

HL 7153   Theme Songs:
                    Sunrise Serenade

HL 7166   A Frankie Carle Piano Bouquet:
                    One Dozen Roses
                    Roses Of Picardy
                    Only A Rose
                    My Wild Irish Rose
                    Rose Of Washington Square
                    Stumbling
                    Deep Purple
                    Chopin's Polonaise In Boogie
                    Stardust
                    Twelfth Street Rag

CL 2520   Caressin' The Keys:
                    Margie
                    The Glow-Worm
                    Prelude In C-Sharp Minor
                    Sweet Sue-Just You
                    Barcarolle from "The Tales Of
                      Hoffman"
                    Honeysuckle Rose

CL 6002   Carle Comes Calling:
                    Star Dust
                    I'll Get By
                    Runnin' Wild
                    Deep Purple
                    Penthouse Serenade
                    I Want A Girl
                    Chopin's Polonaise in Boogie
                    If You Were The Only Girl

CL 6016   Theme Songs:
                    Sunrise Serenade

CL 6018   Frankie Carle And His Girl Friends:
    Ida
    Charmaine
    Margie
    Louise
    Liza
    Diane
    Rose Marie
    Josephine

CL 6032   Frankie Carle Presents Roses In Rhythm:
    Roses Of Picardy
    Mexicale Rose
    Honeysuckle Rose
    Only A Rose
    My Wild Irish Rose
    Rose of Washington Square
    Rose Room
    One Dozen Roses

CL 6047   Frankie Carle Dance Parade:
    Carle Boogie
    Oh! What It Seemed To Be
    Penguin At The Waldorf
    Sunrise Serenade
    Missouri Waltz
    The Glow-Worm
    Sunrise Boogie
    Sweet Sue-Just You

CL 6057   Popular Favorites:
    Cruising Down The River

CL 6075   At The Piano . . . :
    Twelfth Street Rag

	Sweet Lorraine
	Barcarolle from "The Tales Of Hoffman"
	Prelude In C-Sharp Minor
	Sunrise Serenade
	A Lover's Lullaby
	Hindustan
	Estelle
	Stumbling
CL 6085	Carle Meets The Masters:
	Carle Meets Donizetti
	Carle Meets Mozart
	Carle Meets Chopin
	Carle Meets Tchaikowsky
	Carle Meets Beethoven
	Carle Meets Schubert
	Carle Meets Grieg
	Carle Meets Albeniz
LN 3120	For Dancers Only:
	Roses Of Picardy
LN 3127	Pick Up The Beat:
	Runnin' Wild
LN 3136	Dancing With the Stars:
	Moondust Rhapsody
Set C-23 (35570 - 35573)	At The Piano . . . :
B-23 (4-35570 - 4-35573)	A Lover's Lullaby
EP B-23 (5-1105 - 5-1106)	Sunrise Serenade
	Hindustan
	Stumbling
	Estelle

          Twelfth Street Rag
          Sweet Lorraine
          Barcarolle from "Tales Of
             Hoffman"
          Prelude In C-Sharp
             Minor

Set C-70 (36331 - 36334)   Frankie Carle Encores:
          Somebody Loves Me
          I Know That You Know
          Swingin' Down The Lane
          The Love Nest
          I Can't Believe That You're In
             Love With Me
          After You've Gone
          The One I Love Belongs to
             Somebody Else
          Sweet And Lovely

Set C-97 (36689 - 36692)   Frankie Carle And His Girl
    B-97 (4-36689 - 4-   Friends:
36692)
          Ida

EP B-97 (5-1113 - 5-1114)   Liza
          Charmaine
          Diane
          Margie
          Rose Marie
          Louise
          Josephine

Set C-129 (37315 - 37318)   Carle Comes Calling:
    B-129 (4-37316 - 4-   Star Dust
37318;
      4-39087)   Canadian Capers; Runnin' Wild
EP B-129 (5-1202 - 5-   I'll Get By
1203)   Deep Purple

	Penthouse Serenade
	I Want A Girl
	Chopin's Polonaise In Boogie
	If You Were The Only Girl
Set C-140 (37539)	Theme Songs—Volume 11:
B-140 (4-37539)	Sunrise Serenade
EP B-140 (5-1304)	
Set C-174 (38330 - 38333)	Frankie Carle Presents Roses In
B-174 (4-38330 - 4-38333)	Rhythm:
	Roses Of Picardy
EP B-174 (5-1306 - 5-1307)	My Wild Irish Rose
	Mexicali Rose
	Rose Of Washington Square
	Honeysuckle Rose
	Rose Room
	Only A Rose
	One Dozen Roses
Set C-193 (38580 - 38583)	Carle Meets The Masters:
	Carle Meets Donizetti
	Carle Meets Albeniz
	Carle Meets Mozart
	Carle Meets Grieg
	Carle Meets Chopin
	Carle Meets Schubert
	Carle Meets Tchaikovsky
	Carle Meets Beethoven
Set B-365	Late Music—Volume III:
	Moonlight Whispers
Set B-387 (5-1828 - 5-1829)	Frankie Carle's Piano Party:
	Sunrise Serenade
	A Lover's Lullaby

                        Charmaine
                        Swingin' Down The Lane
                        I Can't Believe That You're In
                           Love With Me
                        After You've Gone
                        The One I Love Belongs to
                           Somebody Else
                        Sweet And Lovely
                        Rose Room

Set B-461 (5-2003)   Columbia "Dance Party" Series
                        Saturday Night Mood:
                          Can't You Hear Me Callin'
                          Caroline

Set B-686 (5-2218)   Music for Bachelors:
                          Penthouse Serenade

B-1611   Boogie Woogie:
                            Carle Boogie

B-2039   Frankie Carle And His Girl
                          Friends:
                            Mexicali Rose
                            Sweet Lorraine
                            Estelle
                            If You Were The Only Girl

B-2535   Hall Of Fame:
                            Sunrise Serenade
                            Carle Boogie
                            Penguin At The Waldorf
                            Rumors Are Flying

EG 7100   For Dancers Only:
                            Roses Of Picardy

EG 7110   Pick Up The Beat:
                            Runnin' Wild

EG 7124	Dancing With The Stars: Moondust Rhapsody
50024	Sunrise Serenade
4-50024	Carle Boogie
5155	Chico's Love Song It's A Whole New Thing
5241	Night Glow Blue Fantasy

The following were the Frankie Carle orchestra immediately (Jan. 1945) starting after the recording ban settlement in late 1944.

36760	I Had A Little Talk With The Lord A Little On The Lonely Side
36764	Evelina Right As The Rain
36777	Carle Boogie Saturday Night
36805	Counting The Days Missouri Waltz
36826	I'd Rather Be Me I Was Here When You Left Me
36848	I'd Do It All Over Again Last Night I Had That Dream Again
36888	Prove It By The Things You Do Don't You Remember Me

36892	As Long As I Live Oh! What It Seemed To Be
36906	I'm Glad I Waited For You No, Baby, Nobody But You
36978	One More Tomorrow I'm Gonna Make Believe
36994	Cynthia's In Love I'd Be Lost Without You
37069	Rumors Are Flying Without You
37146	Either It's Love Or It Isn't It's All Over Now
37194	What've You Got To Lose Easy Pickin's
37222	We Could Make Such Beautiful Music Too Many Times
37252	Roses In The Rain You Are There
37269	Sunrise Serenade Carle Boogie
37311	The Man Who Paints The Rainbow In The Sky Unless It Can Happen With You
37337	Rockin' Horse Cowboy Midnight Masquerade

37484	There's That Lonely Feeling Again (Love's Got Me In A) Lazy Mood
37567	The Glow-Worm Penguin At The Waldorf
37819	—And Mimi For Once In Your Life
37930	Peggy O'Neil I'll Hate Myself In The Morning
37972	Corabelle Who Were You Kissing
38036	Beg Your Pardon The Dream Peddler
38050	My Promise To You Tell Me A Story
38090	Dreamy Lullaby Lost April
38130	Laroo Laroo Lilli Bolero Someone Cares
38175	Moondust Rhapsody Sunrise Boogie
38203	That Five O'Clock Feeling I Don't Want To Meet Any More People
38222	Somebody Else's Picture On The Little Village Green

38291	October Twilight A New Kind Of Song
38354	Little Jack Frost Get Lost I Couldn't Stay Away From You
38361	Little Jack Frost Get Lost (For Dreyer Music Corp. only)
38372	An Old Magnolia Tree Congratulations
38388 3-38388	Let A Smile Be Your Umbrella Sweet-Sue—Just You
38411	Cruising Down The River Mississippi Flyer
38429 3-38429	The Little Old Church Near Leicester Square Sault Ste. Marie
38457 3-38457	Tulsa Save A Piece Of Wedding Cake For Me
38518 3-38518	Love Is A Beautiful Thing Rue De Romance
38529 4-38529	Missouri Waltz That Naughty Waltz
38573 3-38573	Why Oh Why? I'm Gonna Let You Cry For A Change

38594	Vieni Su
3-38594	I Want You To Want Me
38646	The Blossoms On The Bough
3-38646	My Rose Garden
38690	Whistling In The Dark
3-38690	I Still Care
38783	Tell Me
3-38783	Dream A Little Dream Of Me

Label	*Record/Album No.*	*Title*
Coronet	CX 280	The Magic Artistry of Frankie Carle
Dot	DLP 3789	Frankie Carle
Dot	DLP 25847	Era: The 30's
Dot	DLP 25877	Era: The 40's
Vocalon	VL 3622	Frankie Carle At The Piano Ridin' High
RCA Victor	CAL 950	Great Honky Tonk Piano Favorites
RCA Victor	CAL 987	Easy To Love
RCA Victor	CAS 478(e)	The Piano Style of Frankie Carle
RCA Victor	CAS 963(e)	April in Portugal
RCA Victor	CAS 2118(e)	Cocktail Time
RCA Victor	CAS 2370(e)	Frankie Carle: Let's Do It
RCA Victor	CPL 2-0362	The Big Band Cavalcade Concert

RCA Victor	CSP 112	Frankie Carle Plays Cocktail Piano
RCA Victor	LPM 19	Frankie Carle Plays Frank Loesser (First RCA album)
RCA Victor	LPM 1064	Frankie Carle Plays Cole Porter
RCA Victor	LPM 1153	Frankie Carle's Finest
RCA Victor	LPM 1188	Honky Tonk
RCA Victor	LPM 1221	Cocktail Time With Frankie Carle
RCA Victor	LPM 1222	Frankie Carle's Sweethearts
RCA Victor	LPM 1275	Mediterranean Cruise
RCA Victor	LPM 1499	Around the World
RCA Victor	LPM 1559	Frankie Carle and His Beautiful Dolls
RCA Victor	LPM 1963	Show Stoppers in Dance Time
RCA Victor	LPM 2142	Take Me Along
RCA Victor	LPM 2148	A Carle-Load of Hits
RCA Victor	LPM 2233	Top of the Mark
RCA Victor	LPM 2288	The Fabulous Four Hands
RCA Victor	LPM 2491	Honky Tonk Hits By the Dozen
RCA Victor	LPM 2540	Honolulu Honky Tonk
RCA Victor	LPM 2592	30 Hits of the Tuneful '20's
RCA Victor	LPM 2721	3 Great Pianos (Carle-Cramer-Nero)
RCA Victor	LPM 2881	30 Hits of the Fantastic 50's
RCA Victor	LPM 2915	12 Double-Barreled Hits of '64
RCA Victor	LPM 3300	Short and Sweet
RCA Victor	LPM 3425	Frankie Carle Plays the Great Piano Hits
RCA Victor	LPM 3469	The Best of Frankie Carle

RCA Victor	LPM 3489	The Best of Frankie Carle
RCA Victor	LPM 3609	The Tropical Style
RCA Victor	LSP 2139	Golden Touch
RCA Victor	LSP 2594	30 Hits of the Flaming '40s
RCA Victor	LSP 2920	Frankie Carle Plays the Big Imported Hits
RCA Victor	LSP 3518	The Latin Style of Frankie Carle
RCA Victor	VPS 6081	This Is Frankie Carle
Reader's Digest Pleasure Programmed	RDA 85-A	Frankie Carle Plays Music for Dancing
Reader's Digest Stereo Tape	Stereo 8	Stardust Memories

PICTURE CREDITS

Page 39, Yohe's Shelatone orchestra photo by Photographic Laboratories, Inc., Latham, Mass. P. 55, Mrs. Frankie Carle portrait by Brown Studio. P. 62, Mound City Blue Blowers photo by Alpeda. P. 82, Mal Hallett orchestra photo by Fred Hess & Son. P. 98, Frankie Carle 1935 band photo by Brown Studio. P. 114, photo by Vitaphone. P. 124, Frankie Carle Seven Gables orchestra, courtesy of Evie Vale. P. 140, Heidt band photo by Alpeda. P. 141, Theatre photos by C. Oscar Lindquist. P. 147, Heidt Herald photos by Ned Scott. P. 152, photo by Lue Denet. P. 163, Official U. S. Navy photo. P. 164, Official U. S. Navy photo. P. 168, Strand photo by Arsene Studio. P. 169, Heidt-Macrae photo by Arsene Studio, Heidt personnel photos, courtesy of Olga Dunbar estate. P. 170, Finale photo by Arsene Studio. P. 174, Frankie Carle Rouge debut photo by Metropolitan Photo Service. P. 177, Carle-Barber-Jones photo by CBS. P. 181, Boys Town photo by Ralf. P. 201, Mary Lou Columbia Picture photo by Christie. P. 202, Frankie Carle personnel photos, courtesy of Olga Dunbar estate. P. 204, Theater Date photos by Paul Winik. P. 205, autograph seekers photo by Joseph Marbello. P. 207, Rhythm Section photo, Official U. S. Army photo, Stagedoor Canteen photo by Paul Oetjen, Bond Rally, WXYZ, photo by Robert Newman.

INDEX

Aaronson, Irving, 85
Accevedo, John, 31
Adams, Cedric, 180
Adams, Peggy, photo, 140
Adams, Stanley, 230
Addeo, Arthur, 22, 29, 73, 122
Ahern, Ollie, 85; photo, 82
Alexy, Robert "Bob", 85, 108
Allen, Paul, 172, 189
Amato, Joe, photo, 202
Ames, Leon, 194
Anderson, Stuart, 85, 86
Andrew Sisters, 14, 110, 115, 189
Andrews, Ernie, 97
Armstrong, Louis, 71
Arnheim, Gus, 172
Astor, Mary, 182
Autrey, Gene, 13
Avola, Al, 172, 194, 229

Backenstoe, Hugh, 182, 192, 193
Bacon, Roger, 172, 173; photo, 174
Baker, Bob, 65
Baker, Bonnie, 13
Bancroft Hotel Orchestra, 64
Barber, Red, 175; photo, 177
Barbour, Dave, 111, 160; photo, 209
Barnet, Charlie, 12, 15, 184
Bartholemew, Freddy, 145
Barton, Bernie, photo, 98
Barton, Joan, 194
Barton, Phil, 230
Basie, Count, 10, 105, 110, 115, 184
Bates, Carrol "Cal", 63
Bellamy, Richard, 184
Benjamin, Ben, 189, 192, 229
Benoit, Mac J., 58

Benoit, Maria, 58
Benvenuti, Augustus "Gus", 84, 99, 123; photos, 98, 124, 202
Berger, Irving, 123; photo, 124
Berigan, Bunny, 105
Berle, Milton, 16, 145
Berman, Fred, 46
Bernie, Ben, 48
Bilder, Bob, 229
Bishop, Jim, 182
Blake, Arthur, 176
Blake, Sunny, 84
Block, Martin, 112, 115, 145
Bloom, Harry, 30
Bonney, Betty, 172, 173; photo, 174
Booth, Percy, 105, 123, 160, 171; photos, 124, 169, 174
Borshard, Jerry, photo, 140
Boswell, Connie, 34
Bowden, Chris, 229, footnote, 143
Bowne, Jerry 231
Brannick, Eddie, 165
Breese, Lou, 145
Brice, Fanny, 17
Brinkman's Society Orchestra, 64
Britt, Elton, 14
Brown, David, 231
Brown, George, 231
Brown, Les, 110, 115, 179, 189
Buie, Dr. Louis, 149
Buntman, Al, 108
Burns, Bob, 145
Burr, Franklin, 66, 70
Burr, Henry, 17, 66, 70
Bush, Lou, 10
Bushkin, Joe, 105, 158

255

Busse, Henry, 65, 76, 77, 78, 102
Byrnes, Frank, 41, 44, 46

Caesar, Sid, 16
Cagney, James, 199
Cagney, Jeanne, 180
Calloway, Cabell "Cab", 13, 77, 102, 145, 182
Carbonero, Joe, 85, 86, 108; photo, 82
Carmichael, Hoagy, 77
Carney, Art, 138, 159; photo, 140
Carpenter, Imogen, 229
Carter, Benny, 10
Casillo, Joe, 123, 125, 126
Casillo, Lenny, 126, 150
Cavallaro, Carmen, 14, 105
Cecil, Chuck, 12; footnote, 110
Christy, June, 16
Clinton, Larry, 81, 105, 115, 118, 145
Coca, Imogene, 16
Colangelo, Nicholas "Uncle Nick", 9, 18, 19, 20, 22, 23, 25, 26, 28, 29, 32, 33, 43, 45, 73, 128; photo, 27
Cole, Nat "King", 14
Columbo, Lee, 172, 173; photos, 174, 202
Columbo, Russ, 77
Como, Perry, 14, 15; photo, 208
Condullo, Pete, 31, 34
Confrey, Zez, 112, 113, 157
Contino, Dick, 138
Cook, Jerry, 10, 38, 40-46, 48-51, 59, 60, 76, 77, 78, 80, 92, 95, 97, 99, 102, 103
Coon-Sanders, 46, 48
Corelli, Alan, 176
Cotton, Larry, 142, 143, 146, 151; photo, 140

Cotton Pickers, 46
Covington, Warren, 166
Cremer, James, 229
Crosby, Bing, 5, 12, 14, 15, 77, 109, 162, 184, 189; footnote, 109
Crosby, Bob, 10, 102, 103, 105, 161, 171
Cugat, Xaviar, 173
Cullen, Fred, 49

Dailey, Frank, 112, 151
Damone, Vic, 14
Daniels, Eliott, 231
David, Mack, 229
Day, Doris, 231
Delaney, Jack, 25
DeMio, Jimmy, photo, 140
Dessinger, George, 231; photo, 140
DeVol, Frank, 127, 138, 231
Diamond, Charles, 46
Dibert, Doc, 99; photo, 98
Dice, Charmaine, 229
DiSantis, Eddie, photo, 202
Disney, Walt, 3
Dixon, Dick, 85; photo, 82
Dolan, Bert, 64
Dolen, Francis, 229
Dolen, Tade, 229, 231
Don Juans, 159
Dorsey Brothers, 10, 71, 102, 103, 109, 125
Dorsey, Jimmy, 10, 14, 108, 125
Dorsey, Tommy, 13, 102, 145, 182, 184, 196
Douglas, Ralph, 229, 231
Drane, Mary, photo, 140
Drane, Virginia, photo, 140
Dube, Paul, 184
Duchin, Eddy, 35, 102, 162, 165
Dunbar, Olga, 198
Dundee, Johnny, 25
Dunham, Sonny, 145, 173

Duren, Joe, 99, 105; photo, 98
Durocher, Leo, 58

Eaton, Jimmy, 231
Eberly, Bob, 14
Eckert, Harold C., 159
Edwards, Ralph, 182; photo, 183
Ellington, Duke, 71, 117, 182, 184

Falvey, Jerry, 64
Farnsworth, Ken, 46, 63
Farrell, Charles, 70
Farrell, Lisa, 229
Father Flanagan, 3; photo, 181
Fazola, Irving, 159, 160, 166
Ferdinando, Felix, 91
Fidler, Jimmy, 134
Fiedler, Arthur, 12
Fields, W. C., 17
Finnegan, Bill, 166
Fisher, Ham, 182
Flewelling, Norman, 103, 105, 106, 121, 122, 123
Fones, Randy, 229
Forrest, Helen, 191
Fowlkes, Harry, 46
Frisch, Al, 231
Fulford, Tom, 105
Funk, Ben, 123; photo, 124
Funk, Larry, 86, 90, 91, 125

Gallagher, George, 46, 63
Gamelli, Vincent (Jimmy James), 57, 97, 105; photo, 98
Garber-Davis (also Jan Garber), 48, 71, 77, 85, 172
Geist, Harry, 173
Geist, Morty, 7
George, Betty, footnote, 173
Gil, Emerson, 59

Gillman, Butler "Butch", 5, 56, 57, 58
Goddard, Paulette, 194
Goldkette, Jean, 48, 99
Gonier, Chet, 85
Goodman, Benny 10, 12, 13, 14, 16, 81, 86, 102, 106, 182, 184
Goodwin, Bill, 209
Gordon, Irving, 231
Grace, Teddy, 84, 86; footnote, 120
Graham, Ann, 84
Granato, Frank, 97, 98, 123; photo, 124
Grancey, Clarence, 46, 70
Gray, Glenn, 10, 81, 86, 102, 105, 132, 134, 135, 154; footnote, 173; photo, 136
Green, Bud, 231
Green, George, 84
Green, Homer, 46
Green, Urby, 195, 196; photo, 202
Griffin, Merv, 12
Grundy, James, 115
Guarnieri, Johnny, 158

Hackett, Bobby, 138, 160, 165; photos, 140, 169
Hall, Howard, 10
Hallett, Mal, 5, 9, 10, 59, 80-92, 95, 99, 108-116, 120, 121, 125, 128, 130-132, 138, 144, 158, 171, 176; photos, 82, 114; footnote, 120
Hampton, Lionel, 115
Handy, William C., 28
Harrington, Dan, 46
Harris, Phil, 145
Hayes, George, 231
Haymes, Dick, 14, 191
Heidt, Horace, 5, 9, 10, 13, 14, 105, 127, 128, 135,

137-172, 176, 179, 180, 184, 187, 193, 198; photos, 140, 147, 155, 168, 169; footnote, 182
Henderson, Fletcher, 48, 59, 66, 70, 90, 91
Henry, Tal, 99
Herman, Woody, 12, 13, 14, 172, 182, 184
Higgens, Joe, 153
Hines, Earl, 59, 71, 77
Hirt, Al, 135
Hoffman, Irving, 191
Hopfner, Ray, photo, 202
Hopkins, Claude, 85, 86, 91
Hornung, Paul, 178
House, Anne, 50
House, Art, 50, 54, 72
House, Floss, 50
House, Frank, 50, 72
House, Fred, Jr., 50
House, Fred, Sr., 49, 50, 52, 56
House, Gert, 50
House, Loretta, 49, 50, 51, 56
House, Nellie, 50
Howard, Eddie, 145, 198
Howard, William W., 178
Humphrey, Stepson "Doc", 161
Hunt, Pee Wee, 134
Huntington, Alice, 231
Hutchins, Hugh, 159
Hutton, Marion, photo, 208

Ink Spots, 14, 182
Ivonelli, Harry, 31

Jackson, Chubby, footnote, 17
Jacobson, Henry, 29, 31, 32, 58
James, Harry, 12, 13, 81, 115, 182, 184
James, Jimmy (see Gamelli)
James, Lewis, 66, 70

Jarvis, Al, 145
Jenney, Jack, 83, 84, 85, 108, 121; photo, 82
Jessel, George, 77
Johns, Julian Pete, 85, 86, 172; photos, 82, 174
Johnson, Austen-Croon, 118, 229
Johnson, Jim, 84
Jolson, Al, 14, 15, 145
Jones, Alan, 175; photo, 177
Jones, Isham, 46, 59, 86
Jones, LeRoi, footnote, 16
Jones, Spike, 14
Joplin, Scott, 28
Jordan, Frank, 84
Jordan, Louis, 14
Joy, Leonard, 134, 135
Jurgens, Dick, 102, 109; footnote, 109

Kapp, Jack, 134; footnote, 109
Kardos, Gene, 117, 132
Kasper, Jerry, photo, 140
Katz, Al, 97
Kaye, Sammy, 5, 115, 153, 175; photo, 155
Kemp, Hal, 77, 90
Kemper, Ronnie, 146, 231
Kenny, Nick, 156, 197
Kenton, Stan, 179
Kilgallen, Dorothy, 134, 182, 191
King, Wayne, 40
Knight, Bob, 160; photo, 140
Knight, Evelyn, 14
Krupa, Gene, 10, 81, 84-87, 89, 91, 105, 108, 121, 153, 176, 184; photos, 82, 94, 155
Kuppe, Waino, 46
Kyser, Kay, 13, 153

Lackenbauer, William "Bill",

108, 116, 117, 120, 131-135, 149-154, 160; photo, 152
Laine, Frankie, 14, 91
Lamb, Gil, 179
Landis, Carol, 161
Landry, Art, 85
Lang Sisters, 106
Lanin, Sam, 48, 59
Lawrence, Greg, 197; photo, 202
Lawrence, Jack, 231
LeAnn Sisters, photo, 140
Lee, Peggy, 14; photo, 209
Leveen, Raymond, 231
Lewis, Sterling, footnote, 109
Lewis, Ted, 89, 90
Lewis, Wayne, 232; photo, 140
Lieber, Dave, 229
Link, Ernie, 84, 85
Little, Little Jack, 73
Logan, Cal, 86
Lombardo, Art, 108
Lombardo, Guy, 5, 13, 14, 17, 48, 71, 77; footnote, 81
Loman, Jules, 230, 232
Long, Johnny, 13
Lopez, Vincent, 48, 65, 182
Lorraine, Ted, and Minto, 36
Lowery, Fred, 138, 159; photo, 140
Lown, Bert, 85
Lucas, Eddie, 172; photos, 174, 202
Lunceford, Jimmy, 90, 91
Lund, Art, 14
Lyman, Abe, 48
Lynne, Phyllis, 172
Lyon, Nancy, 182

MacGreggar, Chummy, 10
Mack, David, 232
Macrae, Gordon, 138, 156; photo, 169
Madrequera, Enric, 103
Marcus, Abe, 173
Marks, Frankie, 46, 63
Marsh, W. Ward, 159
Martin, Freddy, 7, 13, 102
Martin, Mary, 161
Martin, Phil, 195
Matthewson, Bernie, 140, 160
Marvin, Johnny, 66, 70
Maxwell, Marilyn, 196
Mayfair, Mitzie, 176, 178
Mazur, William, 99, 101
McCabe, James, 166, 167, 171
McCoy, Bob, photo, 140
McCoy, Clyde, 12, 70, 117, 132
McDonald, Bob, 123; photo, 124
McEnelly, Edwin J., 5, 9, 10, 18, 38, 40-50, 53, 56-72, 75, 76, 77, 79-87, 95, 102, 105, 117, 128, 139, 144, 159, 171; photo, 67
McHugh, Johnny, 195; photo, 209
McKelvey, Lige, 232
McKenzie, William "Red", 59, 117, 118, 230; photo, 62
McKimey, Edward, 161; photo, 140
McMickle, R. Dale "Mick", 85, 86; photo, 82
Meadows, Fred, 232
Melcher, Irving, 230
Mendelsohn, Artie, 171; photo, 174
Mercer, Johnny, 189; photo, 209
Merrill, Bob, 232
Methot, Andy, 97, 105; photo, 98
Miller, Glenn, 9, 10, 12, 13, 15, 16, 81, 102, 108, 134, 135, 151, 153, 154, 161, 166

Miller, Jim, 70
Mills Brothers, 14, 197; photo, 204
Mills, Jack, 118, 133
Mills Music, 65, 76, 78, 92, 118, 120, 131, 156
Milton, Burt, 232
Minton, Leo, 37
Mitchell, Bernie, 172; photo, 174
Mondello, Toots, 83-86, 91, 108, 121; photo, 82
Mondello, Vic, 85; photo, 82
Monroe, Vaughn, 14, 91, 172, 198
Mooney, Art, 7
Morgan, Helen, 77
Morgan, Russ, 172, 195
Morris, Lee, 192
Mound City Blue Blowers (see also Red McKenzie), 61, 117; photo, 62
Munn, Frank, 70, 77
Murphy, Lyle "Spud", 5, 81, 83, 85, 86, 108; photo, 82
Murray, Billy, 18, 66, 70
Murray, Jan, 178
Murray, Maurice, 230
Musette, Glahe, 13
Mustard, Bill, 159

Neiburg, Al J., 232
Neigher, Harry, 186
Nelson, Ed G., 230
Nelson, Ozzie, 91, 102, 103, 145
Newcomb, Dick, 64
Nichols, Red, 71, 137
Niesen, Gertrude, 145
Noble, Bob, 105
Noble, Ray, 77, 102
Nordstrand, Van, 10
Norvo, Red, 102

O'Brien, H. L. "Hack", 5, 32, 57, 105, 123, 166, 172, 194; photos, 169, 174
O'Connell, Helen, 14, 125
O'Keefe, Corky, 125, 134
Old Dixieland Jazz Band, 28
Oliver, King, 71
Olsen, George, 60
Olson and Johnson, 36
Osborne, Will, 102
O'Shea, Jerome, 193, 194
O'Toole, Ollie, 159, 178
Owens, Jack, 232
Overman, Ralph "Slim", 99, 101, 105; photo, 98

Page, Patti, 193
Parish, Mitchell, 232
Parker, D., 232
Paxton, George, 191
Pearl, Warren, 172, 173, 193, 194, 195
Perrin, Beatrice, photo, 140
Perry, Joe, 109; footnote, 109
Petrillo, Caesar, 11; footnote, 11
Peyton, Doc, 100
Pied Pipers, 108
Pollack, Ben, 71, 77, 86
Powell, Mel, 158
Praeger, Bert, 172; photo, 174
Prima, Louis, 102, 172
Publicover, Louis, 46, 71
Puglia, Ben, 105, 123; photo, 124

Quinn, Frank, 230
Quinn, Fred, 232
Quinn, Grace, 128
Quinn, Johnny, 128-131

Ranney, Omar, 197
Rapp, Barney, 97
Raskin, Milt, 105
Raye, Martha, 145

Razaf, Andy, 232
Reisman, Leo, 46, 60
Renth, Herbert, 97, 105;
  photo, 98
Rey, Alvino, 184
Rich, Buddy, 36
Rich, Lou, 232
Riddle, Nelson, 194; footnote,
  194
Robillard, Paul, 97, 105;
  photo, 98
Rockwell, Tom, 125, 166, 167,
  171
Rogers, Dick, 172
Rogers, Will, 17
Rooney, Pat, 30, 36
Roy, Maurice, 172; photo, 174
Russell, Bob, 232
Russell, Henry "Hank", 156,
  159, 230, 232; photos,
  140, 169
Ryerson, Frank, 85, 90, 108,
  132; photo, 82
Rylander, Al, 173, 188
Riedel, Bob, photo, 140

Salomone, Sam, 123; photo,
  124
Santin (Santoniello), Dudley,
  172; photo, 174
Schneider, Charles, 189
Sears, Jerry, 133
Shaftel, Selig, 230
Shaw, Artie, 10, 13, 105, 115,
  150, 172
Shaw, Elliot, 66, 70
Shearing, George, footnote,
  110
Shore, Dinah, 14, 184
Shribman, Charlie, 59, 78,
  80, 81, 85, 99, 100, 107,
  108, 112, 113
Simms, Ginny, 176, 178, 189;
  photo, 190
Simon, George, 12, 88, 166,
  173

Sinatra, Frank, 14, 184, 191
Sinay, Joey, 230
Sister Kenny, 3
Skylar, Sunny, 192, 233
Small, Danny, 172; photo,
  174
Smith, Kate, 14, 182
Smith, Ken, 139, 157, 165
Smith, Pinetop, 71
Snow, Russell, 120, 233
Sokol, Bill, 97
Spears, Doc, 108
Spitalney, Phil, 85
Spivak, Charlie, 172, 184
Stacy, Jess, 105, 158
Stanton, Frank, 230, 233
Stearns, Marshall, footnote,
  16
Steele, Lois, 233
Stein, Alan, 173
Stephens, Dave, 111, 160
Sterling, Ray, 230
Stevens, Bob, 109, 110;
  footnote, 109
Stevens, Gary, 173, 187
Strasek, Frank, photo, 140
Sullivan, Ed, 16, 182
Switzer, Bob, 77

Tasillo, Bill, 64
Tatum, Art, 158
Taylor, Dick, 108
Taylor, Irene, 86
Teagarden, Jack, 84-86, 91,
  108, 121
Their, Henry, 99
Thomas, Terry, 233
Thompson, Chet, 233
Totten, Hal, 139
Travers, Andy, 173
Three Stooges, 50
Trestman, Irving, 172;
  photos, 174, 202
Trotta, Ray, 230, 233
Troup, George, 84, 89
Tucker, Orrin, 13

Tucker, Sophie, 36
Tucker, Tommy, 172

Unger, Stella, 233

Vale, Evie, 123, 194; photos, 124, 202
Vallee, Rudy, 65, 102, 103
Von Tilzer, Harry, 30

Wade, Fred, 58, 64, 66, 70
Wagner, Larry, 132, 133, 151, 230
Walker, Danton, 134, 196, 197
Wallace, Oliver, 233
Waller, Fats, 48, 74, 75, 113, 157
Walsh & Faye, 38
Walsh, Irene, 24
Warde Sisters, 37
Waring, Fred, 46, 48
Warren, Harry, 195; photo, 209
Waters, Ethel, 77
Wayne, Dottie, 233
Webb, Chick, 105
Webb, Wayne, photo, 140
Weems, Ted, 13, 46, 145
Weiss, George, 189, 192, 230
Weiss, Sammy, 111, 160
Welch, Ray, 34, 35
Welcome, Buddy, 108
Welk, Lawrence, 5, 17

Weston, Cliff (Wetterau), 85; photo, 82
Weston, Paul, 192
Whalen, Joe, 153
White, Jim, 86, 90
White, Vic, 230
Whiteman, Paul, 46, 48, 65, 66, 70, 75, 86, 182, 184
Whiting, Art, 161
Whiting, Margaret, 14; photo, 209
Whittaker, Ray, 31
Wilson, Earl, 134
Winchell, Walter, 134, 180
Wise, Fred, 233
Wood, Donna, 159; photo, 141
Wood, Gloria, photo, 141
Wood, Guy, 233
Woodbury, Mitch, 159

Yeager, Buddy, 59
Yohe, May, 35-38, 41, 44, 76, 128
Yokum, Clark, 84, 108
Youngman, Henny, 178

Zamborano, Dr. U. E., 122
Zaremba, Mitch, photo, 202
Zeile, Harry, 167, 172; photo, 174
Zissu, Leonard, 144, 148, 173, 184
Zurke, Bob, 10, 105